CW00673564

DELUSIONAL
POLITICS

ADVANCE PRAISE FOR THE BOOK

'Hardeep Singh Puri has, among other attributes, that rarest of qualities: lucidity of mind. If you want to learn about current events, read his accounts in *Delusional Politics*. Every chapter is a summary that cuts through the journalistic noise to give you the pure signal. Like a classical chronicler, he manages to provide clarity about what happens in our time, put things in context, and deliver to you the proper context to make up your mind. It is as if a historian is covering the present with the same filtering one can possibly apply only to the past'—Nassim Nicholas Taleb, scholar and author of *Skin in the Game*, *Antifragile* and *The Black Swan*

'*Delusional Politics* is a sophisticated and deep reflection on the technological, political, economic and social forces driving this tumultuous era in global affairs. As a diplomat, policymaker and politician, Hardeep Singh Puri cuts through common opinion to reveal new insights into our present malaise. Rich in both historical and contemporary examples, it argues a number of thought-provoking and controversial propositions. This is an important contribution to the debate about the future of the global order—and how we might fix it'—The Hon. Kevin Rudd, former prime minister of Australia, and president, Asia Society Policy Institute

'Hardeep Singh Puri's book *Delusional Politics* is insightful, thought-provoking, superbly researched and deftly crafted. While it's an engaging story on global politics and global governance—and a textbook battle plan for anyone who wants to formulate foreign policy in today's world—it is also much more . . . it's a fascinating read! The lucid, open-hearted account makes interesting and informative reading for academics and practitioners alike. Puri's unique experience and brilliant writing brings out the authentic richness of the world we are living in. The book could well be the key to all our futures'—Amitabh Kant, chief executive officer, National Institute for Transforming India (NITI Aayog)

'This is a diplomat–politician's unsparing political scrutiny of the rise of populism and a bruising shift from facts to belief-based politics in the post-truth era. The book looks at how Donald Trump's rise has more to do with white working class woes than with racism; and how Narendra Modi's popularity is a break from the culture of impunity that existed before him. While populism has been a reality in democracies for long, he says, social media can be its force multiplier. This results in delusional politics, and delusional decision-making'—Shekhar Gupta, senior journalist

DELUSIONAL POLITICS

HARDEEP SINGH PURI

PENGUIN
VIKING

An imprint of Penguin Random House

VIKING

USA | Canada | UK | Ireland | Australia
New Zealand | India | South Africa | China

Viking is part of the Penguin Random House group of companies
whose addresses can be found at global.penguinrandomhouse.com

Published by Penguin Random House India Pvt. Ltd
7th Floor, Infinity Tower C, DLF Cyber City,
Gurgaon 122 002, Haryana, India

First published in Viking by Penguin Random House India 2019

Copyright © Hardeep Singh Puri 2019

All rights reserved

10 9 8 7 6 5 4 3 2 1

The views and opinions expressed in this book are the author's own and the
facts are as reported by him which have been verified to the extent possible,
and the publishers are not in any way liable for the same.

ISBN 9780670090259

Typeset in Adobe Caslon Pro by Manipal Digital Systems, Manipal
Printed at Replika Press Pvt. Ltd, India

This book is sold subject to the condition that it shall not, by way of trade
or otherwise, be lent, resold, hired out, or otherwise circulated without the
publisher's prior consent in any form of binding or cover other than that in
which it is published and without a similar condition including this condition
being imposed on the subsequent purchaser.

www.penguin.co.in

For Himayani, our first born and one of god's greatest gifts to us. Himayani is a celebration and inspiration of Lakshmi's and my life.

Contents

Author's Note

This, my second book, *Delusional Politics*, draws inspiration from an early phase in a long career when I started to observe, across the world, public figures who seemed perfectly rational, exhibiting tendencies in their decision-making that could only be described as delusional. As I note in the Introduction, this phenomenon is not new—Adolf Hitler, Pol Pot, Attila the Hun, Joseph Stalin, Maximilien Robespierre and many more have gone down this path, leading to catastrophic outcomes for the rest of the world. Given the scale and scope of disruptions taking place the world over, I was tempted to study contemporary politicians and their decision-making, which in many cases displayed a delusional streak. I chose to study three countries, the UK, the US and India, only because I am more familiar with the internal dynamic in these than I am with political nuances elsewhere. The chapters on global governance, terror and trade must be read in line with the experiences of these three countries, for each of them has implications, in one way or another, to influence the contours of the world order.

Delusional Politics was written prior to my joining the council of ministers in September 2017. While statistics have been updated and developments post September 2017 have been incorporated in the text, my conclusions in each of the chapters remain unaltered. To summarize each of these briefly, I would like to begin with the UK.

It is now widely recognized that the decision to hold the 'Brexit' referendum was, at the very least, taken in haste. With the benefit of hindsight, it is clear that PM Cameron, sitting at a pizza parlour at Chicago airport, came up with the idea in an attempt to undermine his party colleagues. Prior to the vote, he was feeling the heat from within the Conservative Party as new challengers threatened his position. 'To smoke them' out, he decided to call a referendum, not realizing that he was providing a platform to 'Brexiteers' such as Nigel Farage, leader of the UK Independence Party. To make matters worse, having lost the referendum, the leaders of the UK decided to double down on delusional decision-making. PM May, who succeeded Cameron post the results, called a snap poll in order to strengthen the position of the Conservative Party as they negotiated the terms and conditions of Brexit. The result? Conservatives were left weaker, barely managing to form a government, and the Labour Party, under the leadership of Jeremy Corbyn, won more seats than it previously had. My own analysis is that the UK is descending into what is now called FUKEW or the Former United Kingdom of England and Wales. Their fortunes, particularly at the international stage, are dwindling, and will continue to do so unless the status ante is restored, and this is not even in the realm of consideration, or so it would seem.

The Brexit referendum results were followed a few months later by the election of Donald Trump as the forty-fifth President of the United States (POTUS).

I was able to read the writing on the wall. Donald Trump beat sixteen other Republican candidates and two Democrats, each with far more governance experience and better credentials than him, to the top job. What explains this phenomenon? While a number of factors can be cited, the most fundamental one, clearly overlooked by the other candidates— the angst of the white, working class American who felt disadvantaged as a result of globalization. Trump was able to build a narrative that struck a chord with them. He made them believe that under President Obama, their interests had either been ignored or short-changed. A Hillary Clinton presidency was projected as an Obama 3.0 narrative. Trump instead emphasized the need for someone who spoke like them. This is not to suggest the Democrats did not make mistakes or that there were no external factors at play—Hillary Clinton paid a huge price for calling large sections of the American population deplorable. The revelations by former FBI director Comey too played their part.

It was perhaps a given that a Trump presidency would be unconventional. A number of decisions he has taken—including the nuclear deal with Korea, pulling out of the Iran Nuclear Deal and the Paris climate agreement—stand out. However, the allegations regarding his dealings with Russia, both during the campaign and the presidency, are striking and most crucial to his presidency. Impeaching a President is never easy, and Trump will most likely avoid that fate. He will, however, be indicted for acts of omission/commission prior to the elections, and perhaps be charged for obstruction of justice during his tenure. The Russia problem is not one that will easily go away and will continue to cast a shadow throughout the duration of his term in office.

I would like to conclude by stating what I believe has now become self-evident—the results of the 2014 general election in India brought with them a paradigmatic shift in the country's politics and economic governance. I make this claim for two reasons—first, the ten years of the Congress-led UPA governments brought India to a standstill. Corruption, economic mismanagement and lethargy in international affairs characterized those years, particularly the last four. The party that played a pivotal role in ensuring India's freedom has been reduced to a fiefdom, headed by the Gandhi family. India was crying out for a second independence. The results in May 2014 and the state assembly elections over the past four years only proved this point. By winning just forty-four seats in the Lok Sabha in 2014 and thereby not being able to have one of its leaders elected as the leader of opposition, the grand old party of India faces serious existential questions. Any suggestion that Congress's victories in three Hindi heartland states in December 2018 erases this existential threat needs to be examined. In all three states, the BJP was the incumbent, and yet, in two of these states, the Congress barely managed to scrape through. In Madhya Pradesh, for instance, the BJP was the incumbent for fifteen years, and still managed to receive a slightly higher vote share (41 per cent) than the Congress (40.9 per cent). In fact, the Congress by itself did not even reach the halfway mark, and needed the support of the BSP to form a government. The suggestion therefore that the phoenix has risen from the ashes could still be premature.

The year 2014 also provided, in several respects, India the last chance to reform the structural inefficiencies of its economy. The overwhelming nature of the verdict meant Prime Minister Modi's government was able to deliver what all Indians wanted i.e. basic goods and services. Programmes like Swachh Bharat Mission, which seeks to make India open defecation free and provide 100 per cent waste management; Pradhan Mantri Awas Yojana, or Affordable Housing for All, wherein the PM has promised that every Indian will have a home they can call theirs; Jan Dhan Yojana, which is perhaps the world's largest financial inclusion programme; Goods and Services Tax and the Insolvency Bankruptcy Code, which have made doing business in India easier; and the GiveItUp scheme, where households have been encouraged to voluntarily give up subsidies, are just some of the achievements of the Modi government I point out in the book. I have no qualms in predicting that these measures will hold the BJP in good stead going into the general election in 2019. There is widespread acknowledgement among India's citizens that the days of *khichdi* politics are over, and the proposed 'mahagathbandan' or a grand coalition is nothing more than an alliance of opportunists.

According to Cambridge historian Angus Maddison, India's contribution to global output in 1700 stood at 27 per cent. By 1950, this had come down to 3 per cent, and today stands at approximately 13 per cent. The advent of imperialism, followed by sixty-odd years of Congress rule meant India was never able to reclaim its rightful place as one of the world's leading economies. Under PM Modi, India is poised to become a $5 trillion economy by 2025, and a $10 trillion one by 2030. This increase in GDP, along with substantial increase in per capita income, requires stability at the very top of the decision-making system.

India needs another ten years of PM Modi to reattain its pre-colonial economic strength. It is well on its way to regaining its rightful place in the universe.

The Setting

'Be humble, for you are made of earth.
Be noble, for you are made of stars.'

—Serbian Proverb

'Are you psychic or what? First Brexit and now Trump!' This was the essence of a crisp message from our younger daughter Tilottama on the morning of 6 November 2016 when it became abundantly clear that Donald Trump was going to carry the electoral college.

No, I am certainly not a psychic. However, forty years of professional life has taught me to see the fault lines in a flawed narrative. My instincts have, over the years, been sufficiently honed to see through a situation in which a narrative is contrived. Producing an erroneous narrative is bad enough. But then to market it as the dominant mainstream narrative suggests a more serious underlying problem. Anyone can get an assessment wrong or make a wrong prediction. But if the expertise is suspect and the analyst or commentator has a vested interest in producing a flawed narrative, then the very essence of the democratic process stands undermined.

My friend Nassim Nicholas Taleb, the author of *The Black Swan: The Impact of the Highly Improbable*, *Anti-fragile: Things that Gain from Disorder* and so many other brilliant books, called this 'a global riot against pseudo-experts'.[1] 'Learned' commentators the world over got both the Brexit and the Trump victory wrong. Many reputations should have been destroyed, including those of CNN and the *New York Times*. But instead of gracefully accepting their mistake(s), they dug in and decided to join the battle. They refused to come to terms with the fact that Trump could or, more importantly, should be allowed to win. Brexit and the election of the forty-fifth President of the United States (POTUS) were just the beginning of a process. Social media had already altered the dynamic. Once Trump began to settle down, well before he completed a hundred days in office, the battle to set the narrative started in the right earnest. Facts—as per the normal way they are understood, as being empirically verifiable—appeared no longer sacrosanct. Their 'alternatives' began to enter and occupy considerable space in the lexicon and the framing of narratives. The era of alternative facts and alternative narratives had finally arrived. It had been in the making for some time.

The world was in sufficient disarray and already in an advanced stage of entropy well before Brexit. Brexit and Trump, however, signalled the unveiling of an entirely different narrative—one only partly anchored in domestic mismanagement and influenced to a considerable extent by the processes of globalization.

Over the past quarter century, I have failed to be persuaded that the Western liberal democratic order represents the closest approximation to what is best for human civilization. The emphasis on human rights is laudable. The gains of globalization are also truly impressive. The model based on the processes of globalization—the Washington Consensus and trade liberalization, which in turn produced unprecedented economic growth—is, however, not without problems. Trade certainly helped individuals and nations to grow wealthy but has never been entirely 'free' but 'managed'. The so-called 'magic' of markets is, at a certain level, a camouflage for rigging by elites.

That globalization produces winners and losers is a no-brainer. What has so far been underestimated is the angst of the marginalized and alienated voters among the losing segment. It is that angst which the intelligent politician taps into for political advantage. Taking advantage of something like public anger for short-term gain to seek political power for a larger good is one thing, quite another if that angst is used to unravel a society and country and to facilitate uncertainty and turbulence.

What is that trend and, if it is so, the process called? For want of a better term, populism, which is on the rise globally. Why? There must be several explanations. In order to outline the 'Setting' for this book, I will confine myself to only a few.

Populism provides a vehicle, at one level, to secure power quickly. This vehicle is not powered and driven by intellectual rigour and careful analysis of facts and trends. Nor is there any attempt to sift facts from fiction, to distinguish between objective reality and contrived narratives.

In a limited sort of way, social media has changed the texture of politics; revolutionized the processes of communications and simplified and dumbed down serious discourse. More seriously, it has also provided a platform to hurl invectives, hatred and divisiveness.

Participating in a meeting on 'Next Generation Democracy' of the Club de Madrid in Dili, Timor Leste, one of the world's newest nations, from 30–31 July 2017, I gained several interesting insights. Some clearly merit mention.

There was an agreement among us participants that the global swing of the pendulum is such that it must necessarily be much more sensitive to the voice of the marginalized and dispossessed, the poor. A very relevant point that emerged from our discussion was that the poor of today are very different; they have access to information, which gives them empowerment. It is their access to social media that has unleashed a new politics.

Traditional democratic governance, on the other hand, has been handicapped by disillusionment borne of inequalities produced by globalization, and the absence of genuine icons and heroes who can speak for and advocate the virtues of liberal democracy. The youth, in particular, are sceptical about politics. It is this cynicism which led one of the leaders, an ex-prime minister from South Asia to stress the need for civic education and to reform the three 'P's: Politics, Politicians and Political Parties.[2] Elections now are regrettably beginning to work like processes designed to choose masters rather than public servants. Is it any surprise, therefore, that sections of voters who feel left out now express themselves with such clarity and vengeance?

Equally, the Brexit and Trump phenomenon have demonstrated that such angst that expresses itself across party and ideological lines, can produce a geographical demographic divide, and that the angry continue to provide a support base to maverick governance. In the case of Trump, this support base has remained by and large relatively stable, if not seen a steady rise in 2018 as compared to 2017,[3] his failure on or as per traditional governance norms notwithstanding.

A leader who anchors his/her appeal on populist sentiment or angst invariably does well in the short term but produces devastating consequences in the medium to long term. Because institutions are stronger and more resilient in the 'advanced' world and less so in the poorer developing countries, a leader indulging in populist politics makes a greater contribution to arresting and derailing economic development that is so necessary for the welfare of people. Short-term populism is the worst enemy of long-term development. This lesson does not appear to have been learnt even by the systems that are normally associated with more mature governance.

The so-called Western liberal democratic order received a rude wake-up call with Brexit and election of Trump. In some respects, the trailer for this movie actually did a test-run in India in May 2014, when the political party that had been in power for most of the seven decades of India's existence as an independent country, including the last decade, found itself completely eclipsed at the polls. While India has made impressive strides, post Modi's spectacular victory in 2014, the prospects for the UK, post-Brexit, are gloomy. The jury is still out on what the outcome will be of the turbulence unleashed by Trump's election as the forty-fifth President of the United States.

Rewind to May 2014. Unlike Brexit and Trump, in some respects, I did not get May 2014 entirely right. No one had any doubt that the Bharatiya Janata Party (BJP) led by the then chief minister of Gujarat, Narendra Modi, would by far be the single-largest party in the Lok Sabha and also that he would be the next prime minister of India. He set the narrative, and sustained and dominated it entirely. The previous ten years of the United Progressive Alliance (UPA) coalition were widely perceived as being characterized by policy paralysis, corruption and a diarchy of political control and power.

As noted by Sanjaya Baru, Prime Minister Manmohan Singh's media advisor during 2004-2008, '. . . the Indian

National Congress is a party of our national movement. It's a more than 150-year-old political party. And this is the political party that made India a free country. And I think it's done enormous damage to Indian democracy that this national party, that this historic party, has been taken over by a family, so that it's just a mother, daughter, son-in-law, son, that become the key figures of the party. Everybody else is secondary, including the prime minister.'[4]

To put it mildly, a powerful stench enveloped the political system during the UPA rule. An amendment to the Congress party constitution in 2004 transferred political power effectively from the prime minister to the party president, Sonia Gandhi. Ten years of UPA rule witnessed many positives, especially in the first five years. The narrative was, however, vitiated in the second half of the second term, particularly from 2011 to the end of 2013. Policy paralysis, corruption and toxicity helped produce the backdrop for the meteoric rise of Narendra Modi.

Like many others, I didn't get it entirely wrong either. I underestimated the scale of the Modi victory. Back-of-the-envelope electoral arithmetic is a favourite pastime for most students of Indian politics. A Modi victory and a BJP government was a foregone conclusion. To achieve the 272 seats required for majority in the Lok Sabha, some of us thought the BJP would comfortably win more than 240 seats, and require the help of one or two, if not more, smaller coalition partners to cobble together the requisite 272 seats. Arun Jaitley[5] said many times that this was not about arithmetic but chemistry.[6] The people of India had made up their mind. The BJP got 282 and an absolute majority on its own, for the first time in 37 years.[7]

We were not wrong in predicting an increase in the BJP's vote share. We underestimated the collapse of the Congress Party. But why did analysts and commentators get it wrong?

Quite simply, they were lazy and out of sync with the popular sentiment at the grass-roots level. More seriously, they allowed their judgment to be influenced and shaped by a media that had ceased to be independent, a media that was now a 'participant' in the political process. The media in New Delhi reflected the ideological biases and preferences of Lutyens' New Delhi. An otherwise educated, now retired, member of the Indian Foreign Service and subsequently member of the Congress party was so bold as to suggest that Narendra Modi could not ever become the prime minister of India, and invited him instead to sell tea at the All India Congress Committee session, clearly referring to the now PM's humble origins.[8]

A retired senior colleague from the foreign service, in a column, wrote that every opinion poll had declared that Hillary Clinton would be the likely winner, amongst other predictions.[9] Any person making such a glaring mistake in terms of a prediction should normally go into an extended phase of hibernation or retire. CNN and the *New York Times*, in particular, disgraced themselves. The attempt to make amends from the publisher/editor, through their publication's editorial calls, soon after the election of the forty-fifth President of the United States, was insipid and only added to the growing erosion of the *NYT*'s credibility.[10] The intellectual icons of our times from the US, Europe and Asia joined Fareed Zakaria on his show on CNN to pontificate on American democracy. They failed to realize how ridiculous they looked and sounded. The US electoral system, such as it is with all its flaws, elected Trump as the forty-fifth POTUS. An analysis of how and why this happened and how this might play out would have been far more relevant then and now. That is what provides the 'Setting' for delusional politics, in this, my second book.

Introduction

'Great minds discuss ideas; average minds discuss events; small minds discuss people.'

—Eleanor Roosevelt

These words, popularly ascribed to the first lady of the United States, Eleanor Roosevelt, more than half a century ago, are unexceptionable as an aspirational exhortation to raise the intellectual level of public discourse. Even though their copyright has never been established beyond doubt, it is widely believed that Roosevelt wrote these lines and was given credit for this wisdom.

She went on to make a seminal contribution to the drafting of the Universal Declaration of Human Rights, which was adopted in 1948.

There is, however, a small problem: Who are the so-called 'great minds' and who will define or characterize them as such? A high IQ, it has been established, does not guarantee success. However, the prospects for failure are high in the absence of EQ or emotional intelligence.

'Greatness' of mind cannot be inherited. It must be nurtured and demonstrated. Some famous people, after having tasted success, became delusional. A brilliant mind can in fact be delusional, ever so often.

An additional problem: Many of these delusional characters are thrown up by democratic systems. Hitler is a case in point. There are hundreds of other examples.

This is why it is all the more important to focus instead on 'ideas'. A good idea needs to be pursued, and when its time comes, it can have a profound and transformational effect.

Great minds alone don't produce ideas that are positively beneficial. Not all ideas are of this genre. Even contrived and flawed narratives take shape in ideas, in deception and falsehood. When individuals persist in producing and perpetuating falsehoods, knowing them to be so, they are at the very least delusional and are attempting to delude others.

Once elected, leaders can mould and shape the popular narrative. If they are allowed to do so without regard to factual reality and through processes that smack of arbitrariness and unilateralism, democracy would be viewed as having facilitated their task and they come to be branded as delusional. Democracy only provides a vehicle or route for such persons to acquire power.

Why and, more importantly, how did I become interested in studying this phenomenon of 'delusional' decision-making, particularly in politics? In 2013, I stepped out into the open world after nearly four decades in the Indian Foreign Service. The life of a diplomat is interesting and diplomacy as a profession can also be exciting and professionally rewarding. However, decision-making in diplomacy, as indeed in most other governmental activity, takes place in a controlled environment and follows a top-down model.

If the person entrusted with the decision-making authority, usually an elected official in a democratic system, is not fully sure and confident of his environment and displays some signs of diffidence, then the established bureaucracy, the mandarins, will take over. And because the civil service is hierarchical, cautious and risk-averse, the advice to the sovereign will be couched in a status-quoist 'no risk' envelope. Several layers of bureaucracy will ensure that a diffident political leader will hear what he/she wants to hear: usually, that the choice(s) of not taking any action, is also a policy option which will be rationalized ex post facto by scribes is encouraged by the status-quoist bureaucracy.

The alternate scenario is also equally interesting. The elected representative is a strong personality, and the mandarins buckle under and are not able to speak truth to power. Delusional decision-making or delusional politics can and does take place in both scenarios.

It is only when I had the time, intellectual freedom and ability to think outside the framework of a formalized system, that the full implications of what was going on in the world became clear. I was part of a think tank in New York around that time and had the unique privilege of watching another extreme variant—various delusional characters in full play in the geo-political sphere. Unhinged characters giving advice to poor unsuspecting governments—which, for the most part, was self-serving—and offering to use their 'margin of persuasion', a euphemism for 'lobbying'. Looking out of my corner fourth-floor office with a full-frontal view, across First Avenue of the headquarters of the United Nations with the flags of the 193 member states fluttering majestically, I was reminded ever so often of what Bertrand Russell said: 'The trouble with the world is that the stupid are cocksure and the intelligent are full of doubt.'

A casual conversation between David Cameron, the then prime minister of the United Kingdom, and his foreign secretary, William Hague, at Chicago's O'Hare airport in May 2012, unleashed events that led to the holding of a referendum and subsequently Brexit, for which there was no constitutional requirement. It effectively succeeded in beginning the end of the United Kingdom, which, by virtue of the series of actions and reactions unchained and likely to follow, could end up, if corrective action is not taken, as the United Kingdom of just England and Wales.

At the height of military success in World War II, Hitler decided to take his army to Russia in the middle of severe winter. In effect, he opened not one but two additional fronts in 1941. He was not the first. Napoleon had done much the same more than a hundred years earlier in 1812.

In Nepal, an entirely bizarre action on 1 June 2001 by the heir apparent of the ruling family resulted in fratricide, regicide, matricide and suicide.[1] Whether the queen, mother of the heir apparent, was solely responsible, or the former was egged on by a devious and scheming uncle is less than material.[2] A country was thrown into disarray and chaos. It is still reeling from that one action when the crown prince went berserk because he had been denied permission to marry the young woman of his choice.

In each of these cases, it is necessary to ascertain why the concerned persons took the actions they did. Were they aware of any other choices or decisions whose consequences could be anticipated and evaluated? Were they of sound mind? Were they on opiates? Did they just underestimate the consequences of their actions and took these decisions without factoring in the consequences?

Many examples of delusional politics are available in South Asia, including in India itself. In Sri Lanka, an elected president decided to define his legacy by erecting huge white elephants in his home district Mattala, a port in Hambantota, and the Mattala Rajapaksa International Airport.[3] What purpose do these mega infrastructure projects serve? They provide an ego boost to the leader. But what else? He succeeded in driving up his country's debt. Sri Lanka now faces the prospect of more than 90 per cent of its GDP being earmarked for debt repayment.[4]

Since this is not sustainable and the Chinese are not into philanthropy or altruism, the debt has been converted into equity and parts of Sri Lanka have been sold to the Chinese.[5] That could also be the pattern in Pakistan on account of the China–Pakistan Economic Corridor (CPEC), unless better sense prevails.[6] My colleagues familiar with the dynamics of the bilateral relationship between China and Pakistan, variously described as 'all-weather' and 'time-tested,' try to convince me that it will all be smooth-sailing. In my view, this is more likely to evolve in an asymmetrical fashion, converting Pakistan into a client state of China.

However, my intention here is not to catalogue or list all the delusional politicians of our time or their delusional decision-making. It is a much more limited exercise to take three case studies of three important democracies: United Kingdom in 2015 post Brexit; the United States in 2016 post Trump; and the story of India which I attempt to trace on a wider historical canvas.

Who was 'delusional'? The Congress party which facilitated India's freedom struggle and was in a governance role during the bulk of its existence as an independent country? Or its leaders during the last ten years of providing a quality of governance which resulted in its winning less than 10 per cent of the seats in the Lok Sabha—the threshold required to be recognized as the designated 'opposition' in parliament? Or a self-made man of humble origins, who called for a Congress-*mukt* (Congress-free) India, whose campaign produced an absolute majority in the Lok Sabha after an astonishingly large gap of thirty-seven years?

Then again, a probing question: Why did voters reject the more qualified of the two presidential candidates in the United States? The voters didn't opt for the candidates' experience and credentials in governance but instead for a man who during the course of the campaign and after being elected behaved in the most unconventional manner. What explains the Trump phenomenon?

And, in between, what was the need for a referendum on Brexit? Only delusional politicians act against their own and their country's best interest in the belief that they are making history.

How will these three democracies reconcile their own internal fault lines, their delusional politics? Countries, like institutions, have to be assiduously built, step by step, brick by brick. Lest there comes along a delusional politician who either out of a fit of hubris, megalomania or bad advice takes one or more decisions that can have long-term adverse consequences and can result in the unravelling of countries.

Why choose India, UK and the US? Quite simply because they are democracies; they are countries I know and have had the privilege of living in and have been able to study in some detail.

At the centre of delusional politics, invariably, is the delusional politician who, in turn, is often encouraged and egged on by pseudo expertise, and self-serving and motivated advice. With the benefit of hindsight, it is tempting to characterize and dismiss such historical figures just as 'delusional' or 'intelligent but unhinged'. Deeper analysis, however, shows that all of them had serious character flaws. Such leaders pursue delusional policies that can only prove catastrophic. The interplay between the so-called great 'minds' and 'ideas' often produces toxicity.

I do realize that this runs the risk of straying into the study of individuals. Having defined greatness in terms of great minds and ideas, one is gravitationally pulled down or dumbed down to what average minds do—discuss events—and what small minds do—talk about 'people'.

To define the compass, this book is about the greatest gift of mankind, a great idea: democracy. Unfortunately, that great idea has to be comprehensively surveyed for the sake of its survival in terms of individuals who have to provide leadership. And this must necessarily cover events.

Another caveat, delusional politics is not confined to the actions of delusional politicians at the level of the nation state. Governance at the level of the multilateral system has much to answer for—hence a chapter on this subject. There is a chapter each on the fight against international terrorism and the politics of trade. Delusional decision-making in both of these areas has severely impacted and influenced the advanced state of entropy the world finds itself in today.

My first book, *Perilous Interventions: The Security Council and the Politics of Chaos*, looked at the genesis of flawed decision-making in the United Nations Security Council in 2011 and 2012, and thereafter, the use of force and the arming of rebels. Those policies led to the unravelling of countries. This book, *Delusional Politics*, looks at the dynamics within three democracies. What will the leaders of these three do to their own countries and the world around them?

An interesting question that continued to come up during the exercise of writing this book was whether there is any link between mental illness and delusional politics in general. Do those who hold extreme political views and/or are known to act irrationally suffer from some form of mental disequilibrium or illness? As far as I am aware, there is no scientific or medical evidence for this. Totalitarian states have had little or no hesitation in locking up dissidents or opponents of the regime for the simple reason that they refuse to conform to the prevailing political philosophy and oppose the ruling dispensation.

Sluggish schizophrenia, a diagnosis that was in use in the erstwhile Soviet Union, was formulated in the Soviet psychiatric establishment. The psychiatrists who developed this perhaps genuinely believed that one had to be psychologically delusional to oppose or question the Bolshevik project of building a socialist state.

Interestingly, I found little empirical evidence to establish a difference between people suffering from delusions and those with mental illness. I was astonished and alarmed to know that behavioural science or psychology does not focus on how seemingly normal persons, without any known history of mental illness, can display delusional behaviour in their actions on a regular basis. The people around them come to accept this as normal. Such behaviour then tends to be rationalized as part of a 'belief' devoid of objectivity and facts.

Policies followed by Adolf Hitler, Pol Pot, Attila the Hun, Joseph Stalin, Maximilien Robespierre and several others brought death and destruction to tens of millions of people. Examples of evil incarnate in history are not confined to the past. Many democratically elected leaders of the twenty-first century display streaks of recklessness, megalomania, bizarre self-obsession and political views that are difficult to characterize. Are they mentally unstable and, therefore, delusional? Or, are they delusional without being mentally ill?

Is being pathologically delusional less serious or more serious than being just delusional?

Perhaps each recipient of a mention in history's hall of shame would have to be carefully analysed and studied separately.

In the case of Hitler, new research based on the papers of his private physician shows that as the war progressed he became progressively more dependent on drugs. Three phases are mentioned by Norman Ohler in his new book, *Blitzed, Drugs in the Third Reich*:[7] 'The first one are the vitamins given in high doses intravenously. The second phase starts in the fall of 1941 with the first opiate, but especially with the first hormone injections. Then in '43 the third phase starts, which is the heavy opiate phase.'

The crucial question that arises is the following: Could the war have had a different outcome if Hitler's doctor, Theodor Morell, had not put him on a vitamin injection therapy and then graduated him to opiates subsequently?

CHAPTER I

The Credibility Crisis

'I covered two presidents, LBJ and Nixon, who could no longer convince, persuade, or govern, once people had decided they had no credibility, but we seem to be more tolerant now of what I think we should not tolerate.'

—Helen Thomas[1]

Is 'truth' finally dead? Not really. It has been in a coma for quite some time. We've have just been reluctant to take it off life support.

The most telling examples of the need to refer to 'truth' in the past tense can be found in the deteriorating and toxic relationship between the government and the media in most 'democracies'.

Partisan media outlets have been on a steady increase since the late 1980s. These allow consumers to enjoy the self-constructed confines of their own ideological bubbles. This 'homophilous sorting', as the *Economist* terms it,[2] allows like-minded people, in a sense, to form their own realities. So, when public figures—be it celebrities or politicians— who are viewed favourably in these ideological clusters are positioned under unfavourable light, the credibility of the allegation lies not within the facts but within emotions. The 'truth' is not determined by facts; 'truth' is determined by what *feels* true, regardless of whether or not those feelings have any basis in facts.[3]

This combination of increasingly polarized media outlets and tight-knit ideological communities whose beliefs are shaped by preference over fact lies at the core of truth's decline. This trend is evident in each of the three democracies discussed in this book—the United States, United Kingdom, and India—and in all these cases, the trend is signalled by a divergence of political reality from the dominant political narrative.

As I discuss in this chapter, these democracies have fallen into the dangerous comforts of 'post-truth' politics. The Oxford Dictionaries named 'post-truth' as their 2016 Word of the Year. They define post-truth as: 'Relating to or denoting circumstances in which objective facts are less influential in shaping public opinion than appeals to emotion and personal belief. '[4]

The year 2017 has its own variant of this. 'Fake News', a term heavily popularized by US President Donald Trump, has been named the word of the year by Collins Dictionary due to its widespread use around the world. Defined as 'false, often sensational, information disseminated under the guise of news reporting',[5] fake news takes over from Brexit—which was named the definitive word last year after the June 2016 referendum in favour of the UK's exit from the European Union (EU).

For societies to accept 'post-truth' politics as the norm—which has not happened yet in totality but is on the horizon in the US, UK, and India—there must be a fundamental shift in the basis for political beliefs from fact-based credibility to belief-based credibility. In other words, in the post-truth era, people's realities are moulded not by evidence but by whichever narratives complement their pre-existing biases. As historian

Daniel J. Boorstin wrote in 1962 in his book *The Image: A Guide to Pseudo-Events in America*:

When 'truth' has been displaced by 'believability' as the test of the statements which dominate our lives . . . ingenuity is devoted less to discovering facts than to inventing statements which can be made to seem true.

The post-truth era is indeed upon us, as is manifestly apparent from two historic tests of democratic politics recently: the 2016 referendum to determine the fate of the United Kingdom's membership in the EU and the 2016 US presidential election. In both instances, we witnessed a surge in populist rhetoric, capitalizing on the public's economic or social angst by appealing to the public's emotions rather than their rationale. Politicians on the campaign trail morphed public discourse by tampering with truth. As author of *The Post-Truth Era* Ralph Keyes describes, 'we "massage" truthfulness, we "sweeten it", we tell "the truth improved".'[6]

In the run-up to the 2016 presidential election in the United States, several studies looked at the media coverage of the campaigns. Consensus across the various studies was that policy discussion on the campaign trail was largely absent, overshadowed by discussion on the candidates' personalities and controversies.[7] News media, of course, exacerbated this problem, choosing, for instance, to focus on Hillary Clinton's blunders with her email server rather than her policy proposals.

Priority issues for political campaigns have been shuffled, both in terms of candidates' talking points and coverage thereof. As Keyes explains, 'On our media-driven scale of values, celebrity trumps honesty.'[8] The value of truth is in decline. As a result, we are replacing political reality with political narratives. The irony is that in the media coverage of the Trump/Clinton election contest, their character and integrity became issues, only to be jettisoned conveniently to fit ideological preferences.

Political Narrative vs Political Reality

I am a student of history. Historians essentially like to contextualize and organize events in order to provide a better understanding and meaning of those occurrences. They create chronologies and narratives. Creating narratives is relatively straightforward. Given enough evidence, a certain degree of consensus can be reached. Historians, however, are definitely not without their biases or ideological preferences. There is no such thing as clinical empiricism. The assertion that 'facts speak for themselves' is open to questioning. What is a 'fact'? My favourite example is taken from E.H. Carr's *What Is History?*[9]

The fact that Caesar crossed the Rubicon is a fact. Was he the first to do so, how many did so before him and thereafter? Were these numbers in hundreds, thousands or millions? In short, the historian has to give shape to facts. This is where his/her preferences, biases and ideological predilections become important in the shaping of his/her product. Even a chronological listing of facts need not be entirely free from deliberately introduced impurities. And yes, there is a greater propensity of such externally introduced elements for slant, twist or distortion in narratives of a political nature.

Narratives constructed in the context of politics—whether by politicians, governments, or pundits—are 'necessarily the product of a particular perspective'.[10] Thus political narratives cannot by any means mirror the clear-cut process of preparing clinical historical narratives.

Political narrative, in its simplest form, is a mere retelling of events which are then woven together into a timeline. Even in this case, narratives can be distorted by cherry-picking particular elements to include or exclude from the narrative. In media coverage of the 2016 US presidential election, for instance, even if one were to overlook the political charge of news stories produced by partisan media outlets, the sheer number of articles focusing on a story rewrites political narratives. Such was the case when former Federal Bureau of Investigation director James Comey reopened the investigation in Democratic presidential candidate Hillary Clinton's emails some days before the election. The story was on the front page of all news outlets; regardless of how the story was covered, the volume of coverage itself was enough to influence the electoral calendar. Even absent deliberate political bias, political narratives cannot help but promote a particular perspective.

The closest that political narrative can reach neutrality is if it were to present all possible political perspectives. Given the near unlimited number of probable views, it is unlikely and unrealistic to expect such all-encompassing political narrative. Even in the case that this comprehensive narrative is successfully and continuously constructed, the process of an individual absorbing such a rich narrative would favour certain aspects of the narrative over others. Ultimately, political narratives can reduce the bias they contain but they cannot escape it entirely. In fact, the very choice of words used and events covered by the narrative is in and of itself indicative of the subjective element or, for want of a better term, the 'bias'.

Recent trends indicate that an increasing number of media outlets blatantly surrender and do not even make an attempt to achieve impartiality. Instead, they cater to specific political views. Politics and political narratives in such situations serve to stimulate existing biases already held by people. This in turn, serves to bolster pre-conceived prejudices.

Political economist William Davies describes this progression as the 'transition from a society of facts to a society of data'.[11] Data, as opposed to facts, can be easily manipulated and inserted into political narratives as needed. The variability endowed by the vagaries of data ensures that the narrative is not entirely falsified, even if it is not entirely true.

A prime example of this loose use of data is the claim made by the Vote Leave campaign and its supporters in the lead-up to Britain's EU referendum. The campaign, which advocated Britain's withdrawal from the European Union, claimed that the UK sends the EU £350 million a week. Several sources, including the UK Statistics Authority,[12] have refuted this claim, calling it misleading. However, the figure of £350 million did not appear out of nowhere. The sum was based on the gross amount the UK contributed to the EU in 2015—£17.8 billion—calculated for its weekly amount.[13] The figure of course fails to take into account monetary flows from Brussels to the UK.

The Vote Leave campaign's claim was not backed with facts but with data. It was not necessarily true, but the claim contained enough empirical data to not be an outright lie. Despite straightforward evidence that disproved the allegation, the claim served its purpose, which was to spur Euroscepticism.

This tendency of data-based political narratives to trump those that are fact-based is only one half of the trend observed in democracies. The more perplexing half is that this change— this devolution of accountability for telling the truth—is becoming the norm.

We are in the dawn of a credibility crisis.

Post-Truth Politics

The '100-day mark' of a presidency is a benchmark created by the American media to assess presidential achievements, which ultimately bears no significance other than the satisfying roundness of its number. For the Trump presidency, the *New York Times* was inspired to publish a piece titled 'Fact-Checking President Trump Through His First 100 Days'.[14] The article traces Trump's *inaccuracies* in his speeches, interviews and tweets, beginning with his inauguration on 20 January 2017, when he claimed his inaugural crowd to be in the tens of millions, a claim that was subsequently found to have been embellished by computer morphing. The article logged 'at least one false or misleading claim per day on 91 of his first 99 days.'

In his book *Trump: The Art of the Deal*, Trump terms boisterous bragging of this sort 'truthful hyperbole'.[15] Trump dragged this into the Oval Office to serve no political or policy-related purpose. Of course, the President's own popularity is sought to be enhanced. Such efforts do not appear to effectively factor in the negative impact of botched attempts. Misleading the public is not entirely new to the presidency. Post-truth politics has been in play for quite some time.

We needn't look too far back into history to recall when misleading the public was a consciously designed political instrument in pursuance of a political agenda in spite of overwhelming evidence to the contrary. Through a systematic misinformation campaign, the Bush administration created a contrived narrative based on Saddam Hussein's alleged possession of weapons of mass destruction (WMD) and Iraq's links to al-Qaeda in order to justify the use of force and military action in Iraq. Post 9/11 era, Americans were particularly fearful of a potential terrorist threat and were easily swayed.

The US invaded Iraq on 19 March 2003 and found no evidence of weapons of mass intervention resulting in one of the most catastrophic culminations of public misinformation in modern history.

In such cases, the fear-mongering normally pays off. It did in this case as well. Despite the fact that the US troops had returned empty-handed, a substantial portion of Americans continued to believe that the US had discovered WMDs in Iraq. The terrorist attacks on 11 September 2001 had left Americans ready and willing to accept narratives that would offer them some reassurance. And in this case, believing that the US military was striking back at the terrorist-conspirators did just this.

This is a major element of post-truth politics, which prevents it from being classified as outright lying. As author Ralph Keyes argues, 'Post-truthfulness exists in an ethical twilight zone. It allows us to dissemble without considering ourselves dishonest.'[16] For many Americans, the Bush administration reinforced their preexisting biases, prejudices and conspiracies. The administration told the public what they wanted to hear, and truth took secondary importance.

Similar tactics were employed on the other side of the Atlantic in the lead-up to the Brexit referendum. Vote Leave made use of the anti-immigrant sentiments that ravaged the nation (which I discuss in some detail in the chapter on the UK), claiming that if Britain remained in the EU, the Union's migrants could force the British population to swell by 5.23 million by 2030, which would place 'clearly unsustainable' strains on British public goods and services.

This prediction was formulated on the assumption that in the coming years Albania, Montenegro, Serbia, Macedonia, and—most worryingly for them—Turkey would join the EU, granting their citizens unfettered access to British resources.[17] Given Turkey's turbulent descent into authoritarianism, the prospect of its EU membership is murky, to say the least. Absent pre-existing prejudices, Vote Leave's assertions fall short of a convincing scare-tactic. But biases ran and continue to run high in the country, so once the claim was put forth, no amount of counter-claims could reverse the damage it had done.

Support for Brexit or the invasion of Iraq did not, of course, extend entirely through their respective countries. Yet in both cases, there was a build-up of sentiment. In the case of Brexit, it fed on the toxicity of a contrived narrative on immigration perpetuated by the open borders of EU member states. And in the case of Iraq, it was nourished by the false story of its arsenal of WMDs and its links to terrorist organizations—the story itself emanated from small groups but was encouraged to fan out to the larger population. Once out, these sentiments created the conditions for ideological isolationism—which allows people to limit themselves to environments that complement and nurture their worldviews— that ensured the viability of post-truth politics.

Polarized Consumption

Before the turn of the century, television channels originally laid the foundation for pushing tailored content aimed at appeasing specific types of consumers.[18] Newspapers and online content have since followed suit, with the latter offering highly efficient options to filter media consumption to fit the consumer's appetite. These three mediums, in addition to conversation with family, friends and peers, are the main sources of information on politics and government for the average person.

A 2014 study found that amidst growing political polarization in the US, 'there is little overlap in the news sources' of liberals and conservatives.[19] Americans are being fed vastly different political narratives, which only works to further polarize consumers and create hostility towards the other end of the political spectrum. Their beliefs are influenced less by content and more by the source; the credibility of the content is determined by the content's compatibility with the individual's opinions and emotions.

The mainstream media has largely been responsible for creating this polarization. Either implicitly through certain editorial calls, or explicitly by supporting a particular candidate during the electoral process, the mainstream media has largely failed in its duty to remain objective. The internet in turn empowered those whose voice had been drowned out, or entirely overlooked by the mainstream outlets. The notorious Breitbart News Network is an extreme but prime example of how the public's loss of faith in mainstream media has been exploited for ideological gain.

The near-universal use of social media in democracies has further enforced the ability to personalize media consumption. A study conducted as recently as August 2017 by the Pew Research Center reveals that two-thirds of Americans reportedly get their news from social media, including more than half of Americans over the age of 50.[20] The degree to which social media is tailored for individual users cannot be understated. Through complex algorithms that are certainly beyond my comprehension, social media discreetly locks us into tunnel vision.

Within these ideological bubbles, there is a lack of faith in empirically verifiable data, and credibility is derived from emotional reactions. The anti-intellectualism and disdain for so-called expertise in evidence in the United States and United Kingdom of late is being witnessed on a smaller scale but with equal intensity in India. And the encouragement for this comes from both sides of the political spectrum, the right and the left.

In fact, in India it has assumed a *sui generis* dynamic. For most of its existence for seventy years as an independent country, the ruling Congress party has exploited it's so-called 'secular' and 'pro-poor' image to put together a rainbow coalition to access political power either on its own or in coalition with other like-minded parties.

The following graph highlights the Indian National Congress's (INC's) electoral performance in India's general election, using percentage of vote share as the metric, through the decades. It is evident from the numbers that apart from a few general elections, the INC's portrayal of itself as the 'secular' party resonated with the Indian voter. Is this narrative based on political reality?

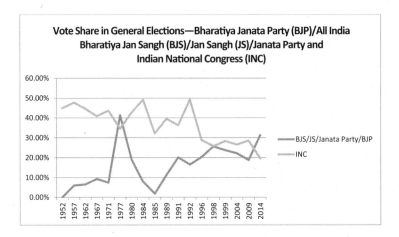

Source: Election Commission of India, http://eci.nic.in/eci_main1/ ElectionStatistics.aspx.

The data clearly illustrates that 2014 was a tipping point. It became evident that the Congress and its allies had done little

by way of social justice. Instead, they had used the secularism
narrative to sow seeds of discontent in India's social fabric for
political purposes. The 31 per cent plus vote share for the BJP
was a paradigmatic shift in India's polity. It resulted in the party
getting 282 seats in the Lok Sabha—ten more than the halfway mark. The NDA as an alliance won 336 seats, close to a
two-third majority in a house with 545 seats.

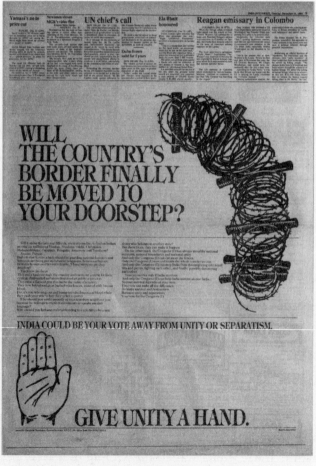

Source: *Indian Express*, 11 December 1984.

Following the tragic assassination of Prime Minister Indira Gandhi on 31 October 1984, the INC ran a diabolical campaign. The party openly fanned communal hatred against the minority Sikh community, to which I belong. In leading national dailies, hate-filled propaganda was published. The image on the preceding page was published on 11 December 1984, in the *Indian Express*, just two weeks prior to the country going to the polls.[21] This is just one example of how the Indian National Congress put fear in the minds of Indians against the Sikh community, purely for political mileage. The fine print of these advertisements illustrates how a concerted effort was made to portray the entire Sikh community as a national security threat—as one that wanted to secede from India, if not the destruction of India. A deliberate attempt was made to raise doubts over the patriotism of Sikhs—an 'us versus them' narrative was propagated, where on the one side were Indian citizens voting for the Congress (I), and on the other 'anti-nationals' who were baying for the breakdown of India.

These attempts to communalize continue to remain a key electoral strategy for the Congress till date. More recently, in the run-up to the Karnataka assembly elections of 2018, the Congress-led government in the state accorded the separate religion status to the Lingayat community—a blatantly communal move just to garner a few votes.

As discussed in more detail in subsequent chapters, the electoral loss of the INC in the 2014 general election, followed by repeated losses in state assembly elections, are clear signs that the tide has finally turned. The people of India no longer buy their pseudo-secularism, and as a result, the INC today faces an existential crisis. As the graph on the previous page shows, the INC, which started off with an over forty per cent vote share in 1952, in 2014 got less than twenty per cent of the votes. In comparison, the Bharatiya Janata Party or BJP (and its previous avatars) started from zero, and in 2014 achieved over thirty per cent.

Is what is *believed* to be true determined by empirical evidence or by prejudices? And how is this shaped? First, there has been this long-encroaching dominance of social media over traditional news outlets. While both platforms are susceptible to political tampering, the former is also vulnerable to a plethora of other risks, including but not limited to cyber threats. Alternatively, media consumption has moved to a platform where polarization is more likely and less visible.

Second, deepening political polarization—induced by conditions discussed in detail in following chapters—has set believability and compatibility with one's beliefs as the source of credibility over evidence. As a result, the variance of political narratives has multiplied, and the era of post-truth politics has taken hold. In the US and UK, this was exposed through the success of Cambridge Analytica, a company credited with influencing the EU referendum and the US presidential elections.

Cambridge Analytica was established in 2013 in order to participate in and influence politics in the US. The company's owners and board members are the same breed of right-wingers and Tea Party supporters, including the infamous Steve Bannon.[22] The company's intentions are made obvious from the company's uniform choice of clients. They originally supported Ted Cruz in the 2016 Republican Party presidential primaries, as well as other conservatives in local elections.[23] After Conservative Cruz failed to secure the nomination, Cambridge Analytica went on to support the Trump campaign.

In a nutshell, the company collects information on Americans, attempts to identify the issues they care about, and mobilizes the right while at the same time demobilizing the left. They do so through micro-targeting, which is the spreading of customized misinformation—information expected to strike an emotional chord with voters—through social media, advertisements, alternative media, and partisan websites. Cambridge Analytica further strategically 'drowns' other messages that do not work to their advantage by flooding their own content.[24]

An offshoot of Cambridge Analytica was reportedly also contracted by Vote Leave and other 'leave' campaigns in the lead-up to the EU referendum,[25] deploying the same methods to spread misleading information that would play to voters' anti-immigrant and anti-EU sentiments.

It is difficult to gauge the extent to which such behavioural profiling companies influenced the referendum and the presidential elections, but the influence itself is undisputable. The success with which people are swayed by false media and content is symptomatic of the current post-truth reality.

And this brings us to the core of the issue. Would this kind of diabolical manipulation of public opinion, of people's mood and calibration of behavioural response be at all conceivable in systems other than democracies? In a totalitarian system, one in which the press is completely absent, this would be unlikely. Cutting off internet services and other means of access to the outside world is more easily undertaken in systems where there is little or no accountability.

Annexure 1

Vote share in general elections: Bharatiya Janata Party/All India Bharatiya Jana Sangh/Jan Sangh/Janata Party and Indian National Congress

1952	
BJS	0.02%
INC	44.99%
1957	
BJS	5.97%
INC	47.78%
1962	
JS	6.44%
INC	44.72%
1967	
BJS	9.31%
INC	40.78%
1971	
BJS	7.35%
INC	43.68%
1977	
Janata Party	41.32%
INC	34.52%
1980	
Janata Party	18.97%
INC (I)	42.69%
1984	
BJP	7.74%
INC	49.10%

1985	
BJP	1.83%
INC	32.14%
1989	
BJP	11.36%
INC	39.53%
1991	
BJP	20.11%
INC	36.26%
1992	
BJP	16.51%
INC	49.27%
1996	
BJP	20.29%
INC	28.80%
1998	
BJP	25.59%
INC	25.82%
1999	
BJP	23.75%
INC	28.30%
2004	
BJP	22.16%
INC	26.53%
2009	
BJP	18.80%
INC	28.55%
2014	
BJP	31.34%
INC	19.52%

Source: Election Commission of India, http://eci.nic.in/eci_main1/
ElectionStatistics.aspx.

CHAPTER 2

Brexit

'I have also always believed that we have to confront big decisions—not duck them . . . And why I made the pledge to renegotiate Britain's position in the European Union . . .'

—Prime Minister David Cameron, 24 June 2016[1]

Context Setting

A poorly calculated and casually reached decision made over pizza at Chicago's O'Hare International Airport in May 2012 culminated, four years later, in this speech outside 10 Downing Street on 24 June 2016.[2]

Prime Minister David Cameron resigned after suffering a devastating loss in a referendum that put the United Kingdom membership in the European Union to a popular vote.

As the story goes, Cameron had been eating pizza at O'Hare while waiting for a commercial flight home following a NATO summit. He was with his Foreign Secretary William Hague and Chief of Staff Ed Llewellyn. The conversation that ultimately led to the unravelling of the United Kingdom apparently went something like this: We have a lot of Euro-sceptics in the party. Let us smoke them out. Let us have a referendum.

Cameron had been on the lookout for an opportunity to reclaim face and leadership, not only in Parliament but within his own party. As leader of the Conservative Party since 2005, Cameron had endured over half a decade of growing pro-Brexit sentiment. This was, however, now becoming increasingly difficult to contain. The final straw, it seems, came some months prior to the conversation in the pizzeria, when in October 2011, eighty-one Conservative members of Parliament (MPs) staged a rebellion, calling for a referendum to determine Britain's relationship with the European Union[3].

Members of Cameron's party had essentially backed the agenda of the UK Independence Party (UKIP). UKIP had, over time, reframed its identity to become the party of the 'left-behinds' of the country's economic development. Their rallying cry became the face of the growing anti-immigrant sentiment that would pull the United Kingdom out of the EU.

The rebel Tories supported Brexit for economic reasons, whereas UKIP supported it, at least in its messaging, for cultural reasons, calling for the UK's identity to be reclaimed.[4] Despite different intentions, the UKIP had a reputation for tilting too far to the right, and the Tory rebellion reflected poorly on the party's leadership.

Cameron sealed the fate of the United Kingdom in his January 2013 Bloomberg speech, pledging to hold an 'in or out' referendum among the British people. The choice, he held, was between 'leaving or being part of a new settlement in which Britain shapes and respects the rules of the single market but is protected by fair safeguards, and free of the spurious regulation which damages Europe's competitiveness.'[5] Voting to remain in the EU, according to Cameron, would be to renegotiate the terms of the relationship to rebalance the 'gives' with the 'takes.' The United Kingdom would maintain full access to the single market, while keeping the Polish worker out. This already indicated, in my opinion, early signs of major delusional thinking and which would in due course lead to a catastrophic decision.

The trends of growing anti-EU sentiments, rise of populism, and increasing nationalism can be tied into the greater shift on continental Europe. In the year prior and in the phase leading up to Brexit, the traction gained by boisterous populist politicians—such as Marine Le Pen of the National Front party in France[6] and Geert Wilders of the Party for Freedom in Netherlands[7]—had been seen to rise and then subside. This offered to the members of the working and middle class a pacifier to their economic frustrations: exit the hazardous EU. Yet somehow, the United Kingdom is the only country in the EU that has now ended up on a path of devolution or unravelling, from an economic and once-territorial monolith, on to a path characterized by fragmentation.

Descent to FUKEW

'I have no illusions about the scale of the task ahead,' Cameron said in his 2013 Bloomberg speech with reference to the referendum he had just announced.[8] This admission, as I discuss in detail in this chapter, is one of the few instances of accurate foresight that Cameron has shown in his political career. The remainder of his tenure as leader of the Conservative Party and as the prime minister is stained with delusion—delusion that has triggered the United Kingdom's descent to FUKEW, the Former United Kingdom of England and Wales.

The seeds of FUKEW were perhaps laid back in 2014, when Scotland conducted a referendum similar to Brexit, to determine whether it would remain part of the United Kingdom.

In 2011, the Scottish National Party (SNP) won a surprising, but overwhelming majority, in the Scottish Parliamentary elections.

Established post a referendum in 1997,[9] the Scottish Parliament had never in its short history seen a party win full majority.[10] Alex Salmond, the leader of the SNP and the first minister, declared on polling day that the mandate his party had received gave it the 'moral authority' to conduct a referendum on Scotland's full independence.[11] David Cameron, a year into his first term as prime minister, retorted, 'If they want to hold a referendum I will campaign to keep our United Kingdom together with every single fibre I have.'[12]

The narrative driven by the 'Yes' camp (i.e. those who advocated for Scotland attaining full independence) during the 2014 Scottish referendum, was much the same as those of Brexiters in 2016.

Scotland has traditionally voted to the left of the political spectrum in the UK—from 2001, it has elected only one Conservative MP into Westminster.[13] Post-Thatcher and with the rise of 'New Labour' under PM Tony Blair in the UK, Scotland had for nearly two decades, felt short-changed by the policies made in London. And following the Conservatives forming a coalition government in 2011, Scotland had reached tipping point in their angst against the British elite ignoring their demands. This was akin to Brexiters referring to the capital of the European Union, Brussels, as one steeped in bureaucratic dogma, constraining and limiting the freedom of London.

Beyond the narrative, the methods used, and the vote-base targeted by the 'Yes' campaign, too should have served as a warning sign to PM Cameron when he hastily announced his decision to conduct the Brexit referendum.

The pro-independence surge and mood in Scotland was largely fuelled by a grass-roots movement which was then capitalized by the political leadership of the SNP. While much of the grandeur of the campaign was largely financed by SNP supporters, it was efforts such as the one by the National Collective, which crowd-sourced £30,000 in under six weeks to stage an arts festival, Yestival, that really galvanized supporters.[14] And these supporters were largely those citizens who had not only not gained by the globalization process of the preceding decades, but were in fact on the losing side, with jobs in manufacturing, construction, and mining, moving eastward. They were predominantly working-class, performing blue-collar jobs, who got their education not in elite British institutions such as Eton and Harrow, but state schools, those funded by the government they had elected.[15] With British wealth moving further south in the UK, concentrating in and around London as the nation's capital became the financial services hub of the world, the disgruntlement among this class of Scotland was palpable.[16]

Alex Salmond, much like Nigel Farage, the leader of the United Kingdom Independence Party in 2016, would leverage this sentiment and champion himself as the messiah of the 'left-behind' Scot. A graduate of the University of St Andrews, which is known for attracting a class of Britain that Salmond now vehemently opposed,[17] Salmond became the face of anti-austerity which had come to dominate the economic discourse around Europe. He advocated a return to the pre-Thatcher days, where socialism and a welfare-state were the bedrock of Britain's economic policy, and steadfastly opposed big corporations, claiming 'The London Cabinet met in private behind the security screen in the HQ of Shell Oil. Big oil meets big government with small ideas.'[18]

And although the 'Yes' campaign eventually lost the referendum by a significant margin, the sentiments it was able to raise during the lead-up to the vote have come to dominate the political discourse in the UK. The 'take back the country' nationalism as propagated by the SNP, aptly predicted what was about to hit the UK two years later.

History

It would be instructive to briefly go into the period prior to and during British colonialism in India and trace its dominion to the present day, which allows for a fitting juxtaposition with the state of modern-day England. The story, in the shortest terms possible, is of how a small-time economic entity became an international corporation-turned-aggressive colonial power[19] within the blink of an eye, and as the saying goes, the rest is history.

On the eve of 1601, Queen Elizabeth I established the English East India Company (EIC), an economic entity which went on to become a corporate entity, which would monopolize trade between England and the countries along the Indian Ocean.[20] By re-exporting Indian goods to the rest of Europe, the EIC exploited and streamed wealth and fortunes from the East to the pockets of the company's officials in London. The company enjoyed the naval military protection of the British government,[21] who saw it in their best interest to stifle foreign competition.

The EIC's involvement with the emergence of urban centres, and financial and economic institutions inevitably gave the Brits unfettered political influence.[22] Over the course of three presidencies, the EIC by 1803 had built up an army of 2,60,000 British and Indian soldiers, which was double the size of the British army.[23]

The EIC was eventually nationalized in 1858 following the so-called Mutiny or the First War of Independence in India in 1857. Back in London, the House of Commons pegged the Indian rebellion and the unmatched bloodshed on both sides of the war on EIC's mismanagement. The company rule ended and the British Crown assumed control of India.[24]

The British empire continued to grow in size, hitting its historical peak after World War I, at which time it 'ruled a population of between 470 and 570 million people, approximately one-quarter of the world's population' and 'about a quarter of the Earth's total land area.'[25]

World War II brought with it the spoils of war. In August 1941, US President Franklin D. Roosevelt and UK Prime Minister Winston Churchill signed the Atlantic Charter, which set the stage for the establishment of the United Nations (UN) some years later.[26] In 1945 at the Yalta Conference, the 'Big Three'—the US, UK and Soviet Union—joined hands to design the structure of the UN, in particular the Security Council, which would be mandated to maintain international peace and security.[27] The Big Three along with two other allied powers, China and France, laid claim to permanent seats on the council.[28]

In the two decades following World War II, the United Kingdom—along with other European countries who are currently witnessing the severest spike in right-wing populism—opened its borders to lure low-wage workers to supplement its manufacturing boom. Workers from eastern Europe, the Middle East and North Africa, and the former colonies trickled into the country. Job opportunities were plenty; absent the competition with natives for employment, anti-immigrant sentiment was practically non-existent, and the immigrants were largely viewed as guest workers.[29] Social welfare was universally accepted among and heeded by all political parties, and it was superbly complemented by the country's economic growth. Brits had 'never had it so good'.[30] The United Kingdom was speeding forward and no one was being left behind.

Then in 1973 came the slowdown.[31] The United Kingdom found itself with a deficit in employment opportunities and a surplus of workers, many of whom were non-European immigrants.[32] The government attempted to incentivize the foreign workers to return to their countries but to no avail. Instead, the workers brought their families and reproduced at higher rates than the natives.[33] Unemployment in the country surged, and suddenly the natives in the UK saw immigrants as competition, as a threat to their national identity, and as unwelcome visitors who were blocking the natives' path to economic prosperity.

In 1979, the Conservative Party leader and newly elected Prime Minister Margaret Thatcher introduced economically conservative tax legislation. Thatcher deregulated and lowered taxes on businesses and the wealthy, which put smaller companies out of business and left fewer industries standing.[34] Despite the eventual redemption of the British economy, the vast majority of the working class felt alienated as the inequality gap widened.

Across the North Sea, communist ideology was being driven further east. The collapse of the Soviet Union in late 1991 fuelled a new wave of immigrants and asylum seekers into Western Europe, where the economy was once again booming.[35] This, paired with Thatcherism, marginalized the voice of the frustrated working class, creating an opening for populist politics.

In the UK, parties on the right capitalized on the blue-collar angst and anti-immigrant sentiments. Right-wing populists maintained their economic agenda behind the scenes, while prioritizing—publicly, at least—anti-immigration.

The UK Independence Party (UKIP) spearheaded this movement, with its primarily less-educated, blue-collar, white-male base at its tail. Founded in 1993 during a transformational point in the UK, UKIP called its base the 'left-behinds' of the country's economic growth and pledged itself as the people's voice against the establishment that coddled the immigrants. UKIP's base expanded in waves, most notably in the mid-2000s, when some Eastern European countries joined the EU, bringing with them another influx of immigrants.[36]

At the head of the UKIP was Nigel Farage, a man who would later gain international notoriety for his leadership style. Farage, a former Tory who left his party after the signing of the Maastricht Treaty in 1992, was elected leader of the Eurosceptic UKIP in 2006.[37] After years of the party seemingly gaining no notable traction, Farage, following the abysmal results of the 2010 general election, reoriented the party's agenda, anchored in pulling the United Kingdom out of the EU—his message essentially being that the UK's immigrant crisis could be mended by closing the country's borders.[38]

Farage was successful. In the 2014 European Parliament elections, for the first time in modern history, UKIP raced to victory over the Conservative and Labour Parties, winning twenty-four seats (Labour won twenty and came in second, while the Conservatives came a close third winning nineteen).[39] Farage's 'political earthquake'[40] was a turning point in UKIP history and a cause for concern for the other two parties that had grown accustomed to a near-two-party system, the Liberal Democrats already having demonstrated their willingness for cohabitation.

UKIP's anti-immigrant, anti-EU populist campaign continued to gain support in areas in which it previously had no political presence. With public sentiment clearly changing, members of the Conservative Party in 2011 rebelled against its party leader and Prime Minister David Cameron, calling for a referendum on Britain's membership in the EU.[41] Euroscepticism was not novel to the Tories; the party had regularly demanded that power be brought back from Brussels to London. But combined with the encroaching Eurosceptic UKIP and its supporters, Cameron was backed into a corner.

Given the populist nature of the opposition, Cameron was for all intents and purposes the least fit among the various candidate to tackle the growing dissent.

Cameron

During the inflection point of the United Kingdom's economic boom in the early to mid-1970s, when Brits were being tossed into unemployment, Cameron was beginning his education at Heatherdown Preparatory School, an exclusive all-boys boarding school reserved for children of the elite.[42]

Amidst a devastating economic recession in England, Cameron, along with classmates from the Royal family, ventured on a three-week trip to South Africa, led by the headmaster at Heatherdown. This trip was followed shortly after by a classmate's birthday party in the United States, where the schoolboys toured around New York, Disneyland in Florida, the Grand Canyon, and Hollywood.[43]

Around this time, the United Kingdom was on a turbulent trip of its own. On 5 June 1975, the UK held a national referendum—the only one of its kind until Cameron's premiership—to vote on whether the country should remain in the European Community. The similarity of the 1975 referendum to the one that would take place forty years later is baffling. Prime Minister Harold Wilson from the Labour Party had announced the referendum as—in Margaret Thatcher's words—'a tactical device to get over a split in their own party'.[44]

The Conservative Party successfully campaigned for the 'Yes' vote to keep the UK in the common market. But unfortunately for Thatcher, her party's successors would make the same mistake precisely forty years later, with far more devastating results.

Upon graduating from Heatherdown, Cameron went to Eton College, another all-boys boarding school. His years at Eton were once again seasoned with opportunities unavailable to his peers, let alone teenagers outside of the institution. His parents' connections laid before him internships and other career openings within the UK Parliament and overseas.[45] In his political career, Cameron has attempted to keep his Eton years in the shadows. As his political opponents argue, Cameron's sheltered life from one elite boarding school to another and his *two silver spoons* put him 'out of touch with the electorate'[46]— an accusation that would later prove true in his years as party leader and prime minister.

In 2015, authors Michael Ashcroft and Isabel Oakeshott released an 'unauthorized biography' of Cameron titled *Call Me Dave*.[47] The biography unveils Cameron's years at Oxford University, portraying the duality of a young man 'destined for a political career'[48] and a student derailed by teenage debauchery. At Oxford, Cameron was part of the Bullingdon Club, a society notorious for its illicit-drug use, an unhealthy drinking culture, and dubious sexual escapades.[49] While Cameron dismissed the rumour of his 'dalliance' with a severed pig's head,[50] the fact that such activities were commonplace in the society is telling of the environment that influenced his formative political years.

Soon after his partying years at Oxford, Cameron started working for the Conservative Party in September 1988, shortly after Thatcher was re-elected for the third term as the prime minister. He began in the Conservative Research Department where he quickly scaled the ranks. Following Thatcher's ouster, Cameron regularly briefed her replacement, Prime Minister John Major, and prepared him for the 1992 general election.[51] With the Tories' victory, Cameron had made a mark among his peers.

The years after, Cameron's career is a mosaic of flirting with parliament seats and the premiership. The Tory loss in the 2005 general election propelled Conservative Party leader Michael Howard to step down, and Cameron, by then an MP, began his campaign.

Cameron was the youngest among the candidates, which is traditionally considered a red flag, but which Cameron skilfully leveraged to his advantage. His resonance with 'youth' was impossible to miss in his campaign. His age and supposed relatability was seen as essential in gaining the support of the under-thirty-fives, who they had not been able to pull in the general elections. In October 2005, a month before the party elections, Cameron delivered a speech to the Conservative Party envisioning a modernized party anchored in, what Cameron described as, the needs of the 'new generation':

> We can lead that new generation. We can be that new generation, changing our party to change our country. It will be an incredible journey. I want you to come with me . . . If we go for it, if we seize it, if we fight for it with every ounce of passion, vigour and energy from now until the next election, nothing, and no one, can stop us.[52]

On 6 December 2005, thirty-nine-year-old David Cameron was announced leader of the Conservative Party, beating his opponent by a margin of more than two to one.[53]

Cameron had wanted to 'switch on a whole new generation'[54] and perhaps he truly believed he had successfully done so in the following years into his premiership. Perhaps he believed the younger generation of social entrepreneurs, businessmen and businesswomen would see the leader as one of their own. Perhaps they would overlook his two silver spoons and see him as a man who had experienced, understood, and sympathized with their struggles.

But when their support was put to the test, Cameron failed.

In the 2015 referendum, the votes of Cameron's 'new generation' were pivotal. Although the young people who did turn up at the booths voted in Cameron's favour—to remain in the EU—their overall turnout was insufficient. As the Liberal Democratic leader Tim Farron put it, 'Young people voted to remain by a considerable margin, but were outvoted.'[55] UKIP and the pro-Brexiters had successfully secured the older, less-educated, working class votes.[56]

This is not to say that Cameron was a failure as a leader. But it is undeniable that Cameron's privileged upbringing, his confines to the upper legions of society, and his rapid-fire ascension up the political ladder detached him from the people he so earnestly desired to serve. Regardless of his intentions, Cameron was a perfectly unfit contender to combat the populist insurgency of the right-wing Eurosceptics.

On the other side of the battle, the Brexit campaign was led by Nigel Farage, a self-professed 'middle-class boy from Kent'[57] with an arsonist tongue characteristic of a populist leader. He correctly felt the mood in parts of the country and rode the anti-immigrant tide. He tethered the resurrection of the British identity—a past-time homogeneous white identity that so many of the Leave voters yearned to return to—to the referendum. Essentially, he convinced enough people that remaining in the EU would put an end to the British national identity.

Privileged though his background is,[58] Farage convincingly painted himself as one of the 'left-behinds' who his party fought for. He fostered a connection with his base that in many ways Cameron failed to do with his. Farage's brazen and open discontent with the establishment resonated with far too many people. Cameron may not have been a failure as a leader of his party, but given his repeated miscalculations leading up to the 2015 referendum, it is difficult to argue that he did not fail as a leader of the Remain campaign.

Delusion Begets Delusion

'I will do everything I can as Prime Minister to steady the ship over the coming weeks and months, but I do not think it would be right for me to try to be the captain that steers our country to its next destination . . . I do believe it's in the national interest to have a period of stability and then the new leadership required.'[59] These were the hopeful words of a defeated Cameron as he delivered his resignation speech shortly after the results of the EU referendum were announced.

Theresa May was elected Cameron's successor, a Remain supporter who previously served as Cameron's home secretary. Given Cameron's delusion-tarnished legacy at the time he left Downing Street, it would be impressive for his replacement to eclipse his time in office. But in the time since May has taken office, the prime minister is well on the path to prove that delusion begets delusion.

On 18 April 2017, in an attempt to gain more power for the Tories in preparation for the Brexit negotiations, May called for general election, which was not due until 2020.[60] Polls at the time had been showing promising figures for the Conservative Party's success, and May thought she could turn these numbers into parliamentary seats.[61] The election, she argued, was 'necessary to secure the strong and stable leadership the country needs to see (it) through "Brexit" and beyond'.[62]

When campaigning for the prime minister's job, Theresa May had pledged to continue in the footsteps of her predecessor. In calling the general election in April 2017, she had succeeded in venturing down the same superfluously tumultuous path as Cameron.

The elections took place less than two months after May's announcement, on 8 June 2017. The Conservatives lost their parliamentary majority, and Labour gained seats. After the embarrassing results, May then resorted to forming a new government with the Democratic Unionist Party in order to secure a governing majority.[63]

Three supreme examples of delusional thinking and politics. One, the calling of a referendum that was not required. Two, allowing the referendum's outcome to be shaped by the uncertainties of democratic politics without due diligence, hard work and safeguards being put in place to ensure the nation's future. And finally, calling an election when it was not due and when the government had a comfortable majority. Where does it say that a larger majority in the legislature strengthens a country's negotiating position? Delusional thinking and taking political decisions based on such flawed analysis are clearly not in short supply in the United Kingdom.

Where to Now?

Already in June 2016, the British pound had plummeted to its lowest level in the past three decades. By June 2017, the UK had become the worst-performing advanced economy in the world, sinking to the bottom of the G7 economies (Canada, France, Germany, Italy, Japan, UK and the US).[64] The city of London is now scrambling to resolve what exactly the 'British position' is.

For the time being, London remains the financial capital of the world. One in seven UK jobs are in the financial sector, which makes up eight per cent of the country's GDP.[65] Within Europe, London houses the most number of large companies' headquarters.[66] London will likely remain the financial capital, at the very least, of Europe for the foreseeable future. But businesses and banks are seeking contingencies outside London, and the competitors are welcoming them in. London's loss of its financial prowess, it would appear, is not an 'if' but a 'when'.[67]

The dark clouds over Britain post its exit from the EU are not confined to the economic sphere alone, and have in fact raised significant existential questions over the 'unity' of the Kingdom.

In Scotland, the demands for another referendum over full independence are only growing. A majority of Scots voted in favour of Britain remaining a part of the EU, and most recently, Nicola Sturgeon has termed 'Hard Brexit', i.e., giving up full access to the single market while making new trade deals, and retaining complete control over British borders, being 'dead in the water'.[68] She went on to cite a report which stated that Brexit would cost each Scot £2,300 a year, and accused the Conservative government in power of being hypocritical in calling her and her party members 'scaremongers' as they themselves knew of these consequences.[69] Some reports, however, suggest that in the event of another referendum to determine Scotland's fate in the United Kingdom, Brexit might actually go against parties like the SNP.[70] It would be premature though to assume that come voting time, Sturgeon, who has been credited with 'doing the absolutely right thing'[71] in advocating for the UK to remain a part of the single market, will not be able to swing votes in her favour.

The situation is somewhat similar in Northern Ireland, which, like Scotland, predominantly voted to stay within the EU. It now finds itself in the midst of domestic turmoil as the two parties that were running the government, the Democratic Union Party (DUP) and the Sinn Féin, have opposing views. The former is a pro-British unionist party that wants to leave the EU along with the rest of Britain, while the latter, a nationalist party, has announced it wants to remain, and has called for its own referendum, for Irish unification.[72]

After spending a year on negotiating Northern Ireland's fate, Sinn Féin pulled out of the coalition government, and the country now faces the prospect of being run directly by its civil servants.

As Inter Press Service founder Roberto Savio succinctly put it, 'Only now the British are realizing that they voted for Brexit, on the basis of a campaign of lies. But nobody has taken on Johnson or Farage publicly, the leaders of Brexit, after Great Britain accepted to pay, as one of the many costs of divorce, at least 45 billion Euro, instead of saving 20 billion Euro, as claimed by the "Brexiters". And there are only a few analysis on why political behaviour is more and more a sheer calculation, without any concern for truth or the good of the country.'[73]

I would like to conclude with three passing observations. One, given that all indicators point to a downward spiral and unravelling of the United Kingdom in so far as its 'Great' and glorious past is concerned, surely the most obvious thought that an attempt be made to restore the status quo ante needs to be expressed. Surprisingly, there appears to be no consensus in this direction. On 18 December 2017, Prime Minister May made a pitch to Parliament whereby, during the transition phase, when both EU and UK iron out a deal, they would both have access to each other's markets. A large section of her own Conservative Party, however, is likely to oppose such a plan, and they baulked at this suggestion when it was made by Finance Minister Philip Hammond.[74]

Two, there seems to be little or no thought being given to the possibility that the collateral damage from Brexit could be much larger than anticipated and in areas least expected. 'Brexit or Remain' offered voters a binary choice, without making them aware, if at all that was possible, that many of the initial presumptions were flawed. To cite just a few: It was not and will not be possible to retain access to the larger European common market without allowing the Polish worker access to Britain's labour market. Two, groupings like the Commonwealth, an association of former colonies, are unlikely to take kindly to their students being picked on as part of an overall anti-immigrant posture and stance. India is a case in point. Those were the years the British mindset was partly conditioned by the ready availability of a strong trans-Atlantic alliance as an alternative, if the bureaucrats in Brussels proved difficult. This thinking did not factor in 'Trump' and finally there is irreversible damage in terms of standing on the global stage.

Is it at all possible to measure a country's international standing? If so, what would be the indicators/template or benchmark for doing so? Institutions and countries take years to build. This needs assiduous hard work, focus and determination, apart from clarity of purpose and vision. The upward journey is time-consuming and can cover generations. Even so, often it is the sacrifice of a previous generation that allows a succeeding one to enjoy the fruits of investments and wise decisions of the past. Equally, it is the astute individual who ever so often places himself, his group or country either on the winning or losing side. Adolf Hitler may well have been on the winning side if he had not made those costly mistakes, covered in an earlier chapter.

The journey downhill is much faster. Even the mightiest of empires can, and do, get unravelled in the shortest period of time. I am personally familiar, as a student of history, with the history of the decline of the Mughal empire whose causation lay in the agrarian crisis. Equally, the Soviet empire collapsed under the weight of its own internal contradictions. Would it have survived if its leadership had opened up earlier or did it collapse because of the opening up? The answer to that question is not as important as it might seem. In fact, it might not be important at all. A simpler working hypothesis might be to accept the position that it is almost impossible to sustain political and economic systems that are closed and inward-working, more so if they are surrounded by a sea of humanity that expresses itself and is anchored in various forms of human freedom.

There is much about the United Kingdom that I admire and greatly value. Its contribution to constitutional governance, starting with the Magna Carta (1215), King in Parliament, and finally democracy itself; from Shakespeare to Adam Smith, UK's contribution to modern political thought and literary culture is perhaps second to none.

At its very peak, the British empire, under the control of Her Majesty's Government, covered twenty-five per cent of the world's land surface area, and at one point or another, ruled vast areas of Asia, Africa, North America, and Australia.[75] Its crowning glory was perhaps its rule over India, often called the British Raj, which embodied all that was 'Great' about British imperialism, namely loot, man-made famines, and abject poverty of its subjects. The Raj is covered, to a limited extent, in the India Chapter.

The loss of India from the empire in 1947 was perhaps the beginning of the end of Britain's greatness. With the rise of the United States and Russia post-World War II, and more recently the increasing influence of China, India, and other developing nations in global affairs, have coincided with a fall in the UK's global standing. The Brexit referendum has perhaps sealed this fate—no longer part of the European bloc, it is difficult to imagine the UK's role in international politics. Worse, the impression one gets, even as the UK unravels, is that the internal dynamics do not seem to be getting any less delusional, at least in the foreseeable future.

CHAPTER 3

Trump and the Global Delusional Order

You know, to just be grossly generalistic, you could put half of Trump's supporters into what I call the basket of deplorables. Right?'

—Hillary Clinton[1]

Till he decided to run for the forty-fifth President of the United States (POTUS), Donald Trump was a relatively unknown entity in the global political arena. As a resident of the Trump World Tower in mid-Manhattan on 47th Street and First Avenue, I met him twice between May 2009 and early 2013, on both occasions at an annual party that brought the residents and Donald together. Like most others, I did not take him seriously. I wasn't impressed with his TV show *The Apprentice* either. This, however, probably reflects more my subjective worldview and prejudices rather than his qualities, i.e., those that impressed his support base. Having spent more than four decades in a profession broadly categorized as diplomacy, I tend to get more easily impressed by a good author, philanthropist or a smart politician, rather than someone who has constructed impressive-looking buildings in Manhattan—the sheer delight of living in apartments 34B and C of the Trump World Tower, owned by the government of India, notwithstanding. So, when he greeted me with, 'Mr Singh, are you enjoying living in the Trump Tower?' I had no inkling I was talking to the man who would be the forty-fifth POTUS less than five years later.

When did he exactly make up his mind to run? Did he always harbour the ultimate political ambition? Was this even partly conditioned by the tongue-lashing he got from the forty-fourth POTUS at the White House Correspondents' Association dinner on 30 April 2011?[2] This requires serious analytical context-setting. The jury is still out.

Context Setting

'Say what you will about Mr Trump—he certainly would bring some change to the White House.'[3] Amidst a symphony of cackle by White House staffers, celebrities and corporate big shots, President Obama took jab after jab at *The Celebrity Apprentice* star. Donald Trump, the reality-television star and face of the so-called 'birther' movement, had been invited to the 2011 White House Correspondents' Association dinner, having gained recent media attention for his tirade against the legitimacy of President Obama's presidency. The camera alternated between the podium—where the President paused in satisfaction between roars of laughter at what was clearly intended as a humiliation of Trump—and Trump, who sat stone-faced, unmoved, blanketed beneath the ridiculing stare of the audience.

The White House released a copy of the President's long-form birth certificate[4] six short weeks after Trump began questioning President Obama's birthplace. The reality television star was silenced. But while the movement died down, its ethos did not.

The birther movement struck a particular chord with the American right. It gave form to the sentiment of Americans who had pegged President Obama's tenure as the source of their growing dissatisfaction with their everyday lives. They suffered 'due to automation, off-shoring, and the growing power of multinational vis-à-vis their workforces,'[5] but they found it easier to blame their President, the first African-American to occupy the Oval Office. They viewed him as disconnected from the people he was mandated to serve. With or without reason, they viewed his trade and immigration policies as being flawed. In their view, these had robbed them of their livelihoods. They saw a cultural revolution led by a President they could not relate to. For these people, the movement served as a vessel to house and voice their unease. It was, in their eyes, a legitimate way to discredit a President whom they did not favour. Rather than risking being labelled as racist or ignorant by the left, they positioned themselves as protectors of the US constitution against a man who held a position to which he was not 'entitled'. To this group, it mattered little that the man they were attacking, though African-American, had outstanding credentials and was resoundingly elected the forty-fourth President of the United States.[6, 7]

Trump's public humiliation by the President of the United States was, in a sense, a harbinger of things to come. It might even have influenced the character of Trump's presidential campaign, which he announced four years later.

In an analysis of the 2011 White House Correspondent's Dinner, Adam Gopnik of the *New Yorker* writes, 'For the politics of populist nationalism are almost entirely the politics of felt humiliation—the politics of shame.'[8] Trump's ensuing presidential campaign did just this. His campaign's populist rhetoric leveraged the humiliation that the American right

believed it had experienced at the hands of the left. He played
to the ears of a populace ignored by the tide of the western
liberal democratic order; a populace seeking freedom from a
growing leftist voice that sought to shame and alter their way
of life.

It is far-fetched to assert that Trump's pursuit of the US
Presidency originated from a single night in the Washington
Hilton hotel in 2011 over some one-liners. In an interview with
the *Washington Post* during his presidential campaign, Trump
stated, 'There are many reasons I'm running, but that's not one
of them.'[9] But as Trump's public persona slowly evolved into a
treasure trove for entertainment and jest, his self-alleged thick
skin grew lean. Stack upon stack of jeers and taunts ushered
Trump towards his eventual realization: 'Unless I actually ran, I
wouldn't be taken seriously.'[10]

The question then remains: How did a satirized businessman's
efforts to gain public stature[11] result in the restructuring of US
politics and policy?

This chapter seeks to trace and understand the hidden
social conditions in the US—conditions predating Trump's
political pursuits—of which Trump was merely an enabler for
public reveal. It attempts to dismantle and examine the post-
Trumpian leftist mantra: Trump is the symptom, not the virus.

It is entirely possible that the United States had not fully
absorbed an internationalist African-American as President
and was not prepared to break the glass ceiling for a first female
president. In the final analysis, the Electoral College was won
or lost on just 107,000 votes in three states in the Rust Belt[12].
What this requires is that the undercurrent of angst be separated
from why the election was won or lost. The 'angst' has to be
addressed. Public opinion, like the proverbial pendulum, will
swing the other way.

Brewing Angst

On 8 November 2016 when it was clear that Trump was going to carry the Electoral College, our younger daughter Tilottama was, like many others, baffled. I had predicted the victory of the presidential candidate. Her disbelief was echoed throughout New York, where I attended an election-viewing party at the house of a former colleague at the International Peace Institute (IPI) and dear friend, John Hirsch and his wife Rita. I had been hesitant to reveal my predictions and under strict instructions from my wife to restrain myself in this group, which was by all standards a diverse but uniformly liberal one. Another colleague from IPI at the dinner reported that I was wearing a red turban, brighter than the fumes of rage that ravaged liberals only a few hours later. A particularly attentive French man, Arthur, reported that this was perhaps my way of signalling either my prediction or political preference. Nothing of the sort. I wear brown or red turbans on Tuesdays to take advantage of the calming effect of planetary configurations, as per advice rendered by Lakshmi early in our marriage. Having been married now for over forty-three years, this advice I have come to greatly value.

The warning signs for the current US political revolution have long been present. In a 2014 survey,[13] the Pew Research Center revealed that 'partisan antipathy is deeper and more extensive—than at any point in the last two decades.' Americans have gradually fortified their political silos, where an increasing number of people believe their opposing political party poses a 'threat to the nation.'[14] Thus for an understanding of Trump, it is crucial to first seek insight into his voters.

Victims without a Language of Victimhood

In *Strangers in Their Own Land*, sociologist Arlie Hochschild travels to the heart of the deep red to understand, with compassion rather than judgement, the factors that have pushed the right further right. Her findings can be split into two categories, discussed in some detail below.

First, the right holds traditions and beliefs that they think government impedes, making a knee-jerk reaction only natural. Second, these traditions, the foundation of their culture and way of life, are increasingly condemned and shamed by liberals. These communities held little to no claim to the changing undercurrents of a liberal, internationalist America, yet were expected to conform to its standards. These two factors, seasoned with a desperation to reclaim the American identity, created the ideological partition that hoisted a populist revolutionary.

For the first category, Hochschild holds that contempt for government is determined through the lenses of religion, hatred of taxes, and loss of honour.[15] In several interviews with Rust-Belt dwellers who identify as Republican, Hochschild highlights their commitment to politicians who 'put God and family on their side',[16] their religious practices overshadowing any other potentially pernicious views they hold. The role of the elected representative/politician in public office as servants to their constituents, then, must be to further uphold and enforce religious customs in public policy. This expectation creates favourable opportunities for Republicans with overarching agendas to harness votes through lesser issues that resonate with religious voters. 'The rich man's social economic agenda,' she writes, 'is paired with a bait of social issues.'[17] Deregulation, fated to harm these communities, is masked by issues such as abortion that easily elicits a guttural reaction from religious devotees. Government intervention in these issues, if not to work in favour of their held beliefs, could 'erode the spirit of a community,'[18] they believe. The cornerstone of their culture is under attack by big government, and it threatens to replace the sense of unity in their communities.

Their sense of unity and tightness in their communities is further put at risk through taxation. The right's hatred of taxes does not stem from a principled refusal to redistribute wealth, as some on the left may argue, but rather from a desire for self-controlled redistribution at the local level. Several of Hochschild's interviewees, despite aversion towards paying taxes, donated regularly to members of their community. Their means are different from liberal income-redistribution, but their intent is the same: 'To give those who are struggling (for) more security and opportunity.'[19] The government taxation system is too distant, too grandiose, and too ambiguous, they would argue. It encourages a practice of *makers and takers*. Hardworking Americans are exploited to pay for freeloaders who make no concerted effort to contribute to the communal pot.

But benefiting from government programmes places them in the same boat as the *takers* and strips them of their honour. The hardworking American does not depend on government handouts; rather than working to reshape the system to work in their favour, they prefer to live without it. In their eyes, the federal government had done little to support them, appearing only to draw from their hard-earned income or to penalize them. If they were not afforded benefits and support from the federal government—even if they themselves refused to accept it—why, then, should they contribute to providing these services to others? They believe the government poses a dilemma for them: walk down a one-way street where they give to the faceless and undeserved for nothing in return; or join the brigade of *poor me's* who live off the toils of other Americans and lose honour.

Hochschild's analysis provides greater understanding for why these communities support Republican candidates who seek to remove the social safety net from which they can, but choose not to, benefit. The result is candidates designing campaigns around fleeting yet sufficiently distracting social issues,[20] all the while discreetly tinkering with socio-economic policies that genuinely affect the standard of living and well-being of their constituencies. This creates, what Hochschild aptly describes as, 'victims without a language of victimhood.'[21]

Then comes the politics of shame. Each political party increasingly gets its news from TV channels and news outlets that lean towards their political views. Republicans rely more and more on Fox News; Democrats tilt towards supposedly non-partisan but reputably left-leaning sources such as CNN, MSNBC, and the *New York Times*.[22] In return, reporting moulds to best allure its audience. Hostility towards the other side festers. The right feels persistently attacked by the left-wing media, and feels it is depicted as racist and bigoted. The right believes the left attempts to instil a sense of humiliation in them, simply to carry on the right's age-old rules and customs. The revamping of the western liberal democratic order excluded the voice of the right, and now expected them to conform to its standards. Under these circumstances, the right sought 'release from liberal notions of what they should feel.'[23] They sought an outlet for their frustration and a voice that would restore their dignity that was robbed by the left.

Their search came to fruition through a candidate for the US presidency who transformed their shame into anger, and who vented this anger through rhetoric shunned by the left. He broke liberal-praised norms and political correctness and spoke to the aggrieved American in their language. The right empathized with the candidate who, himself, was a victim of shame.

I remember when I first came face-to-face with this angst early in 2016, when it was beginning to manifest in subterranean turbulence. During my time as vice-president at IPI, I had grown accustomed to the warm welcomes of the concierge at the UN Church Center, where the IPI headquarters on the corner of 44th Street and First Avenue is located. He enjoyed showing us pictures of his granddaughter, and my colleagues and I shared affection for his positive energy and wit. Then, almost overnight, everyone's favourite grandfather-figure substituted picture-sharing with pro-Trump speeches. At any given chance, he would engage passers-by to enlighten them on the rising champion, the 'man with change in his eyes'. He began taunting one of my dear young friends and close adviser, Omar El-Okdah, telling him to return to his home country of Egypt. It mattered little to him that Omar had as much of a right to live in the United States where he was born and whose citizenship he cherished as much as that of his country of origin, Egypt. Through Trump, the concierge saw a formerly unimaginable bright future for America, and it was one that did not welcome my Muslim friend.

I share this anecdote not to demonize or shame the concierge. Resolution rarely ever comes from tagging the opposition with labels that pose them an exception. Calling the concierge *crazy*, as many in the Church Center did at the time, sets him apart from the nationwide phenomenon. It sets him as an outlier, someone with a deep-rooted psychological problem, rather than a victim of pseudo-populist delusion. But this was a pattern across the United States. The left demonized and shamed the right, as many did the concierge. Dialogue was off the table, which only outcast him further from his liberal surroundings.

In the end, he disappeared from the Church Center. He stopped showing up for work, and few have heard from him since. A brief exchange with the building manager revealed that he was spending more time with his family. The concierge was not an outlier. He was a man filled with angst who held beliefs that were shunned by his peers; a man who bet on the winning horse, while his environment ridiculed him for doing so. So rather than dismantling the mind of the man who placed the winning bet, let's take a closer look at the winning horse, and how and why he snatched the victory.

Trump

At the height of distress in the dawning weeks of Donald Trump's presidency, as panic-driven liberals engraved words such as *unstable*, *vicious* and *aggressive* into Trump's media coverage,[24] historian Stephen Wertheim wrote in the *Washington Post*, 'Trump isn't an isolationist. He is a militarist, something far worse.'[25] As a student of history myself, with an eye trained for historical military leaders, throughout the course of Trump's populist presidential campaign, I had noticed signs of his delusion-ridden military obsession. His fetish can be traced back half a century to his youth as a *rogue-gone-vogue*.

'As an adolescent I was mostly interested in creating mischief, because for some reason I liked to stir things up, and I liked to test people,' muses Trump in his 1987 flagship book *The Art of the Deal*. 'It wasn't malicious so much as it was aggressive.'[26] This statement—which we can now judge as perennial—launched his short-lived military education.

Seeking to discipline his rabble-rouser son, Fred Trump sent Donald Trump to the New York Military Academy, a school reputed to '[whip] rebellious youth into shape'.[27]

Though unimpressive in his earlier years at the academy, by the time Trump graduated in 1964, he had left his mark, earning nicknames such as *big shot* and *ladies' man*,[28] and ascending to the rank of Captain. But the greatest consequence of Trump's time at the academy is not the early signs of his now-amplified public persona. It is, as his co-author of *Art of the Deal* Tony Schwartz asserts, Trump's adoption of social Darwinism. 'Trump felt compelled to go to war with the world,' he argues. 'It was a binary, zero-sum choice for him: You either dominated or you submitted. You either created and exploited fear, or you succumbed to it.'[29]

This sets the baseline for his presidential campaign and ensuing presidency. It was the rallying cry that the time had come for the neglected American right—who by their own account had been submissive, though liberals would argue otherwise—to take the reins. It was the process of converting the right's existential angst into furore and collective action. It was Trump spawning his army for his self-fabricated war with the world.

Failure of the Democratic Party: NObama and ClinDONE

I would be remiss to credit Donald Trump's electoral victory solely to the riled-up, marginalized, white-working class in the Rust Belt. These voters had long remained faithful to the Republican Party. Indeed, candidate Trump reinvigorated their political activism. But according to exit-poll data, the electoral outcomes of the Rust Belt were not swayed so much by an increase in blue votes, as a 'collapse' in Democratic support, with high rates of Democrats opting to avoid the voting booth or to vote for third-party candidates.[30] In almost all income brackets, Democrats lost more votes than Republicans gained them.

Questioning why the Democratic Party was abandoned by its constituents goes hand in hand with the mystery of Trump's ability to attract non-traditional voters.

Demographic changes as a result of globalization misled political pundits, who had, at the turn of the century, prophesied a growing Democratic electorate.[31] This is not an inaccurate statement. There are certain demographic categories—African-Americans, Hispanics, LGBTQ, and so on—whose majority will remain faithful to the Democratic Party for the foreseeable future. The political promiscuity of the minority within these groups, on the other hand, is the point of focus.

Their inability to commit to the Democratic Party may be explained through this question: How long can a campaign of *hope* be sustained until voters realize that *hope* is the end, not the means? At what point, does *hope* become a dead end?

The reality is this. The world's largest industrial democracy has not been able to adjust to a phase of slow growth and the loss of jobs in the manufacturing sector due to imports. The other sectors of the economy have also, in relative terms, registered lacklustre performance. For five decades leading up to the 1980s, the 'lowest 90% of Americans took home 70% of the growth in the country's income'. From 1997 onwards, the 'American people pocketed none'.[32] Trade, or lack thereof, has produced inequality, and Americans are upset. Promoting *hope* got them to get up and dust off their coats, but in the end, they had nowhere to go. As Thomas Frank writes in his 2016 book, *Listen, Liberal*, 'That's where we are, eight years post-hope. Growth that doesn't grow; prosperity that doesn't prosper.'

Given the seeming state of chaos in the United States under Trump's presidency, it is easy to reminisce about President Obama's tenure with appreciation. But absent the juxtaposition of Trump, Obama was not the revered leader he is today. His loss of popularity over the years exhibits a larger trend in US politics. In the mid-term election following his 2008 victory, the Democratic Party lost the highest number of seats in the House of Representatives to the Republicans in sixty-two years.[33] In the mid-terms following Obama's 2012 re-election, the Republicans seized control of the Senate. [34]

Whatever the factors influencing these results—and they are limitless—the downward trend was inherited by 2016 Democratic nominee Hillary Clinton, which further exacerbated her unpopularity that dated back to her early days as First Lady. She clinched the popular vote by nearly three million votes, an indisputable majority.[35] But this is about half a million less than the margin Obama held over Mitt Romney in 2012,[36] and almost six million[37] less than what he held over McCain in 2008. Most remarkably, 'almost one in four of President Obama's 2012 white, working class supporters defected from the Democrats in 2016'.[38]

Considering the social fragility brought on by the existential angst in the American right, Clinton was a prime target for pent-up anti-establishment anger. Looking past the various scandals used to destabilize her campaign, Clinton was viewed as the quintessential Washington 'insider'. She was the heir-apparent of the preceding administration, her presidency being forecast as more or less a continuation of the Obama years. Even Obama himself anointed candidate Clinton as the heiress to his third term in an address at the Democratic convention in July 2016.[39]

The American right sought a change in the status quo, but a Clinton victory would dupe them into another four years of growing uncertainty and into further retreat into their polar end of the political spectrum. This all goes to say that Clinton's loss can be explained in many colourful ways—ways that have merited and received its own dedicated book—but the failure of the Democratic Party must be given due credit. Its popularity has slowly been waning. Its mirage of *hope* can no longer be upheld; the people need action, not abstract promises.

The party's reliance on irregular voters—voters who do not vote unless 'actively inspired' and who 'can be easily discouraged from going to the polls'[40]—ultimately cost them the presidency and the last branch of government they held. Some devotees of the Democratic Party chose to express their discontent by staying at home on election day. Others tried their luck with a third-party candidate. But many decided to take a chance on a candidate who campaigned on deliverables, no matter how egregious the proposals were. The system needed a shake-up, and they were offered a candidate who epitomized a sledgehammer, ready to demolish the system and drain the swamp.

An Alternative Populist: Feeling the Bern

Early on in the election cycle, I had held high hopes for Democrat-pledged-Independent Bernie Sanders. The existential angst that was susceptible to Trump's pseudo-populist rhetoric could have been swayed by Sanders' populist campaign, had he been confirmed as the Democratic nominee. Though the outcome of Clinton vs Trump was murky and too close a call to predict, polls and pundits alike placed a Sanders vs Trump face-off at a Democratic victory.[41] Despite an abysmal turnout for primary elections and a Clinton nomination, Sanders was able to invigorate his supporters in much the same way Trump was able to activate his.

'Populist' is used to describe both of these candidates' campaigns but barring their catalytic potential and a certain degree of *us vs them*-ism, they bear no resemblance. Political analyst John B. Judis's *The Populist Explosion* offers a distinction between right- and left-wing populism. These two different strains of populism are key to understanding how uniquely the two men impacted political culture in the United States.

Candidate Trump followed the textbook formula for right-wing populism, 'champion[ing] the people against an elite they accuse of coddling a third group.'[42] In his case, the third group tend to be immigrants and minorities—the takers—and *the people* the American right—the makers. His campaign targeted Capitol Hill for sympathizing with the undeserving and for robbing honest Americans. He poised himself as the right's defender against the political establishment and pledged his service to hard-working men and women.

Sanders adhered to the left-wing populist approach, 'champion[ing] the people against an elite or an establishment'.[43] He sought to redistribute wealth from the affluent to the working people, to shift power from the concentrated few to the hands of the many, to provide a basic standard of living found in all other developed countries but absent from the United States. He proffered an antidote to inequality through socialist-rooted policies.

He remained faithful to his anti-elitism throughout his campaign, raising funds through appeals for small-dollar sums, the average donation having been $27; he didn't have the sums, but he had the masses, with over four million unique donors.[44] His gestures on the campaign trail confirmed his socialist persona. People used words like *authentic* to describe him—an adjective only otherwise used during the election to describe Trump by his loyalists.[45]

Characteristically, presidential candidates tended to stray far from the extreme ends of political rhetoric, aiming instead for the centre, where traditional votes remained a safe bet.[46] Both Trump and Sanders broke political taboos, venturing into polarized territory. Sanders refused to dance with 'fleeting' social issues and instead plunged headlong into the great plagues of American life, at the seldom-taken gamble of losing votes over politically sensitive topics. He stood at the podium animated with vigour, denouncing the so-called 'economics of exclusion' and fearlessly pointing fingers at elites who held considerable sway over the outcome of elections.[47] He didn't try to win votes through pleasantries or gimmicks. He wanted his voters to know, concretely and transparently, the strides he would take once in the White House. He was as he spoke.

Trump did not abide by the customs of political correctness and used explicit language where he saw fault. The list of his deviations from norms is quite impressive in its extensiveness— colourfully ranging from mocking a reporter with a disability[48] to calling Mexicans rapists.[49] But Trump's now-staunch supporters did not see in him racism, ignorance and bigotry, as the liberals did. They saw a future president who would not hesitate to communicate to his people using language unburdened and untainted by political censorship. Regardless of the sensitivity of the topic, Trump's candour would prevail. He would talk to his people as one of their own.

In this sense, the two candidates forged a personal relationship with the American voters. Sanders was impassioned by the fight for the ever-absent equality, both economical and social, and seemingly held no other motives for the presidency.

Trump was the relatable 'normal guy,' who lashed out when prodded, and whose character, however flawed and delusional, remained unscathed to his support-base.

Sanders' defeat to Clinton in the 2016 primary elections deprived us the opportunity to witness the populist crossroads where the 'hardworking' Americans would have stood. I will not discuss the reasons for Sanders' defeat to Clinton, of which there are many. Nor will I ponder how a Sanders presidency would have differed from the turbulent reign of Trump. I discuss the Trump and Sanders campaigns only to highlight what is all-too-often missing from all sectors of politics—in campaigns, presidencies, legislation, policies, and countless others. The United States, in short, was not ready for a democratic socialist.

In the United States and indeed elsewhere, discourse surrounding politics often falls into the trap of drowning in numbers, debates surrounding the broken political system, gerrymandering, or other such factors that overlook what lies at the heart of democracy: the individual voter. Qualitative analytics or policy analysis is inarguably important. But numbers don't reflect emotions; they can't express existential angst. Trump and Sanders connected to individual voters, and the connection slowly chipped away at the sense of political detachment that gives form to angst.

In the end, both Sanders and Trump were successful in leaving their imprint on American politics. But, as I predicted, the nature of Trump's pseudo-populism has proven most antagonistic towards the shifting sands of the world order. Though he himself may not be an isolationist, his polarized leadership has misdirected the American right's existential angst towards isolationism. The inequalities suffered in the United States will only be heightened, and the angst is destined to return.

Where to Now?

Because Trump is such an unusual President, the usual, run-of-the-mill templates for assessing the performance of past Presidents like the first hundred days or six months in office would not provide a satisfactory and comprehensive explanation. Clearly, if judged in the usual traditional manner, he would be characterized as an unhinged, delusional character completely out of sync with reality. Not surprisingly, less than hundred days into office, there were already whispers of a possible impeachment.[50]

In making an assessment of both the current state of play and the future, i.e., the remaining two years, a few caveats are necessary. He is an unusual President. He comes with no administrative and governance experience. He had not been a particularly successful businessman either. He beat an impressive list of sixteen Republican candidates, many of them highly qualified and with outstanding credentials for the top job. To Trump's credit, he read the national mood and the pulse of the people. What he said resonated with the segment of the population that preferred him over his Republican rival and his democratic opponent. Why this happened has been explained in the previous section. This section looks at the possible scenarios of how the Trump Presidency could possibly play out.

Having said that, we should bear in mind that Trump has a Twitter following of over fifty-two million and has not lost much of his support base of approximately forty-six per cent of the population.[51] He won by the narrowest of margins on account of the peculiar architecture and arithmetic of the Electoral College. Two years into the Presidency, he has not been able to deliver on many of his major promises: healthcare, the Mexican border wall, the immigration ban ('the Muslim ban', currently under consideration by the Supreme Court) and so on. He has also taken some very unpopular decisions such as overturning an Obama-era policy that allowed transgender persons to serve openly in the US armed forces, citing budgetary reasons that were later found to be inaccurate[52] (the policy was subsequently overturned by the US Supreme Court, only to be brought back under the guise of mental and physical health standards).[53] He has withdrawn from the Paris Agreement on climate change—his predecessor's signature international achievement—leaving the US as the only country rejecting the pact.[54] He formally recognized Jerusalem as the capital of Israel, breaking with seven decades of US foreign policy and stripping any prospects of a US-led mediation.[55] He has announced that the US will withdraw from the Iran nuclear deal, breaking away from Western allies and possibly inciting a nuclear arms race in the Middle East.[56] His attempts to earn a Nobel Peace Prize for denuclearizing the Korean peninsula have fallen embarrassingly short. He initially made negotiations with North Korea virtually impossible by threatening to 'totally destroy' the country of twenty-five million and by insulting Kim Jong-Un personally, calling him 'Little Rocket Man' and a 'sick puppy.' He then proceeded to meet with the North Korean leader at a summit in Singapore, where both of them agreed to 'denuke' the Korean Peninsular. A detailed analysis of the summit and its outcomes is provided in the chapter 'Global Governance', but it is safe to say that Trump's walking out of a comprehensive Iran deal and signing a vague and ambiguous agreement with North Korea raises more questions than it answers on his ability to restore stability in East and West Asia.

There are many examples, and surely many more to come. The question is what lies in store for Trump's future.

There are five possibilities: (i) He might succeed despite what is widely perceived as rank incompetence; (ii) He could continue for the remainder of his presidential term as a 'lame duck'; (iii) Given his propensity for gaffes and other costly mistakes, the GOP might replace him; (iv) or as a variant of (iii) above, he might walk out on his own; or (v) He could be impeached.

I spent a fair amount of time in New York, and the most entertaining reality show on TV was the process that led to the election of the forty-fifth POTUS. I have since been a keen observer of the ongoing theatre of the absurd. Clearly, Trump is not the only guilty party. The western liberal democratic order has refused to come to terms with his victory. Within the United States, the deep state and the fourth estate in particular are guilty of gross violations.

Two years on, it seems to me now that the prospects for an impeachment—given past precedent and with the Democrats gaining a small majority in the House of Representatives—appear remote, even if costly mistakes continue to be made. A party in power has little to gain by impeaching its own sitting President. Given the 'friendly' Supreme Court, the prospects for impeachment appear even more unlikely.[57] Any suggestion that the chances of impeachment have increased because of the mid-term elections and success for the Democratic Party[58] should be treated with a degree of circumspection. Impeachment is not possible without a certain level of Republican support, which we should not expect any time soon.

Trump has demonstrated his deep concern over the Russia problem, most notably by firing former FBI Director James Comey. It is almost clear that Trump will face criminal indictment for actions taken prior to his election and, at the very least, charges of obstruction of justice on account of administrative actions as President in relation to the Russia investigations. Five figures with ties to the Trump campaign—his first National Security Adviser Michael Flynn; presidential campaign adviser George Papadopoulos; former lawyer Alex van der Zwaan; former campaign aide Richard Gates; and Richard Pinedo—have pleaded guilty and have agreed to cooperate with the ongoing investigations, while seventeen Trump affiliates have been indicted.[59] More indictments and cooperation deals are likely to follow. Trump's personal lawyer Michael Cohen, who was involved in several of Trump's questionable business dealings (most notably a payment to adult film actress Stormy Daniels), is under investigation for campaign finance violations.[60] Unless Special Counsel Robert Mueller is fired—and even then, possibly despite the firing—the *Russia problem* seems to be the most likely form of the Trump presidency's decline.

Looking at Trump's cabinet appointments, it is clear that those in his administration are striving for the 'lame duck' option. In an article titled 'The Adults in the Room' in the *New York Review of Books*,[61] James Mann profiles three notable Trump appointees: Defence Secretary James Mattis, former National Security Adviser H.R. McMaster, and White House Chief of Staff John Kelly. With their military backgrounds, these men have been considered the icons of stability within a chaotic, incomprehensible administration, and Trump's best bet for a modicum of success during his tenure. However, in the short time since this article was published, H.R. McMaster has already resigned, and while John Kelly has insisted he will remain chief of staff till 2020,[62] given the precedent set by Trump, this might not be the case.

An article in the *Guardian* quotes Frank Luntz, a Republican consultant and pollster, as saying, 'With Donald Trump, every news cycle is a lifetime. Never assume he's dead, because he always rises from the ashes of some political or personal error. And never assume he's safe, because the next political explosion is no more than days away.'[63]

Conclusion

Roberto Savio, founder of Inter Press Service and now its professor emeritus, in a column[64] argues that many of President Trump's policies, like declaring Jerusalem the capital of Israel or withdrawing from the UN Global Compact on Migration, have little to do with American interests. Rather, these decisions are taken as they resonate with a certain section of the population, namely evangelicals, blue-collar workers, and much of rural America, who were left behind in the globalization process. Throughout the campaign trail, President Trump courted this vote bank, and ultimately, it was instrumental in getting him elected to the highest public office in the country. [65]

Given that voter turnout in America is only 55.7 per cent[66] (notwithstanding various measures taken to restrict access to voting), President Trump can ride a thirty-two per cent approval rating,[67] the lowest in the history for an American President, as eighty-two per cent of his voters, would still cast the ballot in his name.[68] Public opinion, and the larger American interest, therefore, matters little to the forty-fifth President of the United States.

At the centre of delusional politics is always the delusional politician. The damage that the delusional politician does will be assessed against the resilience of institutions. In the case of the United States, fortunately, the institutions are strong and will assert themselves hopefully to emerge stronger. Will other countries be able to step in to fill the void created by a

US retreat, either perceived or real? There aren't too many around with the capacity to do so. And even those that have that potential, appear both distracted and unwilling to step up. A certain re-ordering and reset will, however, inevitably follow.

Post Scriptum: The Trump Administration

Fire and Fury: Inside the Trump White House

On 3 January 2018, the *New York Magazine* published excerpts from the book *Fire and Fury* by Michael Wolff.[69]

The excerpts published by *New York Magazine* begins with Kellyanne Conway, the campaign manager for President Trump's bid for the White House, entering the campaign office in a 'buoyant mood', for she was going to have her cake and eat it too. Candidate Trump was going to lose, the blame would be borne by the Republican leadership, and she would in all likelihood land a financially lucrative deal with one of the popular news networks she so prominently featured on.

The excerpt, as much of the book, is predicated on this larger theory—candidate Trump was never expected to 'win' the election. His bid for Presidential office was to make him one of the most famous men on earth, which in turn would add value to his business empire, and everyone associated with him would get his/her own slice of the pie. 'Losing' the election itself was the end game.

Before going deeper into the book, a few words about the author and the tone of the book need to be mentioned.

Described in 2004 as the 'It-boy of New York Media',[70] Wolff rose to prominence as a writer by profiling the lives of the rich and powerful. His most prominent works in fact were focused on those who occupied the high-table in his own profession—the news media.

His reportage has been dubbed unconventional, and that '. . . he absorbs the atmosphere and gossip swirling around him at cocktail parties, on the street, and especially during those long lunches.'[71] A profile of Wolff by the *New Republic* describes his writing as '. . . the scenes in his columns aren't recreated so much as created—springing from Wolff's imagination rather than from actual knowledge of events.'[72]

Given this background, it should come as no surprise that the tonality the book adopts is more akin to a gossip column or even a screenplay for a Netflix special, than a book of either investigative journalism or of academic standing. It is at best a highly dramatized version of the first 100 days of the Trump Presidency, and at worst, a rather long gossip column on the workings of the White House under the forty-fifth POTUS.

Coming back to the contents of the book, the author claims that given that no one on the campaign team, including Donald J. Trump, expected him to win the election, each member(s) proceeded with their respective post-election plans—as mentioned, Conway had laid the foundation to become an expert on TV news; Trump proclaimed he could be the most famous man in the world with the most powerful brand in the world; Ivanka Trump and husband Jared Kushner would be propelled to celebrity status in the international policy community; Reince Priebus would regain control of the Republican Party; and Steve Bannon of Breitbart would come to head the Tea Party.

The author argues that everyone was ready to not win the election, and no one to win it. And it is from this preparedness or unpreparedness that the actions of the team would follow—from allegedly working with Russians during the campaign to the chaos during the transition period; from having no policy or even speech-writing experience in the team to not knowing what was going to be the President's legislative agenda.

The book goes on to suggest that once Trump did take office, his White House was very quickly divided into three rival factions, each with its own independent agenda, which was almost always at odds with that of the others. So, while Bannon tried to amplify the alt-right sentiments (the book suggests he was the architect of the 'Muslim ban'), Ivanka Trump and Jared Kushner wooed the New York elite, pushing for a 'Democrat' narrative. Reince Priebus—whom the book terms the weakest chief-of-staff to an American President in history—tried to anchor the Presidency in the classical, conservative, Republican ideology.

It is the recounting, and detailing, of how each of these factions tried to undercut the other, to mould the Presidency to suit their agenda, that is the most fascinating account in this book. Disagreements between party members, between colleagues in the Cabinet, between members of the West Wing, have always arisen, and will continue to do so. In fact, I would argue, disagreements between colleagues are vital, particularly in a democratic polity, for they ensure a leader is fully informed before making a decision. What is peculiar, and the aspect this book gives a very thorough account of, is the manipulative nature of these factions, and how ruthlessly they have gone after each other, to further their own agenda, with perhaps little regard for American policy. Chapter 20, titled 'McMaster and Scaramucci', which begins with the Trump administration deliberating upon the Afghanistan policy, perhaps best illustrates this point.

Ever since 'The Great Game' of the 1800s, Afghanistan has been front and centre in international politics between great powers. Post-2001, when President George Bush sent in US armed forces to rid the nation of the Taliban, the question of when the war would end loomed large over President Obama's two terms. It came as no surprise then that President Trump too would have to find his answer to this question. He was presented with two options—on the one hand there was Steve Bannon, who viewed American intervention in Afghanistan as a failure of establishment thinking and was steadfastly against the idea of having any American soldiers in the region. On the other end of the spectrum were H.R. McMaster, the National Security Adviser, and the President's son-in-law, Jared Kushner, who wanted to maintain status quo and retain soldiers, if not add more troops on the ground. What ensued between the two camps was a kind of personal war, with both using media outlets to undermine and denigrate one another. Bannon through Breitbart and its associates targeted the National Security Agency (NSA), labelling Kushner a globalist and interventionist, while Kushner, through outlets such as *NYT* and *Washington Post*, upheld the record of Lt. Gen. McMaster, showcasing him as a figure of stability, particularly when compared to Bannon, who was shown as disruptive.

What is interesting in this example, and many others that the author highlights through the book, is that under the garb of ideology, each of the factions inside this White House, is ultimately looking to cut a deal that serves its own interest. And there are no means that they would not use to achieve this end—the Muslim ban, the pulling out of the climate accord, the policy on Afghanistan, the bickering with North Korea, attempts to repeal Obamacare, all serve the purpose of one of these factions, often at the cost of the other, and most notably, at the cost of the nation.

To be fair to the author, he himself cautions the reader against taking the book too seriously. Right at the start, he issues an author's note which reads 'Many of the accounts of what has happened in the Trump White House are in conflict with one another; many, in Trumpian fashion, are baldly untrue. Those conflicts, and that looseness with the truth, if not with reality itself, are an elemental thread of the book. Sometimes I have let the players offer their versions, in turn allowing the reader to judge them. In other instances I have, through a consistency in accounts and through sources I have come to trust, settled on a version of events I believe to be true.'

It is perhaps fitting that the first documented accounts of President Trump's first 100 days in office are based on delusion and exaggeration. The President is known to have made exaggerated claims, whether pertaining to his business dealings or his personality, and the media too has published exaggerated stories of both his past and present. It would seem neither party is ready to shed the delusion and pull back on the hyperbole just yet.

For how long this delusional war goes on is anyone's guess— but its larger impact on creating a divided and increasingly partisan American society has become increasingly clear.

A Higher Loyalty: Truth, Lies and Leadership

Perhaps the most immediate concern for President Trump going forward is the Robert Mueller-led investigation into the President's ties with Russia. The genesis of the investigation was a dossier prepared by a former British intelligence officer, now a private investigator, Christopher Steele, who specializes in Russian affairs.[73] According to the dossier prepared by Steele, evidence suggests that President Trump had colluded with

Russian officials to win the Presidential election of 2016. While there are numerous actors critical to this investigation, none is more important than James Comey, former FBI director, who was hired by President Obama and later sacked by President Trump.

On 5 July 2016, James Comey, director of the Federal Bureau of Investigation made a press statement about the then on-going investigations into the former Secretary of State, former First Lady, and the Democratic candidate for President, Hillary Clinton's use of a personal email server during her term as President Obama's Secretary of State. In his statement, Comey made clear that there would be no criminal investigations against Mrs Clinton. Crucially, however, Comey claimed Mrs Clinton had been 'extremely careless'[74] in how she went about conducting business during her term. Fast-forward to 28 October 2016, eleven days before the country went to vote; Comey confirmed to Congress that the FBI had found further information pertaining to Mrs Clinton's emails while investigating an unrelated case.[75] This new information mandated FBI reopen the investigation into Mrs Clinton's handling of her official emails as Secretary of State.

It was during this period—July 2016 to October 2016— that Comey and the FBI were also investigating the Trump campaign, specifically George Papadopoulos, the campaign's foreign policy adviser, for possible collusion with Russian agents to undermine the electoral process.[76] Unlike the investigations into Mrs Clinton's emails, on which the FBI director so uncharacteristically made public statements, the Russia investigations by the FBI were kept secret from the voters.

Why were different standards followed for what the public should know regarding investigations into the two candidates vying for Presidency? Comey has tried to answer this central question more during the mega-promotion drive of his book, *A Higher Loyalty*, rather than in the book itself.

In an interview which lasted five hours,[77] Comey gave ABC News three reasons for these differing standards: first, he claimed Mrs Clinton's conduct with regards to her email server was made public when the inspector general for the intelligence community notified the department of justice and the FBI of her 'carelessness' and sought an investigation into the matter. However, the alleged collusion of the Trump campaign with Russian officials and the FBI's investigation of these allegations was not public information at the time, and given the premature nature of the investigations, he did not want to alert any of the potential culprits by going public. Second, Comey claims, he made public statements regarding Mrs Clinton's actions because she was directly under investigation. On the other hand, the investigations of any role Russia played in the elections, and whether or not any American individuals from the Trump campaign colluded with Russians, was a much broader investigation and was not specific to candidate Trump. And third, and perhaps most crucially, Comey claims the likelihood of Mrs Clinton winning the election (polls had her leading with a significant margin) was 'a factor' in his public pronouncements—he did not want the American people electing an illegitimate President as that would tarnish the reputation of the FBI as an institution.

Any analysis of Comey's actions, and their impact on the election results, can only take place with the benefit of hindsight. Yet such analysis is crucial to understand his role, for it had far reaching consequences—particularly given he was heading an apolitical institution. While it is meaningless to debate whether he should or should not have discussed either of the two investigations publicly, studying the stated reasons for the actions he took gives valuable insight on the motives behind his decisions.

Beginning with the first: while it is true that the investigations into Mrs Clinton were public knowledge, Comey's press conference in July and his claim that she was 'extremely careless' gave the 'crooked Hillary' narrative further credence. The FBI is an apolitical institution and there is little precedent of the head of the organization speaking in front of the press about any case, let alone one which was so high profile. To then pass value judgements about the accused only made matters worse, particularly given that in the same statement, he made clear that she would not be criminally prosecuted. To claim not doing so would damage the reputation of the FBI is based on a weak foundation, as there was no precedent for such an action to begin with.

The second reason, too, doesn't hold much water. If senior officials of the Trump campaign were colluding with Russian officials to influence the electoral processes, the voters perhaps had the right to know the FBI was investigating these claims— Comey's stand of 'upholding the credibility of the FBI' would have been far more applicable in this case. This is not to say that he needed to conduct a press conference—a simple statement alluding to the role of Russia in undermining the election using fake news, and the FBI's investigation of the same, would have served as a strong warning sign.

The third reason is perhaps the most crucial. For Comey to take decisions based on media polls of the election result makes his actions an act of politicking, a task outside his purview as director of the FBI. Moreover, it does serious damage to the credibility of the institution he was tasked to head, undermining his own principles. Throughout the publicity campaign for his book, and indeed in the book itself, Comey has tried to project himself as the last good Samaritan left in the United States, at a time when political discourse is at an all-time low; and when politicians would use any trick in the book to get elected. To then take decisions based on political arithmetic raises more questions than it answers.

Ostensibly, *A Higher Loyalty* by James Comey is a book about ethical leadership. The author gives a vivid account of the leaders he has encountered through his personal and professional life—from his first 'boss' Harry Howell, the grocery store owner for whom Comey worked as a teenager, to his own wife, Patrice, who he claims has taught him the most about leadership; from the Mafia boss Salvatore 'Sammy the Bull' Gravano, whom he helped bring to book, to Rudy Giuliani, under whom he helped rid New York City of the mafia's control.

It is not hard, however, to gauge the book is more than a manual on what makes leaders ethical. It is also not a memoir of a man who has led an intriguing life, having taken charge of some of the most high-profile public prosecution cases. Rather, the book is an attempt to display the virtuous part of a man's personality, who through his professional career has made attempts to uphold the truth, and bring to book those who took the law into their own hands. Ever since President Trump was elected, the media narrative, to put it mildly, has been unfavourable to Comey. His 'October Surprise' (reopening the investigation into Mrs Clinton just days before the country went to the polling stations) was heavily criticized on the day it was announced, and even more so once President Trump was elected. Comey's decision was seen as an attempt to undermine the candidacy of Mrs Clinton, and many laid the blame for her loss at his doorstep. Nate Silver, founder and editor-in-chief of FiveThirtyEight, and one of America's leading pollsters, writes that Comey single-handedly influenced the outcome of the election: 'Clinton's standing in the polls fell sharply. She'd led Trump by 5.9 percentage points in FiveThirtyEight's popular vote projection at 12.01 a.m. on Oct. 28. A week later—after polls had time to fully reflect the letter—her lead had declined to 2.9 percentage points. That is to say, there was a shift of about 3 percentage points against Clinton . . . In the average swing state, Clinton's lead declined from 4.5 percentage points at the start of Oct. 28 to just 1.7 percentage points on Nov. 4. If the polls were off even slightly, Trump could be headed to the White House.'[78]

Such narratives strike at the heart of a public servant, who holds himself and his office in such high regard. It is an attempt by the author then to share his side of the story, and to assert that the decisions he took came from a place of high ethics, as opposed to political consideration. The book is an unfamiliar place for Comey—a public prosecutor for most of his professional life, he is uncomfortable defending himself against the accusations hurled at him. The post of director of the FBI was supposed to be the crowning glory of his long career in public service—it has, however, become the proverbial albatross that hangs around his neck.

Having read the book, it would come as no surprise to me if closer to the 2020 Presidential elections, Comey decided to join active politics. Individuals of his stature, who take such pride in themselves, rarely go down without a fight. If he does take the plunge into active politics, this book will be regarded as the beginning of his political journey—where he introduces himself to those whose vote he seeks. There are signs in the book to suggest he has already made his decision—the references to him being a family man and his wife's unconditional support throughout his career; how a small white lie he told people would lead to him becoming a serial liar; how he got into public service to take on bullies (a not so subtle reference to President Trump)—are all age-old techniques of American politicians to make themselves look worthy of holding elected office.

The clearest sign of Comey's intent to join politics, though, is when one connects the first line of his book to the last. Channelling perhaps his inner Marc Antony, Comey begins the author's note by questioning 'who am I tell others what ethical leadership is?'; and concludes his acknowledgement section with 'Thank you for the joy and the journey, which isn't over yet'. I am not sure whether the author intended his readers to connect these dots, but nonetheless, they're telling ways to open and conclude his book.

Will we see James Comey run for President of the United States? If I were a betting man, I wouldn't bet against it.

CHAPTER 4

The India Story

'The mass is wiser and more constant than the Prince.'

—Niccolo Machiavelli in *Discourses on Livy*

'Tell your secret to the wind, but don't blame it for telling the trees.'

—Kahlil Gibran

'***K****itnaa hai bad-naseeb "Zafar" dafn key liye do gaz zamin bhi na mili kuu-e-yaar mein* [How unfortunate is Zafar! For his burial not even two yards of land were to be had, in the land of his beloved].'[1]

This was the fate of Bahadur Shah, the last emperor of the great Mughal Empire founded in 1526. At its peak, it extended over nearly all of the Indian subcontinent and large parts of Afghanistan.[2] It was the second-largest empire to have existed in the Indian subcontinent, spanning approximately four million square kilometres at its zenith, after only the Maurya Empire.

Imprisoned and exiled to Yangon, he died on 7 November 1862 at the age of eighty-seven.[3] His last rites were performed without informing anyone, with no vestige to distinguish where the great Mughal rests.

* * *

A Family Business—The Indian National Congress

A political party founded by Annie Bessant[4] and other Indian liberals, like Gopalkrishna Gokhale,[5] in the 1890s served as a vehicle for India's independence after 190 years of colonial rule. In 2017, it faced near extinction.

One of its members,[6] known for his proximity to the 'ruling family', said, on 7 July 2017, that the party had faced an existential crisis as distinct from electoral failures from which it had recovered in the past. "Sultanate gone, but we behave like sultans". This was viewed as open rebellion and he was chastised.[7]

The senior Congress leader stated that the 'Congress had faced electoral crisis' from 1996 to 2004 when it was out of power and also faced a similar situation in 1977 when it lost the elections held immediately after the Emergency. 'But today, I would say that the Congress is facing an existential crisis. It is not an electoral crisis. The party really is in deep crisis.'

He added, 'We have to understand we are up against Mr Modi, Mr Shah. And they think differently, they act differently, and if we are not flexible in our approach, we will become irrelevant, frankly.[8]

On 16 December 2017, in the lead-up to the State Assembly election in Gujarat, Rahul Gandhi, the forty-seven-year-old 'reluctant prince', assumed charge as the president of the 133-year-old party.[9] He became the sixth member[10] of the Nehru–Gandhi family to do so, replacing his mother Sonia who had held the post for nineteen years. The Nehru–Gandhi family has ruled the Congress party for forty years of its 133-year history. Rahul was elected unopposed.[11]

During the nineteen years that Sonia Gandhi was at the helm of the Congress party, the BJP had eight presidents.[12]

Gujarat is also where Gandhi, the 'father' of the Indian nation was born. Thereby hangs another tale, a successfully contrived narrative. Indira Gandhi married a Parsi, Feroze Gandhi, who was not a relative of the Gujarati Gandhi. Many believed, and in fact continue to believe, that with a family name like Gandhi, winning elections is assured. This is a small but significant starting point to study delusional politics in India.

A young colleague in the Indian Foreign Service related an interesting story. Amongst the thousands who came to greet Sonia Gandhi and her children, Rahul and Priyanka, after the Congress Party's unexpected victory in the 2004 elections was a person whom the children recognized as an erstwhile security officer assigned to the family. They could not recall the visitor's name. Before the person concerned had paid his respects and reached home, he had been traced and his appointment to a gubernatorial post was being processed.[13] What, I asked, would have been the reward if they had remembered his name? Pat came the reply, he would have been appointed a cabinet minister.

Many of us have been witness to this almost feudal style of functioning that has come to define the Sonia Gandhi era in the Indian National Congress.

In June 2001, Sonia Gandhi, along with Congress leaders Manmohan Singh, Natwar Singh, Murli Deora and Jairam Ramesh, was to travel to Iceland and the United States. On their way, they made a stop in London, where I was serving as the deputy high commissioner.

Their flight was to land in London in the wee hours, and I was deputed to receive the leader of the Opposition and her party members. Two instances from this meeting still remain with me. I received them at the aerobridge and took them to the Hillingdon Suite at Heathrow. After we had settled down, I noticed that not one of her colleagues had taken a seat on the same sofa as Gandhi—Manmohan Singh and Natwar Singh were seated at one end of the room, while the others stood behind their leader. Unaware of this 'protocol', and finding it rather strange that senior leaders of the party refrained from even sitting on the same sofa as their president, I decided to take a seat across from Gandhi.

The second instance, which I remember vividly, happened when we were leaving the airport for their hotel. As the vehicles we had arranged arrived at the gate, not one of Gandhi's colleagues took the rear seat in the same car with her.

I found this entire episode rather peculiar and was reminded of the 'divine right of kings'. Gandhi was treated and put on the pedestal as though she were a monarch in the sixteenth century, asserting power over her subjects in the Indian National Congress. It is still not clear whether this kind of subservience was demanded or was readily forthcoming. God, for the Congress party, was somehow synonymous with the Nehru–Gandhi surname.

The present day 'cult' status of the Nehru–Gandhi is largely thanks to Nehru's daughter, Indira. Facing a bitter revolt from within the party, she proceeded to systematically destroy the institution.

Much has been written about the legacy of Indira Gandhi. Many praise her for taking the bold decision to take on East Pakistan and liberate the peoples of modern-day Bangladesh; others are rightly unforgiving for she put the tantrums of her son (Sanjay) ahead of the interests of the nation.

Her ultimate 'gift' to Indian politics, however, is the deep-rooted dynastic nature of our polity. The Indian National Congress, which once had presidents of the stature of Subhas Chandra Bose and Vallabhbhai Patel, today cannot look beyond the Gandhi surname.

Under the leadership of another Gandhi, Rahul, and to an extent his mother, Sonia, the Congress party secured a total of only forty-four seats in the Lok Sabha—the lower house where the majority comes at the magical figure of 272—in the 2014 elections. The percentage of seats the Congress party secured was less than the 10 per cent benchmark required to be recognized as the leader of the Opposition.

The party, which was central to India's freedom struggle, and governed the nation for the better part of seven decades, today considers losing an election as a sign of victory and revival. In the 2017 Gujarat State Assembly election, the Bharatiya Janata Party (BJP), battling what was described as '22 years of anti-incumbency',[14] not only won the election, but also increased its vote share compared to the 2012 State Assembly election (up from 47.8 per cent to 49.1 per cent, a 1.3 per cent increase).[15]

The results of the 2018 Karnataka State Assembly election are even more striking. The left-liberal brigade, ever loyal to the Gandhi family, predicted Chief Minister Siddaramaiah faced no anti-incumbency.[16] It is interesting to note that this was the same cabal that had forecasted a strong anti-incumbency wave against the BJP in Gujarat. The Kannadiga people's verdict put to bed any such theory. The Congress party went from 122 seats in the assembly to seventy-eight. Chief Minister Siddaramaiah, unsure of his electoral prowess, stood from two constituencies: He lost one and won by just over 1600 votes in the other; sixteen of his thirty-two cabinet ministers lost their seats. The BJP on the other hand went from forty seats in 2013 to 104 five years later, just shy of the halfway mark. Notwithstanding the unholy and opportunistic post-poll 'alliance' between the Congress and the JD(S), the electoral results in Karnataka are the latest example of India's people demanding a 'Congress-mukt Bharat'; and perhaps a 'Gandhi-mukt Bharat'. A closer look at the electoral data, provided in the New Delhi edition of *Hindustan Times* on 16 May 2018, further illustrates this point.[17]

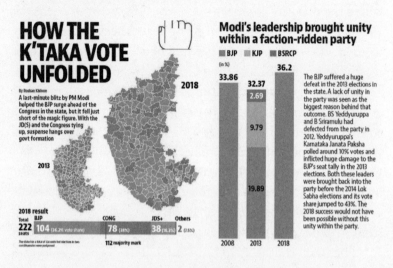

HOW THE K'TAKA VOTE UNFOLDED

By Roshan Kishore

A last-minute blitz by PM Modi helped the BJP surge ahead of the Congress in the state, but it fell just short of the magic figure. With the JD(S) and the Congress tying up, suspense hangs over govt formation

2018

2013

2018 result

Total	BJP	CONG	JDS+	Others
222 seats	104 (36.2% vote share)	78 (28%)	38 (18.3%)	2 (7.5%)

112 majority mark

The state has a total of 224 seats but elections in two constituencies were postponed

Modi's leadership brought unity within a faction-ridden party

- BJP
- KJP
- BSRCP

(in %)

2008	2013	2018
33.86	32.37	36.2
	2.69	
	9.79	
	19.89	

The BJP suffered a huge defeat in the 2013 elections in the state. A lack of unity in the party was seen as the biggest reason behind that outcome. BS Yeddyurappa and B Sriramulu had defected from the party in 2012. Yeddyurappa's Karnataka Janata Paksha polled around 10% votes and inflicted huge damage to the BJP's seat tally in the 2013 elections. Both these leaders were brought back into the party before the 2014 Lok Sabha elections and its vote share jumped to 43%. The 2018 success would not have been possible without this unity within the party.

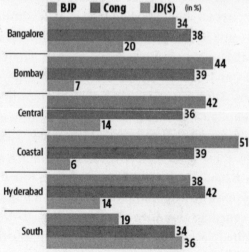

BJP got votes where it mattered

- BJP
- Cong
- JD(S) (in %)

Region	BJP	Cong	JD(S)
Bangalore	34	38	20
Bombay	44	39	7
Central	42	36	14
Coastal	51	39	6
Hyderabad	38	42	14
South	19	34	36

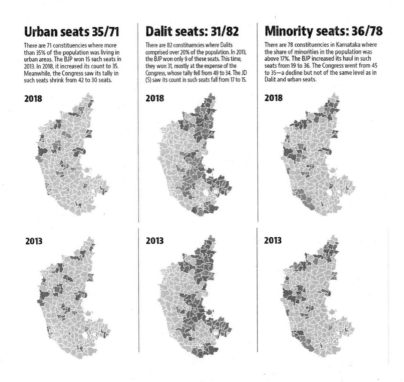

Urban seats 35/71

There are 71 constituencies where more than 35% of the population was living in urban areas. The BJP won 15 such seats in 2013. In 2018, it increased its count to 35. Meanwhile, the Congress saw its tally in such seats shrink from 42 to 30 seats.

2018

2013

Dalit seats: 31/82

There are 82 constituencies where Dalits comprised over 20% of the population. In 2013, the BJP won only 9 of these seats. This time, they won 31, mostly at the expense of the Congress, whose tally fell from 49 to 34. The JD (S) saw its count in such seats fall from 17 to 15.

2018

2013

Minority seats: 36/78

There are 78 constituencies in Karnataka where the share of minorities in the population was above 17%. The BJP increased its haul in such seats from 19 to 36. The Congress went from 45 to 35—a decline but not at the same level as in Dalit and urban seats.

2018

2013

Across demographics and regions, the BJP outperformed both the Congress and JD(S), particularly among the Dalit voters. Television pundits wrongly attributed a Supreme Court verdict, which sought to dilute the Schedule Caste and Scheduled Tribe (Prevention of Atrocities) Act, 1989 that protects those from backward communities, to the BJP. There was a concerted attempt to portray the BJP as an anti-Dalit party.[18] The voters of Karnataka showed they understood India better than the so-called 'experts'.

It is particularly important to note that the Congress's strategy of courting the Lingayat vote through vote-bank politics backfired spectacularly—of the seventy constituencies dominated by the community, Congress won twenty-one seats, down from forty-seven in 2013. The BJP, on the other hand, more than tripled its seats—from eleven in 2013 to thirty-eight in 2018.[19] The message from the people of Karnataka was clear—the age-old Congress technique of divide and rule would no longer work in an India that seeks development and not division.

In the middle of 2018, the BJP and its NDA allies were in power in twenty-one states and governed 70 per cent of India's population—a feat even Indira Gandhi at her peak could not achieve.[20] The Karnataka result was further proof that the BJP has cemented its place as the country's leading national party. There are two overarching factors that have propelled the BJP to this stature. First, under PM Modi, the party has India's most popular leader of the last five decades for it was under his leadership that the BJP won an overwhelming majority in the 2014 Lok Sabha elections. The citizens of this country are intrinsically drawn to his vision that places a premium on development, one in which meritocracy trumps sycophancy to a dynasty. Second, under the leadership of the party president, Amit Shah, the BJP has made a conscious effort to transcend India's social divisions and unite Indians under one umbrella. The BJP is no longer a Brahmin–Bania party, nor is it a party of Hindi-speaking North India. From Arunachal Pradesh in the north-east to Gujarat in the west, from Jammu & Kashmir in the north to Karnataka in the south, over the last four years the BJP has transformed into a party of and for all Indians.

What went so horribly wrong for the Congress party? At a general level, several decisions, which can only be described as 'delusional', need to be mentioned.

Three possible reasons suggest themselves, two of which are apparent: One, a mother's abiding love for and persistence with the less than successful and reluctant leadership qualities of her son; two, a 'dynasticization' of politics, where one family is above the party, and for some Congresspersons, above the country. The third reason, which is not so apparent but more crucial than the first two, is the separation of power and accountability between 2004 and 2014.

An interesting system of 'diarchy' was introduced in 2004 when the Congress won and this was widely regarded as an unexpected victory.

Manmohan Singh was appointed the prime minister but the Gandhis, Sonia Gandhi in particular, wielded political power.

On 27 February 2014, I wrote a piece recalling events ten years earlier.[21] I questioned in my piece, "Does India have an elected or nominated PM?"[22, 23] The reason for writing this article was a change in the constitution of the Indian National Congress, which undermined the foundations of Indian democracy.

As per subsection C inserted in clause 5 of the newly amended constitution of the Congress Parliament Party, a new position was created which was to be headed by Sonia Gandhi. The amendment read, 'The chairperson shall have the authority to name the leader of the Congress Parliamentary Party to head the Government, if necessary.' Thus Gandhi had the power to nominate a prime minister, who was to serve at her pleasure.

What followed had serious and far-reaching consequences— Manmohan Singh was to head a government, without having any political authority to make and execute policy decisions. His own cabinet ministers, who as per India's Constitution he was to lead, wailed and yearned for Gandhi.

'The inner voice of people says you should become the Prime Minister . . . Please don't leave us. Please continue to lead us,' exclaimed a distraught Mani Shankar Aiyar,[24] who later went on to serve as the Union minister for Panchayati Raj; Union minister of petroleum and natural gas; Union minister of youth affairs and sports; and Union minister of the development of the north-eastern region.

Aiyar wasn't the only Congressman to perform theatrics at the durbar of Gandhi. Kapil Sibal who served as the Union minister of science and technology and earth sciences, Union cabinet minister of human resource development and Union cabinet minister of communications and information technology, proclaimed, 'Our faith is only with you.'[25]

Both the above statements were made at the gathering where Sonia Gandhi announced she would not be available for the post of prime minister.

In retrospect and with the benefit of hindsight, it is clear that the interests of the grand old party that had facilitated India's freedom were being subordinated to the interests of one family. This observation has nothing to do with the qualities of Sonia Gandhi as a person or her political strengths and weaknesses. The act of 'renunciation', her decision to decline the leadership of the Congress Parliamentary Party introduced a new distortion in the functioning of parliamentary democracy. It recalled the psychopathic chant of the Indira Gandhi era: 'Indira is India and India is Indira'.[26] The office of the prime minister, to which a person with excellent credentials was appointed, stood diminished.

There were, however, a set of deeper issues which have remained unresolved, and which are being aired seventy years after independence.

At no time since its inception has the Indian National Congress been an ideological monolith. Even among its senior leaders, the ideological spread has covered a vast canvas from the socialists and liberals on the left to what today would be characterized as a conservative centre-right.

The dominant narrative within the party has invariably been set by those in power. In the ten years of the United Progressive Alliance (UPA) government between 2004 and 2014, the government of Prime Minister Manmohan Singh often found itself on a trajectory not just slightly different from but very often at loggerheads with the social activists and left-wing economists in Sonia Gandhi's National Advisory Council (NAC). Deep Joshi, Farah Naqvi, Jean Dreze and Virginius Xaxa were some of the members of the NAC who represented both the categories. If Indira's legacy was to introduce dynasty politics in the Indian National Congress, her daughter-in-law's legacy was to diminish the office of the prime minister and his cabinet, and by extension, the Parliamentary system of democracy practised in this country.

Sonia Gandhi not only introduced a diarchy within the Indian National Congress, but set up and headed a parallel cabinet which was more powerful than the one presided over by the prime minister. It comprised of individuals who were not elected by the people of India, but as per her own whims and fancies.

And as though this parallel government was not enough, the period between 2004 and 2014 saw the establishment of numerous Group of Ministers (GoMs) and Empowered Group of Ministers (EGoMs). In theory, these groups were set up to deliberate upon critical issues before they were placed before the cabinet. In practice, they undermined the leadership of the prime minister. Prithviraj Chavan, the former chief minister of Maharashtra and a member of PM Singh's cabinet, shed light on the heavy lifting undertaken by Pranab Mukherjee during the UPA years:

'In Dr Manmohan Singh's cabinet, Pranabda was the de facto number two. He was the chairman of more than 95 GoMs and EGoMs (Empowered Group of Ministers). I was a member of many such groups dealing with Enron, spectrum, WTO, Bhopal disaster and disinvestment.'[27]

Pranab Mukherjee, the senior most leader of the Indian National Congress in 2004, was relegated to the role of 'de facto number two', when he should have perhaps been the number one, particularly considering he was leading much of the legislative agenda within the council of ministers. In fact, I had the good fortune of working with him when he was the minister of external affairs from 2006–09, and I was serving as the secretary (Economic Relations). His knowledge of India, his relations with leaders across party lines, and his experience in dealing with world leaders, set him apart from most politicians I have come across.

Not only was he unfairly treated within the cabinet, given his stature, he should have perhaps been considered for the post of President back in 2007. The candidate who did eventually hold the highest office in the country, Pratibha Patil was a quintessential Nehru–Gandhi loyalist and in comparison to most political leaders, let alone one of the calibre of Mukherjee, was most unfit for the job. Post her retirement, there have been numerous reports questioning her propriety,[28, 29] and I too have witnessed some such instances first-hand during my days as a senior diplomat.[30]

From senior leaders of the Indian National Congress, to parliamentary democracy as established by the Constitution, no institution was spared. Such is the dynamic of family politics.

Illusion and Delusion—The Early Beginnings

The true architect of India's Independence was Mohandas Karamchand Gandhi. The South Africans enjoy telling us that we sent them a Western-educated barrister (University College London and Inner Temple) and they returned the 'Mahatma'.

Gandhi was also the quintessential politician. He had a 'connect' with the masses. The theory of peaceful social mobilization that he conceived and put into practice transformed the nature of India's independence movement. It was his towering personality and stature that essentially determined the shape of India's freedom struggle and its contours as a nation state post independence. That he chose to anchor the freedom struggle within the rule of law, through agitation by peaceful means, rather than violence and revolution, became the defining characteristic of the nationalist movement and shaped the coordinates of post-colonial India. The Congress party readily welcomed his moral and spiritual leadership and allowed him to provide the broad direction in spite of differences between individual leaders on specific policy issues or on ideological grounds.

Gandhi started, in every sense of the term, as a loyal subject of the Crown. His voice and personal effort to mobilize support for Britain's war effort, during World War I, was very much in keeping with his overall approach. After landing in England on 6 August 1914, Gandhi lost no time in mobilizing support among local Indians for the war effort. Witness this:

> I knew the difference of status between an Indian and an Englishman but I did not believe that we had been quite reduced to slavery. I felt then that it was more the fault of individual officials than that of the British system and that we could convert them by love. If we could improve our status through the help and cooperation of the British, it was our duty to win their help by standing by them in their hour of need.[31]

Two decades later, Gandhi had changed. In a speech at a meeting of the Congress party in Bombay at the beginning of August 1942, Gandhi instructed his followers:

> Here is a mantra, a short one, that I give to you. You may imprint it on your hearts and let every breath of yours give expression to it. The mantra is 'Do or Die'. We shall either free India or die in the attempt; we shall not live to see the perpetuation of our slavery. Every true Congressman or woman will join the struggle with inflexible determination not to remain alive to see the country in bondage and slavery.[32]

The head of the history department at Delhi University, during my final year as a postgraduate student, R.S. Sharma,[33] a bhumihar from Bihar, aptly described Gandhi's style of negotiations as that of a 'bania'. Gandhi, he said, would identify an issue, prepare an agitation and then pursue several modalities to achieve his objective. If his demands were met, he would 'bank' them and proceed to take up another cause. If the authorities felt the demands were excessive, he would be arrested and imprisoned. He would restart the process on his release. In either case/scenario, the people so mobilized and the movement so created, through the agitation, would be disbanded.

I was amused recently then to find some consternation regarding a reference to Gandhi as a 'bania'.[34] Whether he was one by caste is entirely beside the point—what is important to note is his attitude towards caste.

Gandhi was arrested in March 1922 and charged with sedition. Upon being produced in court, he was questioned by the magistrate about his caste or profession, as was the practice under the law back then. Gandhi replied: 'A farmer and a weaver.' Quite astounded by the reaction, the magistrate asked Gandhi the question again, only to get the same reply.[35]

While Gandhi may have been born a bania, his work in Sabarmati Ashram in Ahmedabad consisted of spinning cloth, experimenting with crop and livestock rearing. Gandhi, by transcending the caste he was born into and adopting practices of what were perceived to be of 'others', had a great impact on the social conscious of India. This 'awakening' that he helped achieve was critical to the nationalist movement.[36]

Gandhi was an acute realist. He had the correct feel of the pulse of the population in an economy ravaged by colonialism and characterized by lack of education, malnutrition and poverty. His was a carefully thought-through and deliberate determination that a struggle anchored in and through peaceful social mobilization would help shape the contours of a peaceful post-colonial independent India. In this, he was largely right.

This is not to suggest that there were no other contributing factors that convinced the British to leave India. Chief among these was the open resistance by Indians employed in the British Armed Forces during World War II. The architect behind this revolt was the former president of the Indian National Congress, and the founder of the Indian National Army (INA), Subhas Chandra Bose.

Post the fall of Singapore to Japan in 1942, nearly 50,000 Indian officers,[37] who had earlier pledged their loyalty to the Raj, openly revolted against their imperial masters. Bose's commanding personality and organizational skills reverberated among Indian soldiers, and his war cry, 'Dilli Chalo', became their rallying slogan. While initially the British were sceptical of the potential of this defiance, they would later admit, 'There was substantial popular support from the public in India for the INA.'[38]

Gandhi's role, however, had no parallels. It was his ability to link the liberals in the party and the elitist Congress lawyers to a mass movement that evolved into a broad-based coalition that was essentially responsible for India's freedom. It is not liberal democratic politics that won India its independence. In all fairness, the liberal political leaders had produced an effective critique of the British imperialism, which resonated well with the nationalists. Several of them wrote brilliant analyses of British rule but none were able to galvanize the masses like Gandhi to overthrow the Raj and lead India on the path to independence and self-government. As one of India's top historians Irfan Habib, himself a Marxist, recalls in a recent piece in an Indian weekly.[39]

> By the end of the century, Indian nationalists had produced brilliant critiques of British rule. Dadabhai Naoroji, the 'Grand Old Man' of Indian nationalism, published his *Poverty and UnBritish Rule in India* (1901), a collection of his writings of over some 30 years. R.C. Dutt brought out his two volumes of the *Economic History of British Rule in India* (1901 and 1903), and G. Subramaniya Iyer his *Economic Aspects of British Rule* (1903), all devastatingly critical of British rule, of the tribute Britain exacted, its heavy taxation, and its forcible capture of the Indian market. But they could counterpoise no large vision of a liberated India. *It almost seemed that what was desired was an improved or reformed British rule with larger Indian collaboration.*

In spite of the deep introspection and several fasts that he undertook, he was not successful in preventing the exacerbation of social and communal tensions and the deepening of fault lines. In many respects, the highly divisive policies followed by the colonial power and its manipulation by a section of leaders within the freedom movement led ultimately to a bloody partitioning of the Indian subcontinent which, in many ways, was Gandhi's greatest regret and, with the benefit of hindsight, his one remarkable failure.

The story of partition itself fits the title of this book.

The three actors of this story were Her Majesty's Government (HMG), Muhammad Ali Jinnah and the leadership of the Indian National Congress.

The flailing British Empire post World War II was in search of partners who would abide by HMG's geo-political interests. The Indian subcontinent was crucial as it was the location for the centuries-long 'Great Game' between Britain and Russia (USSR in 1947). HMG wanted to ensure that post 1947 it had enough leverage in the region to counter any Soviet influence in Afghanistan, and by extension India and the rest of South Asia.

However, HMG sensed its influence disappearing when Jawaharlal Nehru, the interim prime minister of India, announced that India was going to be a sovereign republic post independence.

Jinnah, the whisky-drinking lawyer too wanted a larger role in shaping post-independence India. Any objective account written on him illustrates clearly his aversion to extremism, and his desire for an adequate Muslim voice in India and not partition. However, given his diminishing role within the Congress upon Gandhi's arrival in India, he began perpetrating the partition theory.

HMG and Jinnah found in each other the perfect partners to achieve their respective short-term gains. Jinnah conceded the strategic and security autonomy of a to-be-formed Muslim nation to HMG, in return for the title of Quaid-e-azam in Pakistan.

Leaders of the Indian National Congress, largely due to their naivety, and in some parts due to their impatience, were unable to see through the final play in this game of chess. The more power HMG devolved to India's interim government in 1946 (with Nehru as the interim prime minister), the more it strengthened the demands for partition.

'As I have said for some months, Pakistan is likely to come from 'Congresstan' [acceptance of office by Congress party],'[40] remarked N.P.A. Smith, director of the Intelligence Bureau, perfectly summing up the final days of the British Raj in India.

Cyril Radcliffe, a London-based barrister, was flown to Delhi and given forty days to produce the strange political geography of an India flanked by an eastern and western wing called Pakistan. His arbitrary and ham-handed cartography succeeded in sowing the seeds for confusion and political violence in Bengal, Punjab and Kashmir. Just before his death, in 1977, he told a journalist: 'I suspect they'd shoot me out of hand—both sides.' He had good reason to believe so. The job he finished in three weeks resulted in hundreds of thousands of people being slaughtered, millions being mutilated or raped and tens of millions being forced out of their homes and livelihood.

The post-partition trajectory of the two nations too falls under the delusional category. It was predicted that a Muslim-only nation had more chances of remaining united, secure and prosperous, as opposed to a multicultural, multilingual and multi-ethnic country.

How wrong were they? Two countries, born from the womb of the same mother turned out to be radically different from each other.

From repeated coups d'état to the creation of Bangladesh, from being in perpetual civil unrest to being the epicentre of global terror, Pakistan today stands an isolated nation. India on the other hand is a success story of how a post-colonial economy, the world's largest democracy, stands at the cusp of becoming a great power on the international stage.

It is apt that I conclude this section by calling out the delusions of the dominant narrative that persists today about our erstwhile colonizers.

First, if the British Raj was indeed as rapacious as it is made out to be, how is it that we have so easily forgiven our colonial masters? Second, and more important, the manner in which the subcontinent was partitioned opens the colonial power to the charge of mass atrocity crimes and to crimes against humanity.

Gandhian Economics—Rise of the Conservative Right

Seventy-one years later, India and the freedom so acquired stand at a crossroads. Which direction will India now take? Will it take shape broadly respecting the Mahatma's wishes when it celebrates its seventy-fifth anniversary as a nation a few years from now? Or will the India story continue to remain the custodian of its 'elites', who, in an Orwellian way, have dominated the country's narrative for much of the last seven decades.

In 1991, P.V. Narasimha Rao, who was appointed the prime minister after Rajiv Gandhi's assassination, proceeded to thrust India into a globalizing world through wide-ranging economic reforms, lowering of tariffs, removal of non-tariff barriers and adoption of outward-oriented economic postures. He did all this, he claimed, within the framework of Nehruvian socialism.

Changes and reforms carried out over decades notwithstanding, most of the domestic consumption subsidies and other support systems put in place during the long years of Congress rule have remained in place during the four years of the Modi government, as they did during the Vajpayee years (1998–2004). Many of the economic policies followed by the Vajpayee and now Modi governments for poverty reduction and elimination are traceable, for purposes of inspiration, back to those followed by Indira Gandhi (1966–77 and 1980–84). There are, however, significant differences. I stress this for a particular reason. Rahul Gandhi's efforts to project the view that the Modi government represents the rich, the 'suit, boot ki sarkar', therefore, finds no traction.

I have never been persuaded that there is too much of an intellectual divide between the Congress and the BJP on the core economic issues facing the country. What has, therefore, changed now?

Ram Madhav, the national general secretary of the BJP, put it most eloquently in one of his columns:

> For the first time in 70 years, the high constitutional positions are all held today by individuals subscribing to a non-congress ideology.
>
> This time around, the president, vice president and prime minister are all from the same ideological fraternity that is broadly not necessarily correctly, described as the Conservative Right.

We have a new scenario where the ruling party would champion the cause of the 'humble' citizens and the Opposition that of the 'affluent'. But it will be a mistake to assume that the new difference is such a narrow one. It goes much deeper. It symbolizes a more profound and fundamental transition of ideas and ideals.

Many eminent leaders, from Swami Vivekananda to Annie Besant to Mahatma Gandhi, viewed India in ideas that a westerner would perceive as conservative right. Swami Vivekananda described India in beautiful terms as 'Dharma Praana Bharata (Dharma is the soul force of Bharat)'. Gandhi always spoke in his discourses and dissertations about Ram Rajya. They were not theological ideas promoting a theocratic polity in the country. They represent the genius of India, which is rooted in its religio-social institutions like state, family, caste, guru and festival. There is even an economic idea centred round work, sharing, happiness and charity.[41]

These are the very ideals that are now being implemented by Prime Minister Modi.

In an economy such as India, which confronts massive developmental challenges, where vast sections of the population still live in poverty, government support is essential for the livelihood of millions. This kind of support can take one of several forms, including that of consumption subsidies. And it is imperative, in fact it is the duty of a democratically elected government, to support and sustain the lives of these citizens by providing them with the basics for sustenance.

However, no country and most certainly no developing country, can afford to grant subsidies on an indefinite basis. Such support must necessarily be focused on the most-needy and be circumscribed by limitations of need. In other words, digressive subsidies, which provide support in a time-bound manner and ensure citizens are not entirely dependent on such mechanisms, must be the way forward.

The approach and method adopted in providing this support is what distinguishes PM Modi from the Congress party.

The Modi-led government too has continued with the practice of providing various forms of government support to Indian citizens. The difference between what is being done now from earlier periods centres on certain critical questions: What constitutes government support? For what purpose should this support be extended? How should it be provided? Who is the ultimately beneficiary of such policies?

Modi views these as a tool for empowering those at the very bottom of the pyramid.

He has empowered a vast section of the society by providing government support through direct cash transfers, rather than treating them as recipients of government largesse, which is ostensibly how the international community views overseas development assistance. And this has also brought about a change in the mindset of honest tax payers, who now feel their money is actually being used for the benefit of the nation as opposed to capturing votes for a political party, or, worse, for rent-seeking among public servants.

Schemes such as 'Give it Up'—which encourage citizens who do not need cooking gas subsidy to voluntarily forgo the government benefit—have yielded enormous savings for the exchequer, for they have limited government support to only those who need it the most. It has also brought about a behavioural change by creating a citizen-led movement for efficient public policy.

Ultimately, it is the view of the Modi government that government support and subsidies are tools for empowerment, and once more and more people achieve higher standards of living, the quantum of such support would automatically reduce. This is a completely different and new approach as it is anchored in digressive subsidies, and it seeks to change the view of government support—one from handouts and entitlements to one of growth and empowerment.

Unfortunately, at the dawn of our independence, conflict arose between the ideas that had their roots in this country's age-old wisdom and those that were transmitted by the colonizers from the West. Jawaharlal Nehru represented the colonizers' view, steeped in the 'white-man's guilt', while Gandhi became the voice of native wisdom. The conflict reached a flashpoint a couple of years before independence when a sharp exchange of letters took place between the two tall leaders of the freedom movement.

'The first thing I want to write about is the difference in outlook between us,'[42] wrote Gandhi in a sharply worded letter to Nehru on 5 October 1945. He reiterated in that letter his belief that village life in India should get more focus as 'crores of people will never be able to live at peace with one another in towns and palaces'.[43]

Nehru replied from Allahabad four days later on 9 October. His retort was also strident. 'I do not understand why a village should necessarily embody truth and non-violence. A village, normally speaking, is backward, intellectually and culturally, and no progress can be made from a backward environment. Narrow-minded people are much more likely to be untruthful and violent,[44] he wrote.

If the difference (in our outlook) is so fundamental, then the public should also be made aware of it, pleaded Gandhi. Nehru knew the pitfalls of letting people of the country know that he and Gandhi had fundamental differences in their outlook about the direction of the nation. He requested Gandhi not to insist upon making the differences public at this juncture and let them be resolved by the people after independence.[45]

On the seventy-first anniversary of India's independence, it is useful to recall the above. These facts are a pointer to deeper issues that remain unresolved. They raise questions about the nature of the Indian state that is evolving. More importantly, these issues have not been frontally addressed.

For most of the seventy years that it was in power, the ruling party nursed a large constituency of liberal, left-wing 'do-gooders', some with intellectual pretensions, others with well-deserved reputations. They were not against the state *per se*. Perhaps they wanted and continue to want a weak or helpless state that would on the one hand allow individual expression and freedom to flourish, and on the other would institutionalize an entitlement culture where government benefits would be handed to all and sundry. What is even more alarming is that they appear to want the state, already handicapped by limited capability, to be challenged. This is precisely the kind of thinking that was anchored in Western political thought before terrorism hit them full force. The battle for human rights, or so it was thought, was one between a helpless individual and a strong, all powerful state that stifled, undermined and deprived the human being. The rise of the non-state actor, including the non-state military actor, was outside the comprehension of such thinking. Reality has a way of driving home a comprehensive wake-up call, a reality check, which makes this an existential issue, one of survival.

The Secularism Debate—Hypocrisy within Our Midst

Is secularism under threat in India? If yes, since when and from where is that threat emanating?

Those on the left of the political spectrum, who have thus far dominated the political discourse in India, paint the secular discussion as the majority i.e. Hindu, versus minority, i.e. Muslim.

They argue that since a majority of the Indians believe in the Hindu faith, those who practise Islam are under constant threat. They would like the nation to believe the Hindus of the country are out to get the Muslims—whether this is a colonial hangover is best answered by a distinguished sociologist, but in my view, this is pure delusional politics, which uses victimization for votes. Before calling out the hypocrisy of this discourse, it is important to address the issue of lynching of those belonging to the Muslim faith or a lower caste. At one stage, there seemed to have been an increase in the number of such cases.

Even one case of lynching should be roundly condemned and be regarded as one too many. There has to be zero tolerance for such and other acts of bestiality and criminality. That the miscreants drew inspiration and, in some cases, even encouragement from a 'saffronized' authority now in power has been alleged but not conclusively proved. But to focus on just this one aspect of a crime so heinous only helps draw political mileage and doesn't necessarily solve the problem.

The explanation, the real, underlying cause, can be found in the enabling environment characterized by the complete absence of any sense of accountability and a culture of impunity prevalent in large parts of the Hindi heartland, in the very cow belt that has been allowed to go unpunished for seven decades under various governments headed either by the Congress party, or the plethora of parties that call themselves 'secular and socialist'.

Aroon Purie, writing as editor-in-chief of *India Today* on 14 July 2017, stated Ashis Nandy's reference to a 'chartered accountancy of violence'.[46] This is interesting because the people who plan these attacks, he says, are not driven by faith or fanaticism but by calculations of political power. He says lynchings are a manifestation of a new type of abstracted, free floating violence seeking a soft target. The deeper reason is that underlying tensions in society cause such resentments to explode into rage. Social mobility has not gone hand in hand with social cohesion. People are living in cities without imbibing civil values. Anyone who looks, prays, eats and lives differently from the majority becomes the enemy.

Sociologist Dipankar Gupta ascribes it to the imperfect establishment of the rule of law. 'Violence is also endemic where law enforcement officials are ambiguous about their role or are partisan in the performance of their duties'.[47]

And here I would like to point out the hypocrisy peddled by Indian liberals under the garb of strengthening Indian secularism.

As per these individuals, any public display of embracing religion in India is fine, as long as it is not Hinduism. To call oneself a Hindu draws ire and labels such as communal if not worse. The following example illustrates this point:

When Prime Minister Narendra Modi refused to wear a skull cap offered to him by a maulana in 2011, he was chastised by liberals for being disrespectful to Indian Muslims.

Rahul Gandhi too recently was chastised for stoking communalism, but this time for embracing his Hindu faith! On the campaign trail during the 2017 Gujarat State Assembly election, the Congress scion was photographed offering prayers at Hindu temples, and a leaked video showed him telling party workers he was a Shivaite.

In no other country, do we see the faith of the majority so routinely treated as the 'other'. The majority Hindu population, its faith and cultures, are tolerant and have contributed to the peace and harmony such a diverse population enjoys. The public acceptance of one faith over another is a deeply divisive tactic deployed for political gain, and it's time to call out those who have peddled this argument for decades.

More than seventy years after independence, 224 million Indians still live below the poverty line and India accounts for one-third of the world's poor.[48] Much of our physical infrastructure, railways, roads, ports, etc., need huge infusion of capital. More importantly, two of our crucial 'systems'—healthcare and education—are falling apart. They need improvement and reform to give the average Indian citizen a decent chance for a normal subsistence-level existence.

The only real way forward to counter this communal versus secular discourse is to put India in a high growth path and address the challenge of poverty, and abject poverty, of these 172 million.

Prime Minister Modi's Sabka Saath, Sabka Vikas motto—vision of equal development for all sections of society—has the potential to transcend these issues of caste and religion. When the entire country grows, and reaps the benefits of economic development, our peaceful ethos only gets strengthened.

'Sabka Saath, Sabka Vikas'—India's Last Chance

On 9 August 2017, the seventy-fifth anniversary of the Quit India movement, Prime Minister Narendra Modi asked the people of India to take a pledge to free the country of problems like communalism, casteism and corruption and create a 'new India' by 2022.

He saluted all those who participated in the historic movement in 1942 under the leadership of Mahatma Gandhi and asked people to take inspiration from that.

In a series of tweets, he noted that the entire nation had come together under the leadership of Mahatma Gandhi with the aim of attaining freedom.

'On the 75th anniversary of the historic Quit India movement, we salute all the great women & men who took part in the movement,' he wrote.[49]

'In 1942, the need of the hour was to free India from colonialism. Today, 75 years later the issues are different,' he added.[50]

'Let us pledge to free India from poverty, dirt, corruption, terrorism, casteism, communalism and create a "New India" of our dreams by 2022,' he said.[51]

Giving the slogan of 'Sankalp se Siddhi' (pledge to achieve), he urged the people to work shoulder to shoulder 'to create the India that our freedom fighters would be proud of'.[52]

Seventy years later, the political transformation that India is witnessing—following the May 2014 Lok Sabha elections and subsequent state assembly elections—is again anchored, at one level, in a spectacular bid to connect to the masses cutting across ideological, religious and caste divisions which in terms of a framework is inspirationally anchored in development. Will this effort succeed? More importantly, can this effort succeed given that the 'state' which has to deliver on Prime Minister Modi's bold vision for a New India by 2022 and implement the desired transformation continues to display severe limitations? This is, in several respects, India's last chance.

There are two perceptions of India, seemingly contradictory but in reality complimentary, that need to be understood and assessed to obtain a realistic picture of the state of play on the India story as it is unfolding.

India is an old civilization—going back five or even seven thousand years. Prior to British colonization, India accounted, in 1700, for 27 per cent of global output, as pointed out by the Cambridge historian Angus Maddison.[53] Arthur Llewellyn Basham's *The Wonder That Was India* and Sunil Khilnani's *The Idea of India* further elucidate India's syncretic and multi-lingual identity. Moreover, India is the most successful story of post-colonial reconstruction after 190 years of colonial rule. It is today a polyglot, secular country, the world's largest democracy, a 2.8 trillion dollar economy[54] with a rate of growth, which is one of the fastest amongst emerging economies. In a nutshell, India is a country that would appear to have everything going for it.

At the same time, after 70 years of colonial rule, India still falls under the 'developing country' category and is plagued by social fault-lines, particularly along the lines of caste.

In spite of all the praise that is showered on India's performance as a successful example of post-colonial reconstruction, India's large population of over 1.25 billion people has more poor people than there are in all the least-developed countries of the world put together. A graphic illustration of India's poverty lies in the fact that millions of Indians still do not have access to toilets.

A young colleague who worked with me in the Defence Ministry and who is now associated with the Swachh Bharat Mission (SBM) assured me that the total number of persons defecating out in the open has seen drastic reduction. He estimated that in 2017, the figure had come down from 520 million to 320 million, thanks to the efforts of the SBM. I invariably express my admiration to him. The very fact that a task of this nature has been accorded priority by successive governments is in and of itself commendable. There is no escaping the fact that according to my friend's statistics, at the time of my meeting with him, 320 million still went out into the open fields to answer the call of nature every morning. This is more than the entire population of the Brazil, Canada and Mexico put together.

In a short span of four years, the Narendra Modi-led government has secured for India a 62-place jump in the World Bank's Ease of Doing Business Index—from a rank of 142 to 77. Credit rating agencies Moody's and Standard & Poor's have backed the government's reform agenda—with the former improving India's credit rating, and the latter reaffirming the government's sound external accounts position, management of fiscal deficit, and improved monetary credibility set the tone.

The Sabka Saath, Sabka Vikas mantra of the present government is predicated on creating a corruption-free, citizen-centric, development-friendly ecosystem in the country.[55]

What has brought about this turnaround? If one were to cast their minds back to the years 2010–2013, the forecasts for the Indian economy sang an entirely different tune. I would submit that the NDA government has not just reformed, but re-formed three critical areas of both India's society and its economy.

First, there has been an unflinching commitment to literally 'building' India's infrastructure. In the first four years of the Modi government, it sanctioned construction of 51,073 km of national highways as compared to 25,158 km in the preceding four years. The rate of construction achieved in the year 2017 was 27 km per day.[56] In civil aviation, the UDAAN scheme has been a resounding success—India's civil aviation sector has grown between 18 and 20 per cent under the Modi government and, as of May 2018, stands just behind that of USA and China in terms of passenger trips.[57] In urban development, more than 60 lakh household toilets and over 4.3 lakh community toilets have been constructed, and 75 per cent of all wards have door-to-door waste collection under the SBM. Under the Pradhan Mantri Aawas Yojana, the government has sanctioned construction of over 6.3 million homes, of which more than 800,000 have been occupied in four years (as of August 2018). More importantly, the titles of these homes is under the lady of the house or co-jointly, securing her financial future and thereby providing a fillip to women's empowerment. As a comparison, under the Jawaharlal Nehru National Urban Renewal Mission and Rajiv Gandhi Awas Yojana, in ten years, the UPA was able to sanction construction of 1.34 million. As minister for housing and urban affairs, I am confident of meeting my (SBM) target of open defecation-free cities and 100 per cent door-to-door waste collection by 2 October 2019. Under PMAY, 12 million homes will be sanctioned before the end of 2019, much ahead of the target year of 2022.

Second, the government has shown that investment in 'hard infrastructure' need not come at the cost of 'softer' needs. Prime Minister Modi's devotion to achieving swacchata in India is perhaps the best example. While SBM targets building infrastructure, the social movement for swacchata is above all focused on human security. The ethos of the movement stems from the belief that it is only when each citizen of this country is liberated from defecating in the open, will India truly achieve sustainable and inclusive development. It is a shame that our fellow Indians, particularly women, have to go through this indignity, often risking physical harm. As the prime minister noted at a public event in London, the mental distress that open defecation inflicts on a woman is perhaps the biggest disservice our polity has committed to the Indian people.

A human security challenge, therefore, cannot simply be overcome by building infrastructure. I do not discount the need for building toilets; they are after all essential to making India open defecation free (ODF). But more than simply building toilets, it has been the effort to bring about a behavioural and cultural change towards swacchata. When PM Modi terms SBM a people's movement, he is delinking the mission from the din of government and politics. He is asking his fellow citizens to take ownership of swacchata; it is only when every Indian imbibes the sanitation ethos of Mahatma Gandhi that India's march towards sustainability will be successful.

It makes me at once proud and humble to note that swacchata today has become a *jan andolan,* a citizen-led social movement. The union government, in partnership with state governments, has put its full weight behind the mission. NGOs and civil society organizations are empowering citizens to demand cleanliness and are supporting the government's efforts to raise awareness. India's corporate sector too has been instrumental—they have adopted towns and are investing significant sums of money to build and maintain toilets.

The Pradhan Mantri Jan Dhan Yojana is another excellent example of the government's welfare efforts. As of October 2018, 329.9 million previously unbanked individuals have a bank account in their name today. A total of Rs 864.80 billion in deposits shows the scale at which Indians today have access to organized finance which had previously been unfathomable, if not unimaginable.[58] Moreover, the linking of Jan Dhan Yojana with Aadhar has been a game changer in public service delivery. Citizens now receive their dues through a Direct Benefit Transfer (DBT) mechanism, leakages have been plugged, middlemen eliminated, and corruption ceased. As a result, the public exchequer has saved over Rs 570 billion till the FY 2016–17.[59]

It has been argued that no developing country can achieve the developed status without adequate investment in health and education. The government has realized the

Indian reality is no different and taken requisite action. In healthcare, in the budget speech of 2014–15, the Finance Minister announced the establishment of four new All India Institutes of Medical Science (AIIMS). The following year, the government announced six more, and in 2017–18, another two.[60] Perhaps the biggest health sector reform this country has witnessed was announced in the 2018 budget. 'Modicare', or the National Health Protection Scheme (NHPS), will extend health insurance to 100 million families and raise the insurance ceiling to Rs 5 lakh.[61] This is a transformational shift on how health care is viewed in India. Fellow citizens will no longer be subjected to the ordeal of making rounds and standing in long queues at government hospitals. The average Indian now has access to establishments, which provide the finest medical treatment.

In education, within the first year of assuming office, the government announced and established five new Indian Institutes of Technology (IITs), with a sixth one following a year later; and five new Indian Institutes of Management (IIMs).[62]

Further, in an unprecedented move, the UGC granted autonomy to sixty higher educational institutions. These centres of excellence will have the freedom to start new courses, off-campus centres, skill development courses, research parks and any other new academic programme.[63] This has led to a paradigm shift in not just how educational institutes are run, but how they are imagined.

Some have argued that the efforts of the Modi government are neither new nor unique. Many governments in the past have tried to address health and sanitation requirements of the country, as they have tried to build roads, highways, airports, and houses. Those who are more cynical have argued that PM Modi's missions are just a rehash of old schemes.

A ringside view of Indian policy-making for over forty years would make me agree that similar attempts have been made in the past. I would, however, urge those asking these questions to ask another question—if this is simply a case of old wine in a new bottle, why does the wine taste so much better now as compared to the past?

The answer to this question lies in the fact that for much of India's history, following independence, a culture of impunity was nourished, encouraged, and allowed to flourish. Corruption had become the norm rather than the exception— the Commonwealth Games scam, the 2G spectrum allocation scam, and the coal block allocation scam were just the tip of the iceberg. The third intervention of this government, therefore, was to put an end to such practices that undermined any and all efforts for growth and development.

Demonetization and Goods and Services Tax (GST) clamped down on nefarious business activities. The move to make all economic transactions transparent brought a fresh air of accountability to Indian business. The fillip given to digital transactions furthered this effort—today, there exists a backstory to every payment made and received.

Similarly, the enactment of the Insolvency and Bankruptcy Code (IBC) into law in 2016 has dealt a serious blow to India's crony capitalists. The World Bank estimates that insolvency procedures in India take an average of 4.3 years; for China, this number stands at 1.7; for the US 1.0, and for Germany 1.2.[64] The IBC enacted by this government now allows entrepreneurs an exit from their loss-making enterprise and focus their resources on establishing more profitable entities. The effects of the IBC can already be seen—out of fear of losing control of their businesses, 2,100 defaulting companies have settled dues worth Rs 83,000 crore. Further, Tata Steel's bid to acquire Bhushan Steel for Rs 350 billion became the first acquisition under the IBC's insolvency proceedings, making it a 'historic breakthrough' in addressing legacy issues of Indian banks.[65]

Urban development too was not immune to nefarious practices—the real estate sector was perhaps the most notorious of all, and often used to park elicit wealth, i.e. black money. I am certain that when the history of India's urban development will be written, it would be divided into two phases—pre-RERA and post-RERA. The Real Estate (Regulation and Development) Act, or RERA, enacted into law in 2016, is a game changer for the real estate sector. The fact that India did not have a real estate regulator for seventy years is perhaps the biggest injustice that had been committed in the fight against corruption. With the enactment of RERA, the builder-politician nexus has been broken—no longer will citizens, and their hard-earned life savings, be at the mercy of corrupt officials and corporates who are out to cheat them off their dream home. RERA, when seen in conjunction with the Benami Transactions (Prohibition) Amendment Act of 2016, has moved the fight against corruption in real estate from mere lip service, to concrete, on-ground solutions.

After ten years of paralytic UPA governance, India is witnessing buoyancy across government departments. There is a sense of purpose in the policy community to implement what the PM calls 'minimum government, maximum governance' in order to provide Indians with 'ease of living', and ultimately achieve, the motto of this government—'Sabka Saath, Sabka Vikas'.

It is delusional to think that India's economic potential can be realized if the Government of India is led by a 1990s-style coalition government. Such a scenario won't just be a bad dream, but a nightmare—a loosely put together federal government, where 'alliances' are formed not for economic and social progress but merely for political power, is the worst thing that can happen to a country, which is today considered one of the few bright spots in a flailing world economy. I began this section of the chapter by claiming this is India's last chance—the last shot at pulling millions out of abject poverty and empowering them to determine their own future. To fulfil the aspirations of the peoples of our land, we need a strong central government, with a visionary leader at its helm, who is willing to take the required political and economic risks that will deliver prosperity and security to its more than 1.2 billion Indians.

CHAPTER 5

Global Governance

'Turning and turning in the widening gyre
The falcon cannot hear the falconer;
Things fall apart; the centre cannot hold;
Mere anarchy is loosed upon the world . . .'

—*Second Coming* by W.B. Yeats,
written in 1919 in the aftermath of World War 1

Delusional Decision-making at the Multilateral Level

Should it ever become possible to conduct a credible global poll
on the existential questions of life and death, war and peace,
the verdict would be overwhelmingly clear. No matter what the
ideological preferences of the earth's seven billion or so human
inhabitants, they would, cutting across nations with different
political systems, opt for peaceful coexistence. They would
express a preference for economic growth and development,
bread and butter, over weapons, strife and war. And yet nation
states, propelled by their narrow sectarian interests, continue
to pursue misconceived policies. They are leading the planet's
seven billion people into a deepening existential crisis.

The Global Governance Crises

The governance framework of individual nations is predicated
on their sovereign rights over a specific territory. In these

specific territories, referred to as sovereign nations, governments are established, monarchs are anointed, dictators and military heads appoint themselves, to control and coordinate social relations and, when required, enforce decisions.

However, the world doesn't have a single government, monarch or dictator, to oversee its governance, and perhaps it does not need one.

The institution which comes closest to overseeing global governance is the United Nations (UN) which views it as 'the sum of laws, norms, policies, and institutions that define, constitute, and mediate trans-border relations between states, cultures, citizens, intergovernmental and non-governmental organizations, and the market. It embraces the totality of institutions, policies, rules, practices, norms, procedures and initiatives by which states and their citizens (indeed, humanity as a whole) try to bring more predictability, stability and order to their responses to transnational challenges—such as climate change and environmental degradation, nuclear proliferation, and terrorism—which go beyond the capacity of a single state to solve.'[1]

To summarize the UN view, one can say that global governance is required for (i) transborder relations between varying sections of society, interacting with one another on a range of public policy issues; (ii) creating a world order which is peaceful and stable, and one where aforementioned interactions lead to prosperity of mankind; and (iii) to address challenges at the supranational level, i.e. to tackle those issues which one nation or actor cannot solve on its own.[2]

To say then that 2017 was a year of turmoil for global governance would be an understatement. From governance of nuclear security to climate change, from the oceans to the Internet, 2017 witnessed delusional politics all around.

In this book I have addressed four areas of global governance: nuclear security, climate change, terrorism and international trade. Given the complexities of the latter three, and my deep personal engagement in the subjects, I have dedicated entire chapters to them. In this chapter, I will be addressing the first two: nuclear security and climate change.

Nuclear Security and Climate Change: The Trump Years

The Trump presidency's three defining acts vis-à-vis nuclear security and climate action are his handling of the Joint Comprehensive Plan of Action (JCOPA), more commonly referred to as the Iran deal, his negotiations with North Korea and the Paris Accord. And unlike the consequences of his delusional politics at home, his actions in these three spheres have had far-reaching international repercussions.

The Art of Making a Deal: Iran

The Iran deal—agreed to by the five permanent members of the United Nations Security Council, besides Germany, the European Union and Iran—was a significant achievement of the international community to rein in Iran's nuclear ambitions. After extensive negotiations, which were led by the United States under President Obama and his secretary of state, John Kerry, all actors agreed the deal was the best possible outcome at the time, given the instability the Middle East had witnessed post the interventions in Iraq, Libya and Yemen.

In an act of the highest form of delusional thinking, on 8 May 2018, President Trump withdrew from the Iran deal, stating, 'This was a horrible, one-sided deal that should have never, ever been made.' Adding, 'It didn't bring calm, it didn't bring peace, and it never will.'[3]

Ostensibly, the President's decision to withdraw was based on the reasoning that the deal was compromised to begin with.

From the outset, the deal did not guarantee a safer future as it had left enough room for Iran to go nuclear in the future. At its core, however, this line of thinking had little to do with the contours of the deal itself. President Trump, throughout his presidential campaign, portrayed Hillary Clinton as part of an 'establishment elite' that was more concerned with international objectives, rather than American national interest. His disregard for multilateralism and its outcomes had little to do with multilateralism or its outcomes. Rather, it was a campaign strategy to galvanize his support base against the elitist Hillary Clinton and President Obama. When viewed from this perspective, the withdrawal from the Iran deal was a corrective measure he took in the interest of the average American—a delusion he himself believed and fed his support base. He was correcting, he believed, a wrong committed by the 'establishment' and saving America from yet another international misadventure, similar to the interventions in Iraq, Libya, Syria, and Yemen. Moreover, the withdrawal was meant to pander to the strong Israeli lobby in the United States, which was steadfastly against the Iran deal but got little attention from President Obama.

The delusional act of bringing domestic partisanship and one-upmanship to international negotiations, that too to an issue as grave as nuclear security, has had serious consequences.

The United States stands isolated as the countries of the European Union have openly distanced themselves from the President and his decision. Worse still for the United States, its withdrawal has left a vacuum and European leaders have already reached out to Russia in a bid to save the Iran deal. The following statements by the French leader Macron and the Russian President Vladimir Putin, post a meeting in May 2018, are instructive:

I was personally assured that Iran is fulfilling all its obligations, so the question arises what grounds there were to exit this agreement . . . We welcome the efforts of Iran and Europe to preserve this deal, while understanding that it will be hard—Vladimir Putin[4]

This process that was already launched to reduce tensions on the peninsula, and the process with the goal of denuclearisation, this process should continue—Emmanuel Macron[5]

Perhaps what is even more worrying than the domestic political considerations to withdraw from the deal is Trump's conviction that he alone can make a better deal. Only two days after the withdrawal, at a campaign rally, he stated, 'I hope to be able to make a deal with them, a good deal, a fair deal—a good deal for them, better for them.'[6]

It remains unclear what the contours of this 'better deal' will be and how it will be achieved. For now, the deal remains in the realm of delusional decision-making, stemming from delusional thinking.

Rocket Men: North Korea

The following tweet from the personal account of the forty-fifth President of the United States is just one example of the flailing governance of nuclear security in the world:

North Korean Leader Kim Jong Un just stated that the 'Nuclear Button is on his desk at all times.' Will someone from his depleted and food-starved regime please inform him that I too have a Nuclear Button, but it is a much bigger & more powerful one than his, and my Button works![7]

For a better part of the Trump presidency, the US President and the North Korean leader were locked in a bitter war of words, trading personal insults, dropping the 'n' word in these duels more often than anyone would have imagined.[8]

As with most policies under Trump, it was unclear whether this form of 'diplomacy' was part of a larger, long-term, US strategy, or just off-the-cuff remarks by the President.

The conflicting statements by the former secretary of state, Rex Tillerson, complicated the matters further during the time the two leaders partook in these exchanges. Take for instance Tillerson's statement which he made at an event at the Atlantic Council, a think tank in Washington, on 13 December 2017: 'We're ready to have the first meeting without precondition. Let's just meet. And we can talk about the weather if you want. We can talk about whether it's going to be a square table or a round table if that's what you're excited about. But can we at least sit down and see each other face to face.'[9] It took the White House, and Tillerson's own state department, less than forty-eight hours to contradict these views. The state department's spokesperson claimed, 'The secretary was not creating any new policy. Our policy remains exactly the same as it was, the very same policy that we have talked about in this room for months and months now. First and foremost, diplomacy is our top priority'.[10] After these statements were made, the White House spokesperson cautioned against Tillerson's words, claiming 'The president's views on North Korea have not changed. North Korea is acting in an unsafe way, not only toward Japan, China and South Korea, but the entire world. North Korea's actions are not good for anyone and certainly not good for North Korea.'[11]

One might be tempted to suggest that this was the US administration's way of playing good cop, bad cop, where the

POTUS projected a more aggressive stance while his secretary of state offered the North Korean dictator an olive branch. However, this view didn't stand on strong footing, given the press reports that suggested that the secretary of state and the President had serious differences on the subject.[12]

And like most officials in the Trump administration who differed with the President, Rex Tillerson was relieved of his job as the secretary of state. Mike Pompeo, the then director of CIA, replaced Tillerson, and his deputy at the intelligence agency, Gina Haspel, came to head the institution. In addition to these changes, the President brought into the fold John Bolton as his national security advisor, replacing Lieutenant General H.R. McMaster.

Each of these individuals had a common reputation that preceded them—Pompeo was a former member of the Tea Party, and known to have a hawkish worldview. He famously defended the CIA against the senate report that claimed that torture tactics were deployed during the Bush presidency.[13] Gina Haspel, who replaced Pompeo as the head of the CIA, was herself accused of torturing suspects and destroying evidence.[14] Neither of them, however, comes close to the hawkishness of John Bolton, who till day remains one of the few individuals who defends the American invasion of Iraq,[15] and the intervention in Libya.[16]

Having assembled a team of some of America's most hawkish and least internationalist individuals, President Trump performed a 180-degree turn. On 12 June 2018, he met with the North Korean leader, Kim Jong-Un, for a historic summit in Singapore—precisely what his previous secretary of state had advocated all along.

This came as a relief to the international community. Unlike the bitter exchanges online, the in-person meeting at the summit saw the two leaders shake hands and interact in a manner which was warm and cordial. At the press conference following the signing of the joint document, Trump stated, 'I want to thank Chairman Kim for taking the first bold step toward a bright new future for his people . . . My meeting with Chairman Kim was honest, direct, and productive. We got to know each other well in a very confined period of time.'[17]

The delusional aspect of the summit, however, emerges when one studies the following—the popular reaction to the outcome, the outcome itself, and the approach adopted by President Trump to the summit's outcome.

Much of the left-leaning liberal commentariat has framed its personal dislike for Trump on the global governance architecture he is trying to build. He has been questioned and criticized for meeting a brutal dictator and giving the regime legitimacy. It is important here to separate the wheat from the chaff—democratically elected leaders are under no compulsion to conduct diplomacy with only leaders who have been elected through a democracy. As Trump has noted following the summit, he has to deal with whoever his counterpart is and however such an individual may have attained the leadership position in his/her sovereign territory.[18] The legitimacy argument too doesn't hold true, particularly in the case of Kim Jong-Un. There is little to suggest the North Korean leader doesn't already enjoy popular support in his home country.[19] There is even less to suggest he seeks/needs legitimacy from the US-led alliance system, which has over the past few decades lost its own credibility thanks to numerous ill-conceived interventions overseas.[20] Too many in the liberal space have deluded themselves to this line of thought. Nations no longer seek an American stamp of approval—the days of hegemonic powers have ended, and the world has witnessed and accepted what looks like a multipolar international order.

Once we clear the cobwebs around legitimacy, it becomes clear that from a North Korean point of view, the summit was a meeting between two heads of state to address long-standing bilateral issues. The outcome document made no mention of South Korea, Japan and China, making it clear that the purpose of the meeting between Kim Jong-Un and Trump was not to address the North–South issue, but to deliberate upon the future of the US–DPRK[21] relationship.

This is not to suggest that the 'deal' struck by Trump is even close to being ideal—the outcome document is steeped in delusional decision-making itself.

Given the context of the meeting between the two leaders, the outcome document emanating from such a summit cannot be subjected to 'bullet-point diplomacy' as it has come to be realized. While there is certainly virtue in Trump and Kim having better personal relationships than they have had over the past two years, the ambiguous nature of the outcome document has left enough room for each side to interpret the agreement for their own consideration—the phrase 'denuclearization of the Korean Peninsula' has an entirely different meaning for the US and North Korea.[22]

Moreover, this ambiguity has set the precedent for future negotiations. Both Iran and North Korea will see the other as a benchmark. For Iran, a much watered-down (and vague) agreement with the United States sends the signal that to get Trump back on the table, it too needs to expand its nuclear capability, and in return, get a better deal than the one it signed with Obama. For North Korea, if Trump can renege on the Obama-era Iran deal, which was much more comprehensive than the bullet points they have agreed to, there is little value in taking the initiative forward, and in fact, their best play is to continue to retain a nuclear arsenal capable of reaching the United States. When viewed from this prism, the discontinuation of military exercises with South Korea is a win-win solution for Kim Jong-Un. He has demonstrated that he can build intercontinental ballistic missiles, buy time from the US (due to the vagueness of the bullet points) on the future course of action, and have South Korea and Japan on the back foot.

In what can only be described as cognitive dissonance on part of Trump, the withdrawal from the Iran deal and the removal of American military presence from the Korean peninsula has reshaped the world order as was imagined post World War II. The alliances that were forged in the aftermath of the war to uphold the liberal world order no longer hold. 'America first' is now the new normal.

The third layer of delusion witnessed at the end of the summit was Trump's belief that he could personally find a solution to North Korea's nuclear programme, just like in the case of Iran. There is a growing sense that for Trump summit level meetings are not a means to an end, but an end in themselves. Having been an officer in the Indian Foreign Service for nearly forty years, I understand the frustrations shared by many over bureaucratic functioning. But even the harshest critics would agree that to finalize a complex nuclear deal between a reality star-turned President and an erratic and brutal North Korean dictator requires careful consideration and deft handling. Trump, over the course of his presidency, has undermined his state department and the larger national security apparatus. The mass-scale downsizing of these institutions conducted under his watch has meant that there exists little to no resources, both in terms of number of personnel and personnel with the requisite expertise. When the time comes to get down to the nuts and bolts of a larger 'de-nuke' framework, questions over the capacity of United States to see it through are likely to emerge. There is every chance that the President could bring in a seasoned negotiator like Bob Einhorn, who is currently at the Brookings Institutions. That, however, will not be sufficient as the state department has been significantly weakened. There is also no guarantee that the professionals who are brought in would risk damage to their reputations as they are likely to meet the fate of many of their predecessors who were left humiliated by the President. This is a rather unlikely situation for a nation that has for long prided itself for its state capacity, and for a President whose USP is to get things done.

The entire discourse around weaponization of nuclear material under the Trump administration is therefore steeped in delusional politics. There is very little narrative to suggest that there is a vision of how the world can be made a safer place. The United Nations has meanwhile been a bystander, its legitimacy in conducting global governance reaching an all-time low.

June 2017: When Paris Was Lost

Negotiations on climate action, spearheaded by the United Nations Framework Convention on Climate Change (UNFCCC), have exhibited a similar delusional approach from the very beginning and can be summarized as follows: The so-called 'developed countries' of the world have industrialized on coal, contributing the most to climate change. These same countries now expect developing nations, who still suffer from large-scale poverty including energy poverty, to renounce coal and find alternate pathways for their development. Moreover, the developed nations don't want to provide financial or technological assistance in this seemingly herculean task.

At the third UNFCCC Conference of Parties in Kyoto, Japan, in 1997, member nations institutionalized the term Common but Differentiated Responsibility (CBDR).[23] The Kyoto Protocol, as it came to be known, acknowledged the historical responsibility of the developed world towards climate action by drawing up a list of developed countries—then referred to in Annexure 1—which committed themselves to targets for cutting or slowing their emission levels.[24] However, the protocol was hamstrung thanks to a resolution in the US senate according to which Congress would not ratify any international commitment where developing countries were omitted. [25] Thus despite the US signing on to the protocol under President Clinton, it was not ratified by Congress.[26]

Up until 2 June 2017, the biggest setback to climate diplomacy came at COP (Conference of Parties) 15 in Copenhagen. The developing world was left bitterly disappointed at the dropping of the global target of reducing emission by 80 per cent by 2050.[27] To make matters worse, the target of limiting rising global temperatures to 1.5 degree Celsius too was dropped.[28]

President Obama's statement that developing countries should be 'getting out of that mindset' of looking at previous agreements which made a distinction between developed and developing countries served as a serious blow to developing nations, who had for years tried to uphold the provisions of CBDR and Kyoto Protocol.[29]

At the other end of the spectrum, COP 21 at Paris was climate diplomacy's finest hour in almost two decades. The agreement ticked all the boxes—over 190 signatories, check;[30] mention of not just 2 degree Celsius, but also 1.5 degree Celsius as a target, check;[31] making USD 100 billion the minimum amount and acknowledging that far larger sums are needed for climate action, check;[32] and, most importantly, bringing back CBDR, check.[33]

However, the glory days of COP 21 were short lived. On 2 June 2017, Trump withdrew US support to the Paris Accord, claiming he was elected President of the citizens of Pittsburgh and not Paris. He made his contempt for climate action, global governance and multilateral diplomacy clear in one go.[34]

Like in the case of the Iran deal, the withdrawal from the Paris Accord too was a campaign pledge the President had made to his support base. To win the presidential election, Trump had promised to bring back the jobs the coal miners had lost due to environmental regulations imposed by Obama. The pull-out from the Paris deal along with a host of domestic measures was therefore Trump's way of delivering on his campaign promise. The fact, however, remains that these efforts have little to no impact and the jobs Trump tried to recreate are nowhere in sight. Like many of his decisions, this renunciation of the Paris Accord too is steeped in delusional thinking.[35]

With the US out of the Paris Accord, the future of climate negotiations looks bleak at best. While India and China have stepped in, each in their own way, and taken leadership of global climate action, how much can be achieved without the world's largest polluter,[36] which also happens be the world's largest economy?[37]

More worryingly, from the perspective of a developing country, a consensus seems to have emerged from the inability of the world to unite behind the Paris Accord, particularly CBDR. A report—published by the Climate Action Network—which ranks fifty-six countries (along with ranking EU as a separate supranational entity), highlights that it is not just the United States that has failed Paris. Europe, the supposed leader in climate action has not done nearly enough. For instance, Germany (ranked twenty-two, eight places below India) 'still has relatively high GHG emissions with nearly no improvements regarding GHG trends within the last years and is rated low in this category.' EU as a whole is ranked twenty-one, seven places below India, and the report suggests, 'the EU rates medium in emissions, renewables and energy use. EU experts emphasize the union's constructive role in international climate diplomacy but criticize the slow progress in putting in place new and more ambitious policies and targets'.[38] Other nations of the Atlantic system such as Japan, Canada, Republic of Korea and Australia, have all received poor rankings and have been placed under the 'very low' performing country category.

The inability of the developed world to commit towards a globally agreed framework for climate action, where those who have polluted the most take up the larger responsibility, points to the fact that in their constituencies the only response to climate change is poverty. For the time being, it suggests the developed world has reached the consensus that to limit the dangers of rising global temperatures the developmental efforts of the developing world must be constrained. This line of thinking is delusional at best and dangerous at worst.

Actors Governing the Globe

In some respects, this has been the most difficult section of this book to write. I do so with some trepidation and after anguished introspection.

I served as the permanent representative of India to the United Nations in Geneva and New York. I sat in the Security Council meetings when some of the most controversial and sensitive decisions of the past decades were made. At the time of writing this book, I have already spent a total of forty-three years in the profession of diplomacy. If you add to that a dozen or so years when I was witness to the evolution of other events, as the son of a diplomat, that is a long time indeed.

A significant part of my career has been dedicated to an institution which was born in the aftermath of war, created to prevent war and whose legitimacy faltered when faced once again with precisely these conditions. It is the only institution under whose ambit I can envision peace. But it is also an institution that has allowed itself to be steered off course by management failures and mechanisms completely out of line and unresponsive to the challenges of the twenty-first century.

This section is an honest attempt at a realistic appraisal. It is also a reality check on whether there is at all any possibility in today's day and age to rebuild confidence in the United Nations. Its detractors have long believed that it is not central to the conduct of global governance. By virtue of the dominant position the strong find themselves in, they have less regard and need for the multilateral system. They think they can act unilaterally or build and act as part of a 'coalition of the willing'. But can they, really?

A clearing of the global cobwebs at the very outset appears to be called for. The world today is admittedly in disarray and in an advanced stage of entropy. Does this pose a greater danger than those posed by earlier crises? This requires context setting. What are the potential and real dangers for the outbreak of hostilities and war among declared nuclear-armed states. Why does the need for a discussion on global governance assume such critical urgency today?

The current system of global governance was designed as World War II was concluding. It is entirely possible that representatives at San Francisco might have delayed adopting the charter of the United Nations had they been convened in peacetime. The ongoing World War II, in other words, provided an urgent context setting. The first draft of the charter was prepared in the US Department of State.[39]

The charter, cast in a post-Westphalian state-centric model is balanced by the far-sighted and visionary provision 'We the Peoples'. The full significance of this is beginning to be comprehended more than seventy years after the adoption of the charter.

The electoral victory of Donald Trump has had a significant impact on this chapter, and indeed this book, as it marks a significant shift in what has come to be known as a post-war world order. A caveat needs to be entered, however, into the narrative at this time. There are other significant and decisive influences on the shaping of the post-war order. The rise of China is a major factor.

There is a growing sense within America that the 'perilous interventions' of the past decade have not only made the country more unsafe, but they have come at the cost of American tax dollars.

The Trump presidency in a way is the legacy of those interventions and by electing Trump, the United States of America has made it clear that it no longer wants to underwrite international security and is no longer the guarantor of economic prosperity.

The following quotes from President Trump shed a glimpse on what he and his support base think of the country's strongest alliance, the North Atlantic Treaty Organization (NATO):

'I have been very very direct with secretary Stoltenberg and members of the alliance in saying NATO members must finally contribute their fair share and meet their financial obligations.'

'But 23 of the 28 member nations are still not paying what they should be paying and what they are supposed to be paying for their defence.'

'This is not fair to the people and taxpayers of the United States and many of these nations owe massive amounts of money from past years. And not paying in those past years.'[40]

Despite President Trump and his angry proclamations against Global Governance, I would like to urge caution against those claiming an American 'retreat'—the United States is still the world's largest economy, with a GDP of over US 18 trillion,[41] and an industrial military complex that is capable of producing and arming governments and insurgents alike in most of the global trouble spots.

Having said that, there is no doubt that there is a temporary retrenchment on part of the United States as the global leader of security and prosperity, and several actors are trying to fill this space. The foremost among these is the People's Republic of China.

Speaking at the World Economic Forum's annual summit in Davos, the Chinese Premier Xi Jingping made official what many knew was inevitable—the rise of the dragon:

'At present, the most pressing task before us is to steer the global economy out of difficulty. The global economy has remained sluggish for quite some time. The gap between the poor and the rich and between the South and the North is widening. The root cause is that the three critical issues in the economic sphere have not been effectively addressed.'[42]

Such a statement from the leader of both the People's Republic of China and of the Communist Party of China would have been inconceivable a few years ago. So, what's changed?

After two decades of double digit growth, largely predicated on export-focused manufacturing, China as of 2017 is a USD

12.38 trillion economy,[43] with a per capita income of USD 8,826.99.[44] This economic might has allowed the People's Republic of China to embark on a mission to create a Sino-centric world order, often dubbed the 'Beijing Consensus'.

The Belt and Road Initiative (BRI), which is supposedly a regional connectivity project aiming to link East Asia with the Eurasian landmass, Africa, and ultimately to the markets of Western Europe, is at its core, a geo-political project to establish Pax Sinica.

The Sri Lankan Hambantota port,[45] the Gwadar port,[46] and the larger China-Pakistan Economic Corridor (CPEC),[47] are just some of the examples of how, under the garb of 'win-win' and 'pragmatic cooperation', the Chinese model looks to create a world order wherein nations are dependent and beholden to the Middle Kingdom. It is not just hard, on-the-ground, infrastructure that the dragon seeks. By establishing institutions such as the Shanghai Cooperation Organisation, Asia Infrastructure Investment Bank, and Regional Comprehensive Economic Partnership, the People's Republic of China has entered the fore of creating norms and rules around geo-economics, and geo-politics.

Perhaps the clearest indication of China's ambitions to be the leading Asian, if not global, power, was illustrated in the recent stand-off between Chinese and Indian troops at Doklam, Bhutan. China, in an attempt to change the ground realities, started road construction and military patrol of the tri-junction separating China, Bhutan, and India.[48] When faced with the prospects of confronting Indian troops, China launched a vicious media and psychological campaign which reached their peak when the CPC's propaganda outlet, Global Times, called the Indian Foreign Minister a 'liar'.[49] Its outright rejection of the verdict by an international tribunal on illegal expansion in the South China Sea,[50] and its support to North

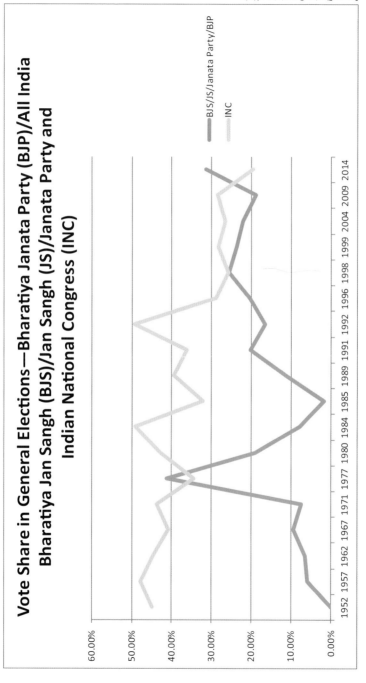

Vote Share in General Elections—Bharatiya Janata Party (BJP)/All India Bharatiya Jan Sangh (BJS)/Jan Sangh (JS)/Janata Party and Indian National Congress (INC)

BJS/JS/Janata Party/BJP
INC

Source: Election Commission of India

This graph highlights the decline of the Indian National Congress and the rise of the BJP in 2014 using percentage of vote share as the metric. It depicts how the BJP, which got less than 10 per cent of votes in 1984, is India's leading national party today. For further reference, see page 13.

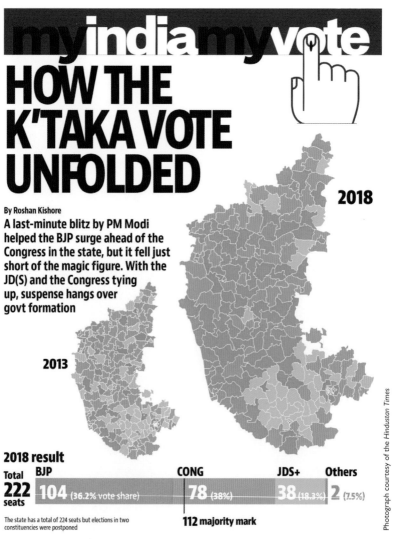

my india my vote

HOW THE K'TAKA VOTE UNFOLDED

By Roshan Kishore

A last-minute blitz by PM Modi helped the BJP surge ahead of the Congress in the state, but it fell just short of the magic figure. With the JD(S) and the Congress tying up, suspense hangs over govt formation

2018

2013

Photograph courtesy of the *Hindustan Times*

2018 result

Total	BJP	CONG	JDS+	Others
222 seats	**104** (36.2% vote share)	**78** (38%)	**38** (18.3%)	**2** (7.5%)

The state has a total of 224 seats but elections in two constituencies were postponed

112 majority mark

Images 2, 3, 4 and 5: A post-poll alliance between the Congress and the JD(S) shows that the electoral results in Karnataka are a classic example of India's people demanding a 'Congress-mukt Bharat'. For further reference, see pages 86, 87.

Photograph courtesy of the Hindustan Times

HOW KARNATAKA VOTED

A mapping of election results on top of data that characterises the socio-economic make up of constituencies throws up interesting details on how certain sections of voters clinched it for the winners. Here are three voting patterns seen in Karnataka.

howindialives.com
howindialives.com is a search engine for public data

■ BJP   ■ Congress   ■ JD (S) +   ■ Others

WHAT BJP'S COMEBACK LOOKS LIKE

222 seats went to the polls, out of 224 assembly seats

224 seats went to polls

2018

2013

Urban seats 35/71

There are 71 constituencies where more than 35% of the population was living in urban areas. The BJP won 15 such seats in 2013. In 2018, it increased its count to 35. Meanwhile, the Congress saw its tally in such seats shrink from 42 to 30 seats.

2018

2013

Dalit seats: 31/82

There are 82 constituencies where Dalits comprised over 20% of the population. In 2013, the BJP won only 9 of these seats. This time, they won 31, mostly at the expense of the Congress, whose tally fell from 49 to 34. The JD (S) saw its count in such seats fall from 17 to 15.

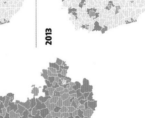

2018

2013

Minority seats: 36/78

There are 78 constituencies in Karnataka where the share of minorities in the population was above 17%. The BJP increased its haul in such seats from 19 to 36. The Congress went from 45 to 35—a decline but not of the same level as in Dalit and urban seats.

2018

2013

Data shows wins/leads as of 5.20 pm, May 15
Data sources: Census 2011 for socio-economic data; Election Commission of India for election results

④

Modi's leadership brought unity within a faction-ridden party

BJP **KJP** **BSRCP**

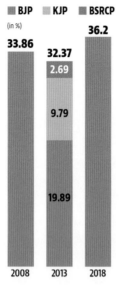

(in %)

33.86 (2008)

32.37 (2013)
- 2.69
- 9.79
- 19.89

36.2 (2018)

2008   2013   2018

The BJP suffered a huge defeat in the 2013 elections in the state. A lack of unity in the party was seen as the biggest reason behind that outcome. BS Yeddyuruppa and B Sriramulu had defected from the party in 2012. Yeddyuruppa's Karnataka Janata Paksha polled around 10% votes and inflicted huge damage to the BJP's seat tally in the 2013 elections. Both these leaders were brought back into the party before the 2014 Lok Sabha elections and its vote share jumped to 43%. The 2018 success would not have been possible without this unity within the party.

Photograph courtesy of the *Hindustan Times*

BJP got votes where it mattered

⑤

BJP **Cong** **JD(S)** (in %)

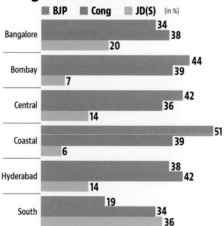

Bangalore — BJP 34, Cong 38, JD(S) 20
Bombay — BJP 44, Cong 39, JD(S) 7
Central — BJP 42, Cong 36, JD(S) 14
Coastal — BJP 51, Cong 39, JD(S) 6
Hyderabad — BJP 38, Cong 42, JD(S) 14
South — BJP 19, Cong 34, JD(S) 36

The Congress is in the unenviable position of having a larger vote share but smaller seat count than the BJP in Karnataka. This is because of the fact that the Congress gets its votes across the state, while the vote share of both the BJP and the JD(S) is concentrated in specific sub-regions. A comparison of average vote shares of the three major parties by sub-regions shows that the Congress is behind either the JD(S) or the BJP in all sub-regions except two.

Photograph courtesy of the *Hindustan Times*

Korean nuclear ambitions are further proof of China's disregard for multilateralism.[51]

While the US is retrenching and the PRC's is growing, two other actors, Western Europe and the Russian Federation, seem to be acting somewhat contrary to their historical roles as global rule-makers.

The European Union faces an existential crisis. Once the promoters of what came to be known as 'European Values', the continent today witnesses widespread bigotry, racism[52] and a complete disregard for human rights, of those fleeing from ISIS strongholds in West Asia.[53] The 'otherization' of resident Muslims, even second and third generation Muslims, has resulted in a wave of support for ISIS-like organizations, and tragic 'lone-wolf' attacks in France and Belgium. Add the economic crisis of 2010 when the PIIGS countries, Portugal, Ireland, Italy, Greece, Spain, almost went bankrupt,[54] and the recent Brexit referendum result, means Europe must set its own house in order, even as it attempts to shape the world order of the twenty-first century. Post the collapse of the USSR, this is perhaps the first time in twenty-eight years that the EU faces this dual challenge. An entire generation or more of Europeans have lived in an era of unprecedented peace and prosperity. How the present generation responds to the dual challenge it faces today, will shape the internal and international future of the continent.

The case of Russia too is unique. At USD 1.578 trillion, its economic size is much smaller than that of the United States, Western Europe, and ranks ahead of only South Africa amongst the BRICS countries.[55] There has been little to no expansion of Russia's domestic industry and it does not feature in too many geo-economic conversations.[56] And yet, thanks to its military prowess, it remains a critical actor in global governance.

No global conflict today can be resolved without Russian participation, as the ISIS challenge illustrates. Moreover, if allegations about its involvement in the American electoral process have any basis in fact, then, at the very least, it shows that Russia is not opposed to intervention in the domestic affairs of other countries.

Russia's 'democratically' elected leader, Vladimir Putin, can certainly not continue with this quasi-hegemony for too long. Having won his second consecutive bid for the presidency (and fourth overall), Putin will soon have to address the economic concerns of his people. As the world enters the fourth industrial revolution, the solutions to decades of economic neglect, might not be as easily forthcoming.

Demise of Multilateralism

It is evident from the preceding analysis that bilateralism or even unilateralism is gaining traction. Member states' façade of a preference for multilateral solutions to global problems has fallen.

Several trends that gave the UN its credibility are now in reversal. In the public's eye—in the eyes of those outside the tight-knit UN community and even some within—the UN appears to be losing the effectiveness and legitimacy it once had. The lexicon now features phrases such as 'greatest humanitarian crisis since World War II' and the 'notion of inter-state and intra-state conflict have blurred and there is no linear path to peace'.[57] Violent extremism and global pandemics race to infect as many minds and bodies as possible.

These are not confined within a state's borders. The interdependency and interconnectedness invited by globalism has made sure of that. When the world is desperately calling out for increased burden-sharing to deal with the multiple crises at hand, faith has been lost in the institution that was created for this very purpose.

In matters of peace and security—the most important of the three founding pillars of the UN—the institution is floundering at best. Created for the purpose of saving future generations from the scourge of war remains, after seven decades, it has become impotent and largely helpless on the major crises facing the world: Iraq, Libya, Syria, North Korea, Yemen and Ukraine, to name a few. The real danger lies elsewhere. Nowhere in these crises does the UN itself believe it has a durable and worthwhile solution to offer.

In December 2015, I wrote 'Multilateral organizations are struggling to adapt to the breadth and pace of the multiple and multi-layered crises. The drafters of the UN Charter could, in all fairness not have anticipated many of the challenges of today's world. The UN is being tested as never before.'[58]

But, in a sense, it is not the UN that is at a crossroads. There are three UNs out there, not one. The 193 member states, the UN Secretariat and civil society, NGOs, think tanks and a vast array of other organizations that collectively shape humanity's consciousness on human rights, humanitarianism, environment and an ocean full of other issues that culminated in the successful negotiations of the Sustainable Development Goals and the adopting of the 2030 Agenda.

If the UN is to remain relevant, the question is whether the UN is fit for purpose as it nears seventy-one years of its existence. The answer is not a straight 'yes'. In many respects, the UN's problems are the creation of its member states, or at least some of them.

In June 2011, participating in an Informal Thematic Debate on 'The United Nations in Global Governance,' I had said:

Let me place before you four propositions. These four propositions, or rather self-evident truisms, apply, to a certain extent, to all organizations created and manned by human beings. First, that organizational lethargy begets structural blind spots. Second, that lessons of history will remain lessons of history if not properly learnt and understood. Third, reform or step aside. Fourth, denial is not a governance response.[59]

Some years later, in 2014, I was appointed the secretary general of the Independent Commission on Multilateralism (ICM). This was a two-year project by the International Peace Institute (IPI), a non-profit think tank, headquartered in New York and with branches in Vienna and Bahrain. The objective was to provide recommendations for the then-incoming UN secretary general to make the UN more 'fit for purpose'. Although I left the ICM before the final report was produced, I spearheaded its activities during the most substantive parts of the project. The findings from hours of discussion and consultation with UN staffers, representatives of member states, NGOs, the private sector and civil society all reinforced the propositions I had made in 2011. As the propositions were relevant six years before this writing, so they will be six years from it. It is thus worth taking the time to deconstruct my arrival at these four propositions.

Which UN?

Only a few days before my departure from the ICM in March 2016, the *New York Times* carried a piece written by the former UN assistant secretary general for field support, Anthony Banbury. The stinging rebuke was titled 'I Love the U.N., but

It Is Failing'[60] and marked his departure from the institution after having served in the UN for over three decades.

In this opinion-piece, Banbury revealed his many grievances with the UN and how they climaxed in his departure from the institution. He criticized the UN's 'sclerotic personnel system' 'minimal accountability,' and debilitating bureaucracy. His frustrations were not ungrounded, and I share some of the sentiments expressed on the UN's 'colossal mismanagement'.

Many have made these criticisms before his exposé in *The Times* and many have made them after. But in his censure of the UN, he failed to clarify, as many often do: which UN is failing?

A main driver of mismanagement within the UN arises from the conflicts of interest of the so-called three UNs and the failure to account for these differences. The 'first UN' is comprised, as observed earlier, of member states, with each state looking to best serve its own national interests. The 'second UN' is made up of employees of the UN Secretariat, working to serve the charter and agenda of the institution; they are committed solely to the organization, and do not, rather should not, answer to any government or authority.[61] The 'third UN' is comprised of organizations on the periphery of the UN, who work independently from the first and second UNs. The third UN is characterized by its impartial influence on the workings of the UN.

At the core of each of the three UNs are ambitions that are at odds with one another and which ever so often work at cross purposes. The three UNs are acknowledged and prescribed roles when forming agendas, reviewing mechanisms, or proposing reform. But their conflict is seldom taken into earnest consideration, as Banbury failed to do in his *New York Times* piece.

Reform is not a one-time affair. It is an ongoing process. Many good things have arisen from the UN's attempts at reform and progress is being made. And yet, the more glaring anomalies remain. It must be accepted that the three UNs paralyse each other. Only after this fact is internalized can we move towards a process that is accommodating to all three and is, above all, sustainable.

2015 Reviews

In 2015, the UN undertook three major reviews to assess whether the institution is fit for purpose in its septuagenarian years, much like our intentions with the ICM. The reviews put under the microscope the UN's peace operations and peace-building architecture, and the implementation of the women, peace, and security agenda. The processes through which these reviews gained concept, form, and implementation follow the same tune and fall into the same trap.

High-Level Independent Panel on Peace Operations

In 2014, the then secretary general, Ban Ki-Moon, created the High-Level Independent Panel on Peace Operations (HIPPO), which in June 2015 released its review of UN peace operations. Peace operations are by and large the costliest gear in the UN machine. The report placed the budget of peace operations at 'more than four times larger than the rest of the UN Secretariat.'[62] Bluntly put, this report was a result of frustrations with a bloated budget, bloated expectations of peace operations capabilities, and a bloating trend in civil conflict.

The high-level panel was comprised of sixteen experts and chaired by Jose Ramos-Horta, Nobel laureate and the highly respected former prime minister of Timor Leste. He was the co-chair of the ICM and is someone I greatly admire. The report, aptly titled 'Uniting Our Strengths for Peace—Politics, Partnership and People' sought to examine the state of UN peace operations.[63]

In terms of the first P of the title, the panel suggested that 'political solutions should always guide the design and deployment of UN peace operations.'[64] This is not to undermine the UN's protection mandates but rather to emphasize their exceptional nature. Any acts of militarism, if or when necessary, must fit into the mandate of the UN mission.

The second P, partnership, emphasizes a 'stronger, more inclusive peace and security partnership.'[65] As I mentioned at the opening of this chapter, we live in an inescapably interconnected, interdependent world. There are goldmines of insight and knowledge at the local, national, and regional levels, which go largely unmined by those who shape the agendas of the UN missions. Sustainable peace is ruled out if local constituents are not consulted in the creation of the peace being delivered; sustainable peace is ruled out if the host country is not consulted in the type of peace it will inherit and must sustain once the UN departs.

The third P reorients peace operations in the direction of being people-centric. The UN has entangled itself in politics and bureaucracy and has lost what the report calls the 'human face' and its ability to connect to local people to 'better understand their concerns, needs, and aspirations.'[66] The UN Charter prioritizes the people; the institution must do the same.

Advisory Group of Experts

In December 2014, the Secretary General nominated seven experts to form the Advisory Group of Experts (AGE) to review the UN peace-building architecture and provide recommendations for its betterment. This review was conducted at the request of the Presidents of the General Assembly and Security Council. The current architecture, they found, left 'peace-building as an afterthought'.[67] In accordance with the UN Charter, which calls for sustainable peace, peace-building should 'inform all UN activities before, during, and after conflict.'

Chaired by seasoned Guatemalan diplomat Gert Rosenthal, AGE delivered the report titled 'The Challenge of Sustaining Peace' in June 2015. A good portion of the recommendations followed the same formula of the HIPPO report, emphasizing the importance of inclusivity, flexibility, and broadening partnerships. The report denounced the silos between the UN Secretariat, the rest of the UN and operations on the field, arguing that this fragmentation only further perpetuated the 'generalized misunderstanding of the nature of peace-building'.[68]

WPS

In October 2013, Secretary General Ban Ki-moon requested a review of the implementation of UN Security Council Resolution 1325 on women, peace and security to mark the resolution's fifteenth anniversary. The review, invited by the UN Security Council, commissioned seventeen experts to study the execution of Resolution 1325. I have had the pleasure of working with and gaining the friendship of several of the appointed experts in my long diplomatic career. Even with biases placed aside, I can say with confidence that the members of the study were chosen wisely.

The pillars of Resolution 1325, in line with the UN's peculiar predilection for the letter P, included prevention, protection, participation, and peace-building and recovery. It doesn't take a group of experts to see that the gender equality in peace processes envisioned in Resolution 1325 has not yet been achieved. But the report highlighted some important global strides in the right direction: more policies to prevent sexual- and gender-based violence in conflict; a representative gender balance at the negotiating table; and the inclusion of women at the decision-making level not extended as a courtesy but rather as a necessity for sustainability.

The report further suggested that alongside lobbying to bridge the gaps in policy at the national level, the UN itself must also undergo some soul-searching. The gender perspective must be mainstreamed and better integrated into all sectors of the institution if it is to lead by example. The commitment and willpower to implement Resolution 1325 must be reflected in the resources and funds allocated to it.

The Paralytic Ps

These summaries are as encompassing of the reviews as can three paragraph abstracts encompass reports numbering more than a hundred pages. All three reviews share a common thread in the recommendations they put forth. But most importantly, the reviews underwent a common process that sheds light on the glaring structural blind spots of the UN. Returning to the concept of the three UNs, all three reviews were commissioned by the second UN (the UN Secretariat), executed by the third UN (independent experts) and laid before the first UN (the member states) for implementation.

With the backdrop of the 2015 reviews, let us look at the paralytic nature of the three UNs using the beloved language of the UN: through three Ps. The reviews originated from the Secretariat, as represented and commissioned by the UN secretary general. The Secretariat's ambitions mark the first P, persistence. The Secretariat is caught between two conflicting roles—one as a shadow-servant to the will of the most powerful of the member states and the other as a charter-abider 'responsible only to the Organization.' It is thus characterized in practice by its persistence in seeking institutional reform to free itself from this debilitating duality.

Upon invitation by the secretary general, the reviews were tasked to the third UN, independent experts unaffiliated with the UN. Absent of influence from the institution or member states, these experts are driven by the second P, progress. The third UN holds no stakes in the UN and works solely to influence and better the institutional mechanism. Their legitimacy is derived from their neutrality (or rather, their assumed neutrality), which in turn allows for exclusive focus on progress. Their independence, however, invites its vices. Their powers extend only so far as to provide recommendations to the institution and to publicly name and shame. Their executive powers are non-existent; they are a brain without a body.

Reform proposals are placed before the first UN, the member states, whose ultimate agenda is the final P, perseverance. In the hierarchy of the three UNs, the member states take the crown. After all, the institution was created by states to facilitate relations between sovereign and equal states. All executive action, including UN reform, is ultimately left at the mercy and will of member states. The status quo within the UN is etched into its foundation, with member states—most importantly the P5[69]—on the winning side. It is fundamentally delusional to expect the greatest benefactors of the current system to shuffle the status quo around to their disadvantage. Thus, there remains little mystery as to why the recommendations were yet to be operationalized.

The troika of perseverance, progress, and persistence holds immense potential to steer the UN towards reform that redeems its cowering credibility. But the three Ps' current matching with the three UNs make for a combination hazardous to the legitimacy of the UN.

The global crises today serve as a litmus test for the effectiveness of the institution in its current form. Clearly, the UN is not succeeding. The only road forward is reform to reconcile the three UNs. If any or all of the UNs are unwilling to commit to a unified agenda, all UNs must accept their obsoleteness and step aside. To do otherwise is to entrench the UN deeper in delusion.

Management Reform

Standing before the General Assembly on 12 December 2016 to take oath of office, Secretary General-elect Antonio Guterres mused, 'Looking at United Nations staff and budgetary rules and regulations, one might think that some of them were designed to prevent, rather than enable, the effective delivery of our mandates.'[70] Addressing the observation by the chief executive of the UN is critical in order to create an environment that facilitates the recommendations of the 2015 reviews.

Secretary General Guterres, since beginning his tenure in January 2017, has kept true to his campaign promise to prioritize management reform and reform of the peace and security architecture.[71]

Management reform has been long-sought, rightfully so. His commitment to management reform has been received popularly in a letter dated 18 July 2017. A group of thirty-seven permanent representatives to the UN—including two P5 representatives from the US and UK—had the following to say to the secretary general:

We encourage you to establish a bold strategy whereby you use
your executive authority to advance organizational reforms.
We will support you fully in exercising such authority—and
urge you to reclaim the powers that have been eroded over
time.[72]

And yet, this is likely to go nowhere in the absence of clear
thinking and a hard bargain. It is almost a cliché to say that
the current composition and architecture of the UNSC does
not reflect the reality of today. Equally, all the efforts in the
final year of the Ban Ki Moon administration to revisit various
peace-related processes, covered in some detail on previous
pages, individually and collectively amount to very little in
the absence of the fundamental reform required of the body
designated to deal with issues related to peace and security and
the only one designated to make a determination of where such
a threat exists. More importantly, it is the only body that has
the formal sanction and authority to do so.

One only has to take a good hard look at all the conflicts
raging around the globe today to get a fairly accurate picture
of the relevance of the UNSC. The fact that nation states are
allowed to wage war either in self-defence or only with the
specific authorization of the Security Council where the council
has been consulted, or in some other way involved, shows the
council in very poor light. In most of these cases—Libya, Syria,
Yemen, Ukraine—the council's involvement, in whatever form,
has had an exacerbating rather than an ameliorating effect. The
only one among these cases—Libya—where the use of force
was specifically sanctioned by the council is in a shambles with
little or no governance. In the case of Syria, the council failed
to act in the light of repeated vetoes by two of its permanent
members.

What is it about the UN Security Council that appears most at risk as we are about to enter the third decade of the twenty-first century? My submission is that what is most at risk is the one unique power that the council has—of being the only designated entity in the international system which can make a determination on whether or not there exists a threat to international peace and security. Having made that determination, it is the council alone that can authorize countervailing measures or the use of force. And this is perhaps the most worrying of all trends. Countries big and small, the powerful and not so powerful, use both covert and overt means to declare war on other countries without feeling the need, let alone the compulsion, to make a reference to the council.

India and the United Nations

India's engagement with multilateral diplomacy began even before we attained freedom from the Raj. On 1 January 1942, India become one of the founding members of the UN as it signed the Declaration by the United Nations in Washington DC.[73]

The context of India's entry into the UN, in fact that of the establishment of the UN itself, needs to be recalled to better understand the relationship that the two share today, and how it can progress in the years to come.

The UN Charter was negotiated during a three-year period when the World War II was still being fought. As the preamble makes clear, the objective of such a multilateral institution, since the time of its inception, has been:[74]

• To save succeeding generations from the scourge of war, which twice in our lifetime has brought untold sorrow to mankind

- To reaffirm faith in fundamental human rights, in the dignity and worth of the human person, in the equal rights of men and women and of nations large and small
- To establish conditions under which justice and respect for the obligations arising from treaties and other sources of international law can be maintained
- To promote social progress and better standards of life in larger freedom

These lofty ambitions resonated with India's own nationalist movement. After two hundred years of imperial rule, which included forced participation of Indian troops in both World Wars, it was only natural that India would not only sign the Charter, but also help shape the foundations of any global institution that resonated with its own civilizational ethos— 'Vasudhaiva Kutumbakam [the whole world is one family]'.

India's post-independence Constitution, anchored in justice, liberty and equality, too echoes much of the idealism of the UN Charter. And given India's multicultural, multi-ethnic and multilingual ethos, it would safe to dub the nation a mini UN of sorts.

Over seventy years on, the significance of a multinational, multilateral institution to India's position in the world, and its growth trajectory, remains seminal. And conversely, the world's largest democracy and a country on the cusp of great power status, is critical to maintain the credibility and legitimacy of the UN.

Global conversations, like the post-2015 development agenda, international cyber norms, UN conventions on terrorism and global finance and trade rules, will have as strong a bearing on India's future as any domestic regulation to reform the country's economic and social landscape. And

India too enjoys a de-facto veto in vital global conversations—the climate negotiation at Paris is one such example. COP 21 would not have achieved the success it did, had India not shown leadership and driven the negotiations towards an outcome which was agreeable to 193 nations.

As a young professional who tasted his first experience of multilateral diplomacy as the first secretary on India's two-member delegation to the General Agreement on Tariffs and Trade (GATT) from September 1981 to 1984, I realized very early on that almost every nation views global issues through the prism of its narrowly defined national interest. This sobering realization only grows as one moves up the ladder. I have served in various capacities at UN since 1981, including as India's permanent representative to the UN both in Geneva (2002–2005) and New York (2009–2013), and can attest to the power play that plays out in these corridors. In fact, one need not look too far back to find an example of high-political drama at the UN—the recent India-UK face-off to get a judge nominated at the International Court of Justice provides ample evidence of the same.

Perhaps the most political of all bodies at the UN is the Security Council for there is clear advantage in sitting around the famous horseshoe table.

One of my eternal regrets has been my inability to persuade decision makers in New Delhi on the need to take Security Council reform more seriously. In all such discussions over the past decade or so, the cautious or the risk-averse bureaucrat succeeded in playing on the fault lines of a less than fully focused political class. Add to it our loss to Japan in 1996, in the election for a non-permanent seat membership representing Asia, which led to delusional thinking within the ranks of the Indian bureaucracy, culminating in specious arguments such as, permanent membership will come without a veto, that it would be a 'second class' membership.

I was deputed as India's permanent representative at the UN in 2009 to organize India's campaign for non-permanent membership. Our win by a record margin (186 votes out of 191) and the subsequent membership in the council for the years 2011 and 2012, has played a significant part in bringing about some change in this mindset back home.

Ultimately, it is only when the Indian bureaucrat realizes that, in the larger scheme of things, even a long term non-permanent membership would be infinitely superior to the present situation, will any reform proposed by India hold weight at this global forum. Else, we will have to wait again, albeit for a shorter time period (ten years since India is up for membership again in 2021),[75] to get our rightful place on the Security Council.

To end this section on a more positive note, I have good reason to believe that with Prime Minister Modi's first term in office concentrated on domestic transformation, as witnessed through the various flagship programmes, a concerted Indian push for expansion and reform of the United Nations Security Council will most definitely come in the second term.

CHAPTER 6

The Politics of Terror

'Either you are with us, or you are with the terrorist.'

—President George W. Bush, 21 September 2001[1]

Just twelve days after the worst terror attack in the history of the United States, President George W. Bush, addressed a joint session of Congress where he laid out the terms and conditions of what came to be known as the 'War on Terror'.

His speech has largely shaped the post-9/11 narrative on terror across the world. The admission that the United States of America was no longer safe from terror attacks perhaps had the most far-reaching impact on world affairs, since the ill-fated Japanese bombing of Pearl Harbour during World War II.

* * *

Nowhere is the delusional streak in policymaking more evident than in the manner in which governments deal with the issue of terrorism. This has been so for a very long time. And this continues to be the case even today.

I have had the privilege, perhaps more appropriately described as a challenge of nightmarish proportion, to deal with issues of terrorism upfront on at least three occasions in a

155

long professional career spanning over four decades. On each
of these occasions, I felt a strong need to de-hyphenate facts
from fiction and to reorient the thinking of those responsible
for decision-making. The evolution of the terrorist threat has
been deeply influenced by delusional thinking and consequently
flawed decision-making. The manner in which governments—
individually and collectively—have responded to, and are
continuing to respond to, this challenge has come to pose
nothing short of an existential threat to mankind.

Let us start with two recent examples: the so-called
victories over the dreaded, hydra-headed monster called the
Islamic State of Iraq and Syria, ISIS or ISIL, and the liberation
of Raqqa and Mosul.

In a statement issued on 20 October 2017, on Raqqa's
liberation from ISIS, the US State Department, inter alia, said:

'In January, ISIS was actively plotting terrorist attacks
against our allies and our homeland in Raqqa. Nine short
months later, it is out of ISIS's control due to critical decisions
President Trump made to accelerate the campaign. Over the
last seven months, millions of people have been liberated
from ISIS's brutal rule and working with our partners on
the ground we are setting the conditions to enable people to
return home.'[2]

'ISIS's cruelty and barbarity cannot be overstated. ISIS is
deliberately and consistently using civilians as human shields
and leaving behind mines to maim and kill children and other
civilians seeking only to return to their homes or schools. The
barbaric nature of ISIS's tactics left many scars and we are
supporting stabilization efforts in liberated areas to help these
communities heal.'[3]

'ISIS's loss of Raqqa does not mean our fight against ISIS is
over. The Global Coalition will continue to draw on all elements

of national power —military, intelligence, diplomacy, economic, law enforcement, and the strength of our communities—until all Syrians have been liberated from ISIS brutality and we can ensure that it can no longer export its terror around the world. The Coalition will continue its relentless campaign to deny ISIS safe haven anywhere in the world, and sever its ability to recruit, move foreign terrorist fighters, transfer funds, and spread false propaganda over the internet and social media. We are confident that we will prevail and defeat this brutal terrorist organization.'[4]

ISIS is the first terrorist group that has demonstrated the ability to hold territory and run its own version of an administration, collecting taxes and dispensing justice. That it was able to do so with the tacit acceptance and, in some respects, the enthusiasm of the population it governed rang alarm bells in the West and its partners—the governing regimes in North Africa and West Asia. To that extent, the liberation of Raqqa, like the liberation of Mosul earlier in July 2017, represents a major victory in the fight against ISIS in several respects.

To dispel the 'caliphate' from its proclaimed physical boundaries needs to be welcomed. That is the point, however, where sober introspection should start. Both Raqqa and Mosul were completely destroyed, millions were displaced and the bulk of the ISIS fighters fled. The sleeper cells, the mined areas and the booby-trapped buildings that remained will only add to the devastation. A more relevant question that needs to be asked is: Do we have a realistic assessment of the extent of the collateral damage caused by the so-called 'liberation' of these two strongholds? The millions displaced are unlikely to be welcomed in the West. The lack of civil liberties in the repressive regimes in the region will continue to provide encouragement and succour to the fleeing fighters. Even if they cannot re-establish the caliphate, it is entirely possible that they will add to the number of the invisible but growing army willing to undertake lone wolf attacks in different Western cities or, for that matter, elsewhere. The victors of the military action in Mosul and Raqqa themselves admit:

'ISIS's loss of Raqqa does not mean our fight against ISIS is over.'[5]

The effort, in retrospect, was:

> . . . to deny ISIS safe haven anywhere in the world, and sever its ability to recruit, move foreign terrorist fighters, transfer funds and spread false propaganda over the internet and social media.[6]

None of the above requires the holding of territory either in or through a caliphate. In today's day and age, all these functions can and will continue to be performed by individuals or groups over the Internet.

The threat from ISIS may just have become more serious.

Prior to the terrorist attacks on 11 September 2001 when nineteen terrorists associated with the Islamic extremist group Al-Qaeda hijacked four airplanes and carried out suicide attacks against targets in the United States, mainstream opinion in the United States and Western Europe viewed terrorism as someone else's problem. And because terrorism had thus far not targeted innocent lives in the West, perceptions and analyses tended to be anchored in a theoretical and philosophical construct that overlooked the fact that a terrorist takes away the most fundamental right of all—the right to life.

In the seventeen years since (2001), the global terror machine has witnessed exponential growth, governments have invariably dealt with and responded to the immediate threat and often employed methods that, over an extended period of time, have exacerbated the problem.

Let me, however, first recount the three occasions when I had to deal with issues relating to terrorism. These experiences shaped my attitude in the most fundamental way.

The first: As a young political officer in the High Commission of India in Colombo, between December 1984 and March 1988, I was assigned duties that required me to maintain contact with Tamil terror groups in general and with the Liberation Tigers of Tamil Eelam (LTTE) in particular. The second: When I was the Deputy High Commissioner of India in London, between 1999 and 2002, I saw jihadi terror networks working the liberal democratic system and taking advantage of the freedoms on offer. Finally, as the permanent representative of India to the United Nations in New York, I had the privilege of representing India on the Security Council in 2011–2012, presiding over the council in August 2011 and November 2012 and chairing the Security Council's Counter Terrorism Committee in 2011–12. The Security Council's Counter Terrorism Committee was established in pursuance of the UNSC Resolution 1373 following the terror attacks in New York on 9/11.

The council is the designated agency in the multilateral system to deal with threats to international peace and security. It is the body designated and authorized to make a determination on whether a particular development does indeed constitute a threat to international peace and security. Having determined that, it alone has the authority to authorize counter measures, or the 'use of force', euphemistically called 'all means necessary'.

On each of these occasions, starting from the mid-1980s to the present, a period spanning over three decades, I was alarmed by the international community's inability to come to terms with the basics of international terrorism.

Let me explain. There are several enduring and abiding myths about terrorism:

- That it is umbilically linked to abject poverty
- That it is linked to, or largely anchored in, a particular religion
- That if only the state could provide good education and jobs, we would be in a position to wean youngsters away from violent extremism and radicalism.

The above are only illustrative. As with other generalizations, the perceptions listed above reflect and capture only a limited segment of the folklore and simplistic understanding of the reality that constitutes today's hardcore terrorism. Equally, they represent the view of the commentator or analyst and, at best, only a myopic and subjective characterization of an event or occurrence. Most often, the characterization is time and context specific.

Terrorism was listed as one of the sixteen thematic issues identified by the Independent Commission on Multilateralism (ICM) for its study of the functioning of the multilateral system, anchored in the United Nations, on its seventeenth anniversary. The multilateral system in and around the United Nations periodically establishes independent commissions to seek a focused review of the dominant concerns/themes. Such a commission has the advantage of in-depth examination without the procedural encumbrances of the UN and the tyranny of experts. Such commissions are invariably headed by a former head of state/government.

As the secretary general of the Independent Commission on Multilateralism (ICM), headed by Kevin Rudd, the former prime minister of Australia, I had the privilege of being personally associated with the drafting of the ICM's discussion paper.[7] Some of the analysis that follows draws on my inputs for that exercise.

It is surprising that even decades after the international community faced the scourge of terrorism, some people continue to spread the enduring and abiding myth that terrorism is linked to abject poverty. If this were true, the parts characterized by abject poverty should have been the epicentre of terrorism. It's possible that poor and uneducated youth can be more easily attracted to a contrived narrative and used as cannon fodder to perpetuate acts of criminality and terrorism. However, analyses show that in each of these cases, other factors and considerations have played an equally, if not more, decisive role to create the terror machine. Targeted provisioning of funds, lack of civil liberties, the role of a pernicious state, which has used terrorism as an instrument of policy, and a variety of other factors emerge through such analyses. Terrorism has found fertile recruiting ground not in sub-Saharan Africa or the other least developed countries of the world but in countries of West Asia, Pakistan and elsewhere. It is not that poverty is not an important factor. However, when a holistic study is undertaken, one which includes all the factors/issues at play, the pattern that emerges is one in which poverty has been a small and most certainly not the decisive determinant for the growth of terrorism in West Asia.

The second proposition, that this has something to do with religion with a finger pointing at one religion, merits careful discussion. If Islam alone had something to do with terrorism then the most populated Islamic countries in the world—Indonesia, India and Bangladesh—should have been the epicentres of inspiring, witnessing and exporting terrorism.

Instead Al Qaeda, ISIS, Lashkar-e-Taiba, Jaish-e-Mohammed are nurtured in a specific political environment where a variety of factors play on religion as the background factor. Like poverty, religion alone cannot provide a sufficient explanation and by no means be construed as the important and decisive determinant.

And finally, the widely repeated assertion that if states could provide good education, there would be a greatly reduced desire for potential terrorists to join the jihad and commit acts of criminality. I wonder how easily this somewhat over-simplistic view finds acceptance. This overlooks the fact that some of the world's most notorious terrorists have had the benefit of the best possible education. Like poverty and religion, education, and the kind of education imparted, might play a small role in the larger narrative that begets an individual to follow an extremist value system, but a response which only looks at this aspect is handicapped from its very inception.

Many factors drive and sustain today's terrorism. In essence, it is a phenomenon that stems from a constellation of fault lines. Imbalances caused by exclusionary, unaccountable and ideologically based governance should be the starting point for an analysis. Inequitable distribution of resources and new and emerging forms of geopolitical power rivalries that are reshaping the trajectory of these imbalances and their outcomes provide the second set of viable explanation. Deft use of web-based communication technologies, including social media, has made it possible for terrorist organizations and organized crime networks to make inroads into disgruntled and marginalized communities and rally them on the basis of social injustices and grievances created by these imbalances. Marginalized youth have been a prime target. Armed non-state actors who hold territory, command resources and engage in highly lucrative illicit economic activities have made these youth their primary recruits.

Multilateral efforts, primarily under the aegis of the United Nations Security Council, have provided various forms of capacity development support and other measures to strengthen member states' domestic counterterrorism initiatives. However, certain ambiguities inherent in these measures and in their uneven implementation have provided a convenient pretext for some to pursue double standards in the fight against terrorism. Factors like the 'siloed' approach to the problem and the inability to agree on a universal definition of terrorism have further hampered these efforts.

The notion that the fight against terrorism can be won primarily by military force, law enforcement measures and intelligence operations is losing currency. The debate has slowly turned to the need for a comprehensive and long-term approach, rooted in political and socio-economic strategies that encourage social inclusion, political participation and quality, as well as bottom-up strategies that address root causes at the national level.

Defining Terrorism

The United Nations—and the multilateral system more widely—remains deadlocked when it comes to a universal definition of terrorism. Because of the challenges posed by the lack of a universally accepted definition, the current framework of international law, although prohibiting terrorist acts in multiple forums, is not capable of addressing the full scope and the evolving nature of the terrorist threat.

The norms governing the use of force by non-state actors have not kept pace with those pertaining to states. This is not so much a legal question as a political one. Legally, almost all forms of terrorism are 'prohibited by one of twelve international counterterrorism conventions, international customary law, the Geneva Conventions or the Rome Statutes'.[8] The fifteen major legal instruments and additional amendments addressing terrorism that exist within the UN system are listed in Annexure 1.

It remains elusive—if not impossible—for the United Nations to achieve the same degree of normative strength concerning non-state use of force as it has concerning state use of force. Lack of agreement on a clear and well-known definition diminishes the normative and moral stance against terrorism.

The search for an agreed definition stumbles on two issues. 'The first is the argument that any definition should include states' use of armed forces against civilians. The second objection is that people under foreign occupation have a right to resistance and a definition of terrorism should not override this right.'[9] In the latter case, as the saying goes: 'One man's terrorist is another man's freedom fighter.'

The inability of member states to agree on an anti-terrorism convention, including a definition, has prevented the United Nations from 'exerting its moral authority and from sending an unequivocal message that terrorism is never an acceptable tactic, even for the most defensible of causes'.[10] Nevertheless, there is a question of what impact a universal definition will have on ground realities.

While the debate over a definition of terrorism may continue, there ought to be no ambiguity on what constitutes 'acts of terrorism' and strict implementation of a universal zero-tolerance norm. Overall, consensus on the pre-eminence of universal non-tolerance for deliberate attacks on non-combatants regardless of any justification should surpass the technicalities of a definition.

The Politics of Terror

No matter where the arena, I find it inconceivable that any terror outfit can outgrow its modest beginning without external assistance. Such assistance more often than not is provided by a group of individuals/another state or other entities because it is perceived that provision of such assistance will help further any one or more set of causes: the furtherance of human rights, minority rights, etc.

Sri Lanka offers an interesting case study.

Having enjoyed what was perceived as an unfair advantage in government jobs on account of access to the English language, Sri Lanka's Tamil minority began to witness a turning of the tide and a slow but sure erosion of minority rights following the passage of the Sinhala Only Act in 1956.[11] The political class in New Delhi failed to fully comprehend the implications of the act and initially viewed it as a 'coordination of anti-imperialist sentiment'.[12]

After being subjected to a systematic trampling of their minority rights in subsequent years and the anti-Tamil riots in Colombo in 1983, there was little doubt left in the mind of the average Sri Lankan Tamil that the Sinhala state had decided to provide a cover for the anti-Tamil riots, the colonization of Tamil areas and the not-too-infrequent rape of their women. This is usually the point at which 'fact' and 'fiction' merge and fuse. The Sinhala state, was at the very least, viewed as acquiescing the erosion of Tamil minority rights. This could not in and of itself provide justification for Tamil groups in India, the state government of Tamil Nadu and/or agencies of the central government in New Delhi to begin considering the financing of an enemy of the Sri Lankan state. And yet, this is precisely what happened. The rest is history. The Sri Lankan government maintains, for good reason, that absent support from India, they could have resolved their 'Tamil problem' much earlier.

There was significant evidence of delusional politics on both sides. At a social function hosted by High Commissioner Jyotindra Nath Dixit in Colombo, I recall someone asking Sirimavo Bandaranaike—the wife of S.W.R.D. Bandaranaike and herself a former prime minister of Sri Lanka, and the mother of Anura Bandaranaike and Chandrika Kumaratunga—an interesting question: What would you have done, and how would you have resolved the Sri Lankan ethnic crisis, or the Tamil issue as it is called. The response was instructive: I would have called my sister (meaning Indira Gandhi) and asked her to look the other way.

There was no subtlety, no ambiguity. A clear statement indicating the mindset of using force.

How much more delusional can one get? On the one hand, the Sri Lankan state's use of force to wipe out a struggle for minority rights and, on the other, the decision by elements in India to encourage the taking up of arms to unravel a sovereign state and its duly elected government.

Assigned to the Court of St. James (as the deputy High commissioner of India in London from January 1999 to March 2002), I was personally witness to and often articulated my frustration with interlocutors in the host government because of the visible double standards in play on issues relating to terrorism. It is so very easy to take pride in one's democratic institutions and the freedom these provide. It is also tempting to turn a blind eye to the reality that this freedom is being misused to the detriment of others. It is also counterproductive. As Hillary Clinton famously observed later (in the context of Pakistan), 'You can't keep snakes in your backyard and expect them only to bite your neighbours.'[13]

Traditionally, Western political theory regards the 'state' as an all-powerful and often repressive entity and the individual as helpless, weak and vulnerable. The human rights discourse has been anchored almost entirely on the presumption that it is only this state that commits human rights violations.

London shut its eyes to what was being preached in the mosques, and the JKLF assassination of Ravindra Mhatre, India's representative in Birmingham in 1984. The active participation of British Muslims of Pakistani origin in violence perpetrated in South Asia was only the precursor. The 'use of force' in Libya and Syria in essence sealed the deal and the birth of ISIS heralded the coming of age of the non-state military actor.

Because the UK ignored the rising radical sentiment in its own backyard for so long, it is now faced with an even greater challenge—online radicalism.

The Internet, which has allowed a conglomeration of deviants, does not respect geographical boundaries. Earlier, vulnerable youth had to walk to their neighbourhood mosque to get radicalized but now all they have to do is log on to the Internet and click on a few tabs to join global jihad.

It is a shame that only after a spate of 'lone-wolf' terror attacks on its soil, and across Europe, that the UK decided to finally shed some of its delusions. It recently set up an exclusive police counterterrorism unit which flags content that is deemed going against UK's legislation, with online platforms. Through a collaborative exercise, the police unit and the online platform take down such content.

However, there is still a long way to go on how Her Majesty's government views non-state military actors, particularly those who have their origins in South Asia. Its past history with Pakistan blinds it to the ground realities—organizations such as Jamaat-ud-Dawa are no different from ISIS. In fact, the ISIS has arguably drawn inspiration from a country like Pakistan, which uses non-state actors as a proxy for achieving geopolitical goals.

Delusional Politics at Its Best

The Counter-Terrorism Committee of the United Nations Security Council held a special meeting on 28 September 2011 to mark the tenth anniversary of the adoption of Security Council Resolution 1373 and urged 'all Member States to ensure zero tolerance towards terrorism and take urgent action to combat terrorism in all its forms and manifestations.'[14] As the chair of the committee, I presided over this special session in which the 'zero-tolerance' norm was adopted.

Two developments helped change that narrative: reaction to 9/11, and the use of military force in Iraq in 2003 and Libya in 2011.

It became abundantly clear that organized terror outfits or non-state military actors cannot exist without the active arming and funding by some states, or at the very least acquiescence by them. ISIS, for example, is the unwanted child of a failed, incompetently handled and neglected occupation (in Iraq).

There is a widespread tendency to underestimate the deep emotional and ideological reasons that prompt young men and women to take up arms and even lay down their lives for a cause they believe in, or have been persuaded to embrace. Radicalization and violent extremism need to be understood if they are to be countered effectively. Locking up unemployed and radicalized youths only helps incubate Al-Qaeda in jails.

Much of the global counterterrorism effort is delusional. It is laying the foundation for deeper polarization and radicalization that will make the world less safe than it already is. Why do I make this claim? Well a closer look at the two approaches used in the war against terror reveals that they both fit the delusional category.

First, erosion of the rule of law. As already touched upon briefly, it is now widely accepted that the American-led invasion of Iraq was illegal.[15] There were no weapons of mass destruction, and despite Saddam Hussain's violently dictatorial regime, many more lives were lost as a result of the US invasion of the country. By disregarding international law and without giving due consideration to the international ramifications of such an invasion (the United Nations Security Council was largely ignored prior to the misadventure) the US and its allies created the monster that we today refer to as ISIS. My previous book was on this very subject and studied the cases of Libya, Syria, Yemen, Crimea and Sri Lanka. It was aptly titled *Perilous Interventions*.

The second approach, a spectacular failure, is that of arming terror outfits. Often done under the garb of promoting democracy, the real motivation here is regime change for geopolitical gains. The American-led support to militant political Islamic organizations is well documented, with its crowning glory being Al-Qaeda.

As General William Odom, director of the National Security Agency under President Ronald Reagan, said: 'By any measure the U.S. has long used terrorism. In 1978-79 the Senate was trying to pass a law against international terrorism—in every version they produced, the lawyers said the U.S. would be in violation.'[16]

And it is not just Western nations which are complicit. Other countries in the region such as Saudi Arabia, Qatar, UAE, Iran and Turkey, have also played their part. Turkey is known to provide a safe haven to ISIS fighters, particularly those joining the terror organization from Europe and UK.[17] And the rise of Pakistan's ISI (the mastermind behind terror attacks in India) is predicated on importing Saudi Arabia's Wahhabism, along with a large helping of financial and technical resources.[18]

Moving forward, violent extremism and terrorism can be better countered if it is approached through the prism of dialogue and discourse, and state responsibility.

The war on global terror can only be won through a process of dialogue among nations where the discourse is focused on the international repercussions of what is an international security threat. Such a discourse, which is anchored in human rights, but not constrained by it, must transcend national interest and look at terrorism for what is—a threat to delicately balanced peace and security architecture, effectively established post the devastation of World War II.

In the absence of an agreement over the definition of 'terrorism', what must be made clear is that there is no such thing as a 'good' terrorist, and responsibility for the tragic loss of life and property as a result of this 'good' theory must be affixed on states supporting these claims. Terror plots only come to fruition with the help of governments/agencies that, under the garb of 'non-state' actors, propagate proxy wars and use terror as a tool for achieving their geostrategic goals. Just as no terror plot would be successful without this government support, no Countering Violent Extremism strategy will be successful without state responsibility. Name and shame is, in the words of Victory Hugo, an idea whose time has come.

Annexure I

International Conventions

Fifteen major legal instruments and additional amendments addressing terrorism exist within the UN context, as follows:

1. 1963 Convention on Offences and Certain Other Acts Committed On Board Aircraft (Aircraft Convention)[19]
   o Applies to acts affecting in-flight safety.
   o Authorizes the aircraft commander to impose reasonable measures, including restraint, on any person he or she has reason to believe has committed or is about to commit such an act, where necessary to protect the safety of the aircraft.
   o Requires contracting states to take custody of offenders and to return control of the aircraft to the lawful commander.

2. 1970 Convention for the Suppression of Unlawful Seizure of Aircraft (Unlawful Seizure Convention)[20]
   o Makes it an offence for any person on board an aircraft in flight to unlawfully, by force or threat thereof, or any other form of intimidation, [to] seize or exercise control of that aircraft or to attempt to do so.
   o Requires parties to the convention to make hijackings punishable by 'severe penalties'.
   o Requires parties that have custody of offenders to either extradite the offender or submit the case for prosecution.
   o Requires parties to assist each other in connection with criminal proceedings brought under the Convention.

3. 1971 Convention for the Suppression of Unlawful Acts
    against the Safety of Civil Aviation (Civil Aviation
    Convention)[21]

    o   Makes it an offence for any person unlawfully and
        intentionally to perform an act of violence against a
        person on board an aircraft in flight, if that act is likely to
        endanger the safety of the aircraft; to place an explosive
        device on an aircraft; to attempt such acts; or to be an
        accomplice of a person who performs or attempts to
        perform such acts.

    o   Requires parties to the Convention to make offences
        punishable by severe penalties.

    o   Requires parties that have custody of offenders to either
        extradite the offender or submit the case for prosecution.

4. 1973 Convention on the Prevention and Punishment
    of Crimes against Internationally Protected Persons
    (Diplomatic Agents Convention)[22]

    o   Defines an 'internationally protected person' as a head
        of state, minister for foreign affairs, representative or
        official of a state or international organization who is
        entitled to special protection in a foreign state, and his/
        her family.

    o   Requires parties to criminalize and make punishable 'by
        appropriate penalties which take into account their grave
        nature' the intentional murder, kidnapping, or other
        attack upon the person or liberty of an internationally
        protected person, a violent attack upon the official
        premises, the private accommodations, or the means of
        transport of such person; a threat or attempt to commit
        such an attack; and an act 'constituting participation as
        an accomplice'.

5. 1979 International Convention against the Taking of Hostages (Hostages Convention)[23]

 o Provides that 'any person who seizes or detains and threatens to kill, to injure, or to continue to detain another person in order to compel a third party, namely, a State, an international intergovernmental organization, a natural or juridical person, or a group of persons, to do or abstain from doing any act as an explicit or implicit condition for the release of the hostage commits the offence of taking of hostage within the meaning of this Convention.

6. 1980 Convention on the Physical Protection of the Nuclear Material (Nuclear Materials Convention)[24]

 o Criminalizes the unlawful possession, use, transfer, or theft of nuclear material and threats to use nuclear material to cause death, serious injury, or substantial property damage.

Amendments to the Convention on the Physical Protection of Nuclear Material

 o Makes it legally binding for states parties to protect nuclear facilities and material in peaceful domestic use, storage as well as transport.

 o Provides for expanded cooperation between and among states regarding rapid measures to locate and recover stolen or smuggled nuclear material, mitigate any radiological consequences or sabotage, and prevent and combat related offences.

7. 1988 Protocol for the Suppression of Unlawful Acts of Violence at Airports Serving International Civil Aviation, supplementary to the Convention for the Suppression of

Unlawful Acts against the Safety of Civil Aviation (extends and supplements the Montreal Convention on Air Safety) (Airport Protocol)[25]

o   Extends the provisions of the Montreal Convention (see No. 3 above) to encompass terrorist acts at airports serving international civil aviation.

8. 1988 Convention for the Suppression of Unlawful Acts against the Safety of Maritime Navigation (Maritime Convention)[26]

o   Establishes a legal regime applicable to acts against international maritime navigation that is similar to the regimes established for international aviation.

o   Makes it an offence for a person unlawfully and intentionally to seize or exercise control over a ship by force, threat, or intimidation; to perform an act of violence against a person on board a ship if that act is likely to endanger the safe navigation of the ship; to place a destructive device or substance aboard a ship; and other acts against the safety of ships.

9. 2005 Protocol to the Convention for the Suppression of Unlawful Acts against the Safety of Maritime Navigation

o   Criminalizes the use of a ship as a device to further an act of terrorism.

o   Criminalizes the transport on board a ship of various materials knowing that they are intended to be used to cause, or in a threat to cause, death or serious injury or damage to further an act of terrorism.

o   Criminalizes the transporting on board a ship of persons who have committed an act of terrorism.

o   Introduces procedures for governing the boarding of a ship believed to have committed an offence under the Convention.

10. 1988 Protocol for the Suppression of Unlawful Acts against the Safety of Fixed Platforms Located on the Continental Shelf (Fixed Platform Protocol)[27]
    o   Establishes a legal regime applicable to acts against fixed platforms on the continental shelf that is similar to the regimes established against international aviation.

11. 2005 Protocol to the Protocol for the Suppression of Unlawful Acts against the Safety of Fixed Platforms Located on the Continental Shelf[28]
    o   Adapts the changes to the Convention for the Suppression of Unlawful Acts against the Safety of Maritime Navigation to the context of fixed platforms located on the continental shelf.

12. 1991 Convention on the Marking of Plastic Explosives for the Purpose of Detection (Plastic Explosives Convention)[29]
    o   Designed to control and limit the use of unmarked and undetectable plastic explosives (negotiated in the aftermath of the 1988 Pan Am flight 103 bombing).
    o   Parties are obligated in their respective territories to ensure effective control over 'unmarked' plastic explosive, i.e., those that do not contain one of the detection agents described in the Technical Annex to the treaty.
    o   Generally speaking, each party must, inter alia, take necessary and effective measures to prohibit and prevent the manufacture of unmarked plastic explosives; prevent the movement of unmarked plastic explosives into or out of its territory; exercise strict and effective control over possession and transfer of unmarked explosives made or imported prior to the entry into force of the Convention; ensure that all stocks of unmarked

explosives not held by the military or police are destroyed, consumed, marked, or rendered permanently ineffective within three years; take necessary measures to ensure that unmarked plastic explosives held by the military or police are destroyed, consumed, marked, or rendered permanently ineffective within fifteen years; and, ensure the destruction, as soon as possible, of any unmarked explosives manufactured after the date of entry into force of the Convention for that state.

13. 1997 International Convention for the Suppression of Terrorist Bombings (Terrorist Bombing Convention[30])
   o Creates a regime of universal jurisdiction over the unlawful and intentional use of explosives and other lethal devices in, into, or against various defined public places with intent to kill or cause serious bodily injury, or with intent to cause extensive destruction of the public place.

14. 1999 International Convention for the Suppression of the Financing of Terrorism (Terrorist Financing Convention)[31]
   o Requires parties to take steps to prevent and counteract the financing of terrorists, whether direct or indirect, through groups claiming to have charitable, social, or cultural goals or which also engage in illicit activities such as drug trafficking or gunrunning.
   o Commits states to hold those who finance terrorism criminally, civilly, or administratively liable for such acts.
   o Provides for the identification, freezing, and seizure of funds allocated for terrorist activities, as well as for the sharing of the forfeited funds with other states on a

case-by-case basis. Bank secrecy is no longer adequate justification for refusing to cooperate.

15. 2005 International Convention for the Suppression of Acts of Nuclear Terrorism (Nuclear Terrorism Convention)[32]
    o Covers a broad range of acts and possible targets, including nuclear power plants and nuclear reactors.
    o Covers threats and attempts to commit such crimes or to participate in them, as an accomplice.
    o Stipulates that offenders shall be either extradited or prosecuted.
    o Encourages states to cooperate in preventing terrorist attacks by sharing information and assisting each other in connection with criminal investigations and extradition proceedings.
    o Deals with both crisis situations (assisting states to solve the situation) and post-crisis situations (rendering nuclear material safe through the International Atomic Energy Agency (IAEA).

* * *

Annexure II

Security Council Counterterrorism Resolutions, Committees and Subsidiary Bodies

The presidential statement adopted by the first-ever Security Council Summit held in January 1992 against the backdrop of the end of the Cold War had expressed its deep concern over acts of international terrorism. Since then, acting under Chapter VII in confronting the scourge of terrorism, the Security Council had adopted various resolutions and imposed sanctions regimes that had made mandatory the thrust of non-binding provisions of various terrorism-related conventions. In pursuance of Article 30 of the UN Charter, the Security Council has set up various subsidiary bodies to carry out its work.

The Security Council imposed sanctions against states considered having links to certain acts of terrorism, including Libya (1992), Sudan (1996) and Afghanistan (1999, expanded to include Al-Qaida in 2000 by Resolution 1333).

The Security Council set up the 1267 Committee in 1999 by its Resolution 1267 and tasked it with monitoring the sanctions against the Taliban (and subsequently al-Qaida as of 2000).[33] An analytical support and sanctions monitoring team comprising experts in counterterrorism and related legal issues, arms embargoes, travel bans, and terrorist financing was appointed to assist the committee.[34] Through its Resolution 1269 (1999), the Council urged countries to work together to prevent and suppress all terrorist acts.[35]

The mandate of the 1267 Committee stems from Security Council Resolution 1267 (of 1999). The mandate of the 1267 Committee was subsequently updated including through

Security Council Resolution 1904 (2009), which inter alia established the Office of Ombudsperson to handle the delisting requests from the Consolidated List. The core responsibility of the 1267 Committee is to work with member states to implement sanctions against al-Qaida and the Taliban, and their associated groups such as Jaish-e-Mohammed, Jamaat-ud-Dawa, and Lashkar-e-Taiba.[36]

In the aftermath of 11 September 2001, the Security Council established the Counter-Terrorism Committee (CTC), under Resolution 1373 (2001). The sweeping provisions of this resolution requests all states to: criminalize the financing of terrorists; freeze without delay any funds related to persons involved in acts of terrorism; deny all forms of financial support for terrorist groups; suppress the provision of safe haven, sustenance, or support for terrorists; share information with other governments on any groups practicing or planning terrorist acts; cooperate with other governments in the investigation, detection, arrest, extradition, and prosecution of those involved in such acts; and criminalize active and passive assistance for terrorism in domestic law and bring violators to justice and implement effective border control measures. The resolution also calls on states to become parties, as soon as possible, to the relevant international counterterrorism instruments.[37]

The CTC was established with the ultimate aim to increase the ability of states to fight terrorism. Unlike the 1267 Committee, it is not a sanctions body, nor does it maintain a list of terrorist organizations or individuals. To assist the CTC's work, the Security Council through its Resolution 1535, set up a Counter-Terrorism Committee Executive Directorate (CTED) to monitor the implementation of Resolution 1373 and to facilitate the provision of technical assistance to member states.[38]

Through Resolution 1540 (2004), which calls on states to prevent non-state actors (including terrorist groups) from accessing weapons of mass destruction, the Security Council established the 1540 Committee.[39]

The Security Council in subsequent resolutions urged member states to take action against groups and organizations engaged in terrorist activities that were not subject to the 1267 Committee's review. Resolution 1566 (2004) established the 1566 Working Group made up of all Security Council members to recommend practical measures against such individuals and groups, as well as to explore the possibility of setting up a compensation fund for victims of terrorism.[40]

On the margins of the 2005 World Summit, the Security Council held a high-level meeting and adopted Resolution 1624 (2005) condemning all acts of terrorism irrespective of their motivation, as well as the incitement to such acts.[41] It also called on member states to prohibit by law terrorist acts and incitement to commit them and to deny safe haven to anyone guilty of such conduct.

Through a number of additional resolutions, the Security Council has in the past few years strengthened the work of its counterterrorism bodies. In its Resolution 2133 (2014), it called on states not to pay ransom to terrorist kidnappers.[42] Recently, through Resolution 2178 (2014), it called on member states to prevent suspected foreign terrorist fighters from travelling to member states, and create legislation to prosecute them.[43] The resolution defines foreign terrorist fighters as 'individuals who travel to a state other than their states of residence or nationality for the purpose of the perpetration, planning, or preparation of, or participation in, terrorist acts or the providing or receiving of terrorist training, including in connection with armed conflict.[44]

Annexure III

CTITF Entities

- Counter-terrorism Committee Executive Directorate (CTED)
- Department of Peacekeeping Operations (DPKO)
- Department of Political Affairs (DPA)
- Department of Public Information (DPI)
- Department of Safety and Security (DSS)
- Expert Staff of 1540 Committee
- International Atomic Energy Agency (IAEA)
- International Civil Aviation Organization (ICAO)
- International Maritime Organization (IMO)
- International Monetary Fund (IMF)
- International Criminal Police Organization (INTERPOL)
- Monitoring Team of 1267 Committee
- Office for Disarmament Affairs (ODA)
- Office of the High Commissioner for Human Rights (OHCHR)
- Office of Legal Affairs (OLA)
- Office of the Secretary-General (OSG)
- Organization for the Prohibition of Chemical Weapons (OPCW)
- Special Rapporteur on the promotion and protection of human rights while countering terrorism
- United Nations Development Programme (UNDP)
- United Nations Educational, Scientific and Cultural Organization (UNESCO)
- United Nations Interregional Crime and Justice Research Institute (UNICRI)

- United Nations Office on Drugs and Crime (UNODC)
- World Customs Organization (WCO)
- World Bank
- World Health Organization (WHO)

Observers

- International Organization for Migration (IOM)
- Office of the Coordinator for Humanitarian Affairs (OCHA)
- United Nations Department for Economic and Social Affairs (DESA)
- United Nations Office of the Special Adviser on Africa (UNOSAA)
- United Nations High Commissioner for Refugees (UNHCR)

CHAPTER 7

The Politics of Trade Policy

'Anyone who reads GATT is likely to have his sanity impaired.'

—Senator Milliken, 1951

Thus spoke Senator Milliken back in 1951, at the hearings held by the Senate Finance Committee. John H. Jackson quoted Senator Milliken to introduce his seminal publication *World Trade and The Law of GATT*, the pre-eminent study on General Agreement on Tariffs and Trade (GATT).[1]

* * *

One might be tempted to ask, what is a chapter on international trade doing in a book titled *Delusional Politics*?

Decisions in the area of trade policy, as in the case of foreign and security policies, have to be made by individuals who ever so often show signs of delusional thinking and decision-making.

The following quotes from the forty-fifth President of the United States of America, Donald J. Trump, will provide guidance:

Our politicians have aggressively pursued a policy of globalization—moving our jobs, our wealth and our factories to Mexico and overseas.[2]

We will follow two simple rules: buy American and hire American.[3]

Who would have thought that the President of the United States—the nation of freedom and capitalism; the flag-bearer of an open, liberal, world order—would so viciously attack the very ethos international trade was instrumental in establishing, and whose fundamentals are so closely aligned with its own.

More importantly, the quoted statement of the President overlooks the fact that the US owes its pre-eminent position in the world to the open, liberal world order.

The following quotes from Xi Jinping, the Chinese premier, are further proof of delusional thinking in the international trade discourse:

It is true that economic globalization has created new problems. But this is no justification to write off economic globalization altogether. Rather we should adapt to and guide globalization, cushion its negative impact, and deliver its benefits to all countries and all nations.

Again, who would have thought that Communist China—with a GDP of over USD 11 trillion but one that has sought, albeit successfully, to manipulate the multilateral trading system—would by 2017 come to be the flag-bearer of global economic integration, as founded and exported under Western values?

* * *

'Thus, principal objectives of the WTO [World Trade Organization], as of the GATT, are raising standards of living, ensuring full employment, expanding production and trade, and allowing optimal use of the world's resources.'[4]

The establishment of the WTO on 1 January 1995 ushered in an age of unprecedented global economic prosperity. Opening of borders to goods and services from countries near and far, coupled with the adoption of the aforementioned Washington Consensus across geographies, became the template for growth and development.

The rationale behind trade liberalization and the Washington Consensus was predicated on the so-called comparative advantage theory—if China had the labour and United States the capital, it made sense for American firms to set up their factories in the People's Republic. China would profit by way of increased investment in its economy, employment for its workers and a trade surplus for the goods it would export back to the US. American firms, by employing cheap labour, could produce goods competitively and sell them for higher margins in their own country—a win-win solution.

Let's discuss the three reasons why this rationale is today facing a backlash. First, the rules of trade and liberalization disproportionately favoured the developed world, for these were conceptualized, designed and implemented by them. Moreover, developing nations started off at a disadvantage as their need for international finance, technology and markets was far stronger than the needs of developed countries, which were initially focused on resource extraction.

Second, trade liberalization, while bringing enormous economic prosperity in absolute terms, was unable to address rising inequality, both within and outside countries. Trickle-down economics largely failed, with rich countries getting richer, often at the expense of developing countries. Moreover, the top 1 per cent within both developed and developing countries benefitted exponentially, more than those in the bottom 99.[5]

Third, China's entry into the WTO and its rapid growth as a major exporter of manufactured goods left most other trading nations unprepared for the consequences of this rise.

These fault lines of the international liberal order were brought to the fore when the world underwent a global financial and economic crises (from December 2007 to June 2009). The US subprime crises and its impact on countries across geographies eroded any faith governments and their peoples had in the global economic integration. International trade in that sense was mere collateral damage.

In the context of India, trade liberalization in the past has happened out of compulsion and not necessarily out of conviction or on the basis of national consensus.

Now there appears to be the emergence of a consensus within the country on the need for reform and liberalization in order for the cake to be much bigger so that there is enough for everyone.

This consensus, however, is fragile and is subject to the vicissitudes of democracy, i.e. elections, management of vested interests and of a few clear redlines. It is contingent on the benefits trickling down to a larger number of people. The redlines referred to above are: rural, especially, farmer distress, massive job losses or reforms that further marginalize the 300 million or so people who live in extreme poverty.

Therefore, the challenge for any democratically elected government in India is to see how one can carry out incremental reforms without any of the redlines being crossed.

It is the author's submission that while no redline has been deliberately crossed so far by governments in the past, the 'policy space' which has been won has not been adequately leveraged. A good example is the Agreement on Textiles and Clothing of the Uruguay Round where India, almost single-handedly got rid of the quotas. But while we have taken some advantage of the elimination of quotas, the present situation is characterized by us having to play 'catch-up' not just with China, but also with the likes of Bangladesh, Sri Lanka and Vietnam. So, where did we go wrong?

An excerpt from my paper for Carnegie India, *India's Trade Policy Dilemma and the Role of Domestic Reform*, published in February 2017, summarizes India's inability to capitalize.

Over the years, India has paid insufficient attention to the value of trade policy. In 1996, for example, it was clear that the end of quotas under the Multi-Fiber Arrangement in 2005, would benefit the more competitive exporting developing countries and that modernization of India's domestic industry was critical. Many policy actions the BJP government undertook in 2016, such as the enhanced duty drawback scheme, had been suggested in 1996. Policy paralysis, lack of will, and perhaps even lack of full understanding prevented the required steps from being taken in 1996. Had timely action been taken, India's share of global trade in textiles and clothing would have been much larger . . . Instead, Bangladesh, China, and Vietnam were the big beneficiaries of the expiring of the erstwhile regime. Between 2000 and 2014, China's share of global exports rose from 10 per cent to 36 per cent in textiles and from 18 per cent to 39 per cent in garments.[6]

First, we need a set of good qualified professionals at the helm of the trade policy decision-making ecosystem—it's too important a matter to be left to generalists. Second, it is important to realize that trade liberalization *per se* will not bring benefits unless the domestic ecosystem, such as trade-related infrastructure, trade facilitation and domestic tax and investment regime, is reformed. Third, our private sector must learn and accept the need to compete. While the issue of dumping by Chinese companies may be a case apart, the same cannot be said about our inability to compete against ASEAN countries or other SAARC countries such as Sri Lanka and

Bangladesh. Fourth, India has to become a bigger part of the global value chain. Not only are we a small part of it at present, there is a danger that the global value chain itself may undergo dramatic transformation (Belt Road Initiative, among other things), and we may find ourselves on the fringes once again. Last but not least, the cataclysmic technological changes that are underway, whether it is artificial intelligence, robotics or just the sheer digitalization of the global economy, will have profound transformative effect.

India is one of the few major countries which has the good fortune that the Constitution provides clear powers to the government of the day to enter into international agreements.[7]

Given this, discussion of our stance at multilateral settings, including the WTO, in the Parliament has an overdose of politics. Trade policy is directly linked to national interest and economic prosperity and we need to develop a bipartisan consensus on the subject. This will strengthen the hands of the government of the day in negotiating with our international partners.

Bipartisan consensus should be supported by bringing in trade expertise to the government fold. Rather than generalist administrators, the government needs advice and assistance from the best in the business, whether they are in the commerce ministry or other ministries, Indian trade or economic service or chambers of commerce or think tanks. While the first steps in this process have been taken, the process itself needs to be taken much further.

The idea must be to depoliticize trade policy as much as possible in a democratic polity such as ours.

The important and positive developments that have happened since the Modi government came to power in 2014 pertain to the domains of trade-related infrastructure and ease of doing business. Some of these initiatives are listed below:

- Implementation of Goods and Services Tax to simplify India's taxation regime.
- Deleting obsolete laws and regulations from the books.
- The Delhi-Mumbai industrial corridor to develop twenty-first century smart cities for expanding India's manufacturing and services base.
- Implementation of Make in India Programme to transform India into a global design and manufacturing hub. A core component of this programme is to promote foreign direct investment in India.
- Implementation of National Waterways Act 2016 to promote connectivity and rejuvenate India's inland waterways.
- Implementation of Digital India Programme to ease government-business interface and thereby promote ease of doing business.

The private sector has undeniably played an important role in India's economic development since independence. But the time has come when massive investments are needed from it for both infrastructure and for acquisition of latest technology. Evidence, however, is strong that although massive reforms have been undertaken by the present government, there has not been a corresponding increase in investment by the private sector. How does one explain the reluctance of the private sector, especially in the face of the most industry-friendly government? The reason has to do with the short-term calculations of most of our private sector and the inability to take the leap in terms of technology and market developments. This is not a new phenomenon and the textiles industry displayed this kind of short-term focus in the wake of the Uruguay Round. The result is there for everyone to see.

All short-term considerations are bound to boomerang in the long run and this is something the private sector must reckon with. For the private sector to be a force multiplier, it has to be prepared to take risks in terms of both massive investment and latest technology.[8]

India is on the fringes of the global value chain today. The chief of the Asian Development Bank (ADB), Kenichi Yokoyama, said in November 2017 that 'the heart of the global value chain resides in Southeast Asia at the moment, and that India plays only a small part in that'.[9] He went on to add that ADB is working with Government of India to improve the situation. So, why is India on the fringes of the global value chain today? Well, there are many reasons for this. But we will begin with the issue of trade-related infrastructure.

The best example of this is to take the top twenty container ports of the world.

Rank	Port	Volume 2016 (Million TEU)
1	Shanghai, China	37.13
2	Singapore	30.90
3	Shenzhen, China	23.97
4	Ningbo-Zhoushan, China	21.60
5	Busan, South Korea	19.85
6	Hong Kong, S.A.R., China	19.81
7	Guangzhou Harbor, China	18.85
8	Qingdao, China	18.01
9	Jebel Ali, Dubai, United Arab Emirates	15.73

Rank	Port	Volume 2016 (Million TEU)
10	Tianjin, China	14.49
11	Port Klang, Malaysia	13.20
12	Rotterdam, Netherlands	12.38
13	Kaohsiung, Taiwan, China	10.46
14	Antwerp, Belgium	10.04
15	Dalian, China	9.61
16	Xiamen, China	9.61
17	Hamburg, Germany	8.91
18	Los Angeles, U.S.A.	8.86
19	Tanjung Pelepas, Malaysia	8.28
20	Keihin Ports, Japan	7.61

Source: World Shipping Council, http://www.worldshipping.org/about-the-industry/global-trade/top-50-world-container-ports.

No port in India figures in the top twenty in the world. On the other hand, there are plenty from China, Singapore, Dubai and some other countries in South East Asia. So, the first step is to build massive trade-related infrastructure. This we have finally started doing under the present government as infrastructure development is at the heart of its economic policy. A good example to cite here is the Sagarmala Programme. Predicated on the mantra 'P for P', i.e. ports for prosperity, the project aims to revitalize old ports to make them among the finest in the world.[10] As part of this programme, more than 577 projects, at the cost of Rs 8.57 lakh crore, have been identified for implementation between 2015 and 2035. This will be done across the areas of port modernization and new port development, port connectivity enhancement, port-linked industrialization and coastal community development. As of 31 March 2018, a total of 492 projects, with an estimate cost of Rs 4.25 lakh crore, were under various stages of implementation, development and completion.[11]

The world merchandise trade (valued at USD 16 trillion) can be broadly divided into two parts: small basket (30 per cent value) and big basket (70 per cent value).[12] Ironically, 70 per cent of India's exports belong to the small basket category, i.e. small diamonds, jewellery, rice, buffalo meat, shrimps, etc.[13] These are not only low value but are also at the fringes of the global value chain. At the higher end of the value chain are electronics, telecom and engineering goods. This is what India needs to target. Of course, in both auto components and pharma products we are already part of the global value chain and the challenge is to see if we can move up the chain. In addition to trade-related infrastructure, there is a need for trade facilitation and access to the latest technology. Finally, there is a need for specialized skills and for a massive effort on research and development. This alone will enable India to become a central part of the global value chain in a large number of products and services.

Trade policy also has to prepare for tomorrow's fourth industrial revolution. Artificial intelligence, robotics, cloud computing, automation, 3D printing, e-commerce and blockchain technology are all here to stay. NITI Aayog along with line ministries needs to take a good look at all the possible implications for an economy such as India's. It is already clear that some of these will have a large effect on key sectors which could do with massive improvements in efficiency. These include agriculture, health and education. Again, it is clear that we cannot leave this to generalist administrators. The government needs to listen to experts and specialists in this domain.

In the Indian context, the Fourth Industrial Revolution will essentially be about urban services and this could be a big win-win for India. Seventy per cent of the India of 2030 is yet to be built.[14] The prime minister's three flagship schemes—Swachh Bharat, Pradhan Mantri Awas Yojana and Smart Cities Mission—and their successful completion will introduce a paradigm shift. The affordable housing scheme requires the building of 10 million homes so that every Indian will have a home by 2022. Housing was how China climbed the economic ladder as well.[15] India today is a USD 2.8 trillion economy[16] with a 50 per cent external sector.[17] At the current rate of 7 per cent plus growth, by 2025, India's per capita GDP is expected to reach USD 5000, propelling India to a USD 5 trillion plus economy.

Two other issues are critical for India's trade policy. First, our approach to free and regional trade agreements; and second our approach to multilateral trade negotiations, especially in the WTO.

India has been a reluctant convert to free and regional trade agreements. For a long time under the GATT and even under the WTO, India was the most fervent supporter of the MFN-based (Most Favoured Nation) trade. This was laudable up until the time every major trading nation entered into a free or regional trading agreement. India was almost the only odd man out. To make matters worse, the GATT and then the WTO did not undertake a serious examination of the compatibility of the free or regional trade agreements and just blessed every such agreement reported to it. This, in retrospect, was a mistake since many free or regional agreements were more trade-diverting than trade-creating and actually undermined the open and non-discriminatory nature of the multilateral trading system. This being the case, India had no choice but to join the bandwagon of countries signing such agreements. As of date, India has signed some nineteen free trade agreements (FTAs)/

preferential trade agreements (PTAs), which are highlighted in the table below:

No.	Name
1	Agreement of Cooperation with Nepal to Control Unauthorized Trade
2	Agreement on Economic Cooperation between India and Finland
3	Agreement on SAARC Preferential Trading Arrangement SAPTA
4	Agreement on South Asia Free Trade Area SAFTA
5	Asia Pacific Trade Agreement APTA
6	CECA between The Republic of India and the Republic of Singapore
7	Comprehensive Economic Cooperation Agreement between India and Malaysia
8	India Africa Trade Agreement
9	India Chile PTA
10	India Afghanistan PTA
11	India ASEAN Agreements
12	India Bhutan Trade Agreement
13	India Japan CEPA
14	India Korea CEPA
15	India MERCOSUR PTA
16	India Nepal Trade Treaty
17	India Sri Lanka FTA
18	SAARC Agreement on Trade in Services SATIS
19	Treaty of Transit between India and Nepal

Source: Department of Commerce, Government of India, http://commerce.
nic.in/trade/international_ta.asp?id=2&trade=i.

India's experience with FTAs has been a mixed one. But this may also be because one of the criteria used by most observers is that if imports exceed exports under a FTA, then somehow it is not considered in India's interest. This may be too narrow a view. Imports may exceed exports, but what is important is whether this leads to efficiency, economic growth and job creation. The other yardstick used for arguing India has not gained much is that utilization rates in the FTAs signed so far have been low (a meagre 5 per cent and 25 per cent). Efforts need to be made to understand why this is low and how this can be augmented. The other grievance is that the area of services, where India holds a competitive advantage, is not opened up enough by our trading partners. This is a justifiable argument and our partners must understand that any tariff concessions they obtain from us is significant because of the size of our market. Given this, it is only fair that we get access to Mode 4, i.e., movement of professionals. Lastly, there is also the eternal question of technical barriers to trade (TBT) and sanitary and phytosanitary (SPS) standards of our products, which is difficult to negotiate in the context of FTAs since mutual recognition and equivalence cannot be determined beforehand.

Despite all of the above points, which are indeed valid, there is no getting away from the fact that FTAs are here to stay, and India has to simply find a way to deal with it from a position of advantage. The WTO is under tremendous strain and there is a real danger that MFN-based trade may be seriously undermined by growing protectionist sentiment around the world. Given this, FTAs may be a way out for several countries, and India will have to cope with this trend.

Against this background, a lot rides on India's participation in the Regional Comprehensive and Economic Partnership Agreement (RCEP).

The Association of Southeast Asian Nations (ASEAN) has free trade agreements with six partners, namely People's Republic of China (ACFTA), Republic of Korea (AKFTA), Japan (AJCEP), India (AIFTA) as well as Australia and New Zealand (AANZFTA).

In order to broaden and deepen the engagement among parties and to enhance their participation in the economic development of the region, the leaders of sixteen participating countries established the Regional Comprehensive Economic Partnership (RCEP). The RCEP was built upon the existing ASEAN+1 FTAs with the spirit to strengthen economic linkages and to enhance trade- and investment-related activities as well as to contribute to minimising development gap among the parties.

In August 2012, the 16 Economic Ministers endorsed the Guiding Principles and Objectives for Negotiating Comprehensive Economic Partnership. The RCEP negotiations were launched by Leaders from 10 ASEAN Member States (Brunei Darussalam, Cambodia, Indonesia, Lao PDR, Malaysia, Myanmar, the Philippines, Singapore, Thailand and Viet Nam) and six ASEAN FTA partners (Australia, People's Republic of China, India, Japan, Republic of Korea, and New Zealand) during the 21st ASEAN Summit and Related Summits in Phnom Penh, Cambodia in November 2012.

The objective of launching RCEP negotiations is to achieve a modern, comprehensive, high-quality, and mutually beneficial economic partnership agreement among the ASEAN Member States and ASEAN's FTA partners. The RCEP negotiations commenced in early 2013.

The RCEP negotiation includes: trade in goods, trade in services, investment, economic and technical cooperation, intellectual property, competition, dispute settlement, e-commerce, small and medium enterprises (SMEs) and other issues.[18]

One way for India to approach the RCEP negotiations is to prepare itself thoroughly based on its experience of FTAs with Singapore and ASEAN. These FTAs have given us a lot of experience, both good and bad, and this can be brought to bear on the talks. To walk away from RCEP would be a mistake on our part. It would be in our interest to negotiate and negotiate hard to achieve a deal that defends our national interest. If nothing else, this will keep us in good stead when it comes to negotiating in the WTO at a later stage.

It might be useful to draw some redlines in consultation with stakeholders and then take everyone into confidence so that there are no surprises in the outcome of these negotiations. The features that should not be underestimated while doing a cost-benefit analysis of our participation in the RCEP are: the potential gains of India being a greater part of the global supply chains; the access to technology our industries will gain; and the fact that our products will meet global standards on TBT and SPS.

The Foreign Trade Policy announced by the government (2015–20) had the following to say on FTAs:

Signing an FTA is the beginning, not the end of the process. Recognizing that it is important to review whether the concessions under these agreements are being gainfully utilized and have resulted in meaningful market access gains, an 'Impact Analysis' of FTAs has been instituted. Further, it is necessary to simplify and ease rules of origin criteria to position India effectively in global and regional value chains. The likelihood of duty inversions will continue to be closely monitored to ensure that industry is not put to any disadvantage. A system for capturing preferential data will be put in place at the earliest.[19]

It remains to be seen how quickly the above will be implemented. One welcome development is that a web portal on FTAs has been developed (http://indiantradeportal.in/) that provides both MFN and preferential tariff rates, rules of origin, and SPS and TBT standards under various FTAs signed by India. It also captures the trade flows from major trading partners. The data is provided at the eight-digit level of the Harmonized System of classification. The portal will be maintained and regularly updated by the Federation of Indian Export Organisations.

The Government of India took a laudable initiative in launching the Foreign Trade Policy for the period 2015–20.[20] The vision is to make India a significant participant in world trade by the year 2020 and to enable the country to assume a position of leadership in the international trade discourse. The government aims to increase India's exports of merchandise and services from USD 465.9 billion in 2013–14 to approximately USD 900 billion by 2019–20 and to raise India's share in world exports from 2 per cent to 3.5 per cent.

The FTP for 2015–20 seeks to provide a stable and sustainable policy environment for foreign trade in merchandise and services; link rules, procedures and incentives for exports and imports with other initiatives such as 'Make in India', 'Digital India' and 'Skills India' to create an 'Export Promotion Mission'; promote the diversification of India's export basket by helping various sectors of the Indian economy to gain global competitiveness; create an architecture for India's global trade engagement with a view to expanding its markets and better integrating with major regions, thereby increasing the demand for India's products and contributing to the 'Make in India' initiative; and to provide a mechanism for regular appraisal in order to rationalize imports and reduce the trade imbalance.[21]

The Foreign Trade Policy (2015–20) is an excellent presentation of the objectives and goals of the country's trade policy. If at all there is any point on which it could possibly be criticized is that it does not dwell much on where the resources are to be found, the various functions of the stakeholders and the means of implementation.

This is important because the endeavour to make India a significant participant in world trade by the year 2020 cannot be accomplished by the Union government alone. State governments have an important role to play. But so does the private sector, the chambers of commerce and even the public sector. It has been mentioned that the Indian industry must be ready for the challenge emanating from FTAs such as RCEP. But equally, the private sector must take risks and invest both within the country and outside.

This combined with access to the latest technology is the only way our products and services can become world class and India can become a central part of the global value chain. Again, in order to increase market share of our exports in the world from 2 to 3.5 per cent, the Foreign Trade Policy focuses on engineering, electronics and pharmaceuticals exports. The challenge, however, is not just to make products of world quality; this must be preceded by massive investment in research and development so that innovation can lead to higher positioning in the global value chain—an aspect the Foreign Trade Policy would have done well to address.

Finally, it is important to study our approach to multilateral negotiations and the WTO in particular. India has a long history of negotiating hard and if the occasion so arises, going it alone in multilateral trade negotiations. This is as it should be since

we are a large country with certain *sui generis* characteristics.
But it is also a fact that we have not done too badly where
we have engaged seriously and intensely in negotiations. The
Foreign Trade Policy (2015–20) has this to say on the subject:

> India, a founding member of the World Trade Organization
> (WTO), believes that a rules-based, non-discriminatory
> multilateral trading system is necessary for bringing
> transparency, equity and fair play into global trade relations.
> Such a system ensures discipline and enables members at all
> levels of development to chart out a course in global trade
> that would meet their economic development requirements.
> The multilateral trading system offers the best institutional
> architecture for a developing country. The consensus-based
> decision making in the WTO ensures that even the voice
> of the smallest Members is heard. India also recognizes the
> extraordinary contribution made by the WTO in dispute
> settlement, laying down jurisprudence in areas where the law
> was relatively ambiguous or not fully developed. As a founding
> member, and a country which has evolved significantly since
> the WTO was established, India will continue to contribute
> to the capacities of willing developing members to help them
> to fully participate in the rule making process . . . The need
> to ensure that the FTP is aligned with both India's interests
> in the negotiations, as well its obligations and commitments
> under various WTO Agreements, has been an important
> consideration in framing this Policy.[22]

It is important to undertake a serious examination of our
participation in multilateral trade negotiations and how we
have come through. The Uruguay Round of trade negotiations
took place against the background of India which had yet to

undertake important economic reforms. It was only towards the fag end of the round that India embarked on tariff reforms, more out of compulsion than conviction. Remember, of course, that in 1991 the country faced a precarious situation and had to ship gold to the Imperial Bank of England as collateral for getting a meagre amount as loan. It was therefore understandable that we approached the Uruguay Round negotiations with a defensive mindset. Even so, there were some remarkable achievements to the credit of the Indian negotiators. For instance, the elimination of the quota raj in textiles and clothing was almost entirely the result of the efforts made by India against all odds. That said, there is no denying that the Uruguay Round outcome as a whole was unfair to all the developing countries. There is now a considerable body of literature to prove this.

Because of our negative experience with 'new issues' in the Uruguay Round, especially the Trade Related Intellectual Property Rights (TRIPs), there has been an understandable reluctance on the part of India to agree to new issues. Hence, the tag of a naysayer for India.

While this tag should not and need not bother the country, it is the author's submission that whenever and wherever we have engaged and negotiated in the WTO since then, we have done well to defend our national interests. Thus in the Doha Round of negotiations launched in 2001, India not only staved off unreasonable demands for inclusion of issues, but actually succeeded in coming up with a declaration on TRIPs and public health which, short of amending the TRIPs Agreement, gave valuable guidance for future dispute settlement panels on how to interpret the agreement. This was arguably the most important outcome from the point of view of India and the developing countries since the conclusion of the Uruguay Round. Here was proof, if proof was indeed needed, that Indian negotiators with a clear brief and backed by resolve could achieve positive results in the WTO.

Since Doha, of course, things have changed dramatically in the WTO. For one thing, the Doha Round itself seems to be under intensive care, as it were an ICU! The Doha Round is important for developing countries like India, since it was the first time that the leading Western powers undertook to place the needs and interests of developing countries at the heart of the negotiating agenda. Hence the name Doha Development Agenda! To now say that the Doha Round is dead would amount to burying with it the promise made to developing countries that their interests would be taken care of by the WTO.

It is therefore the author's belief that one last attempt should be made by India and other developing countries to conclude the round. This will involve, however, the following. In return for the Western countries taking into account issues of importance such as public stockholding in agriculture for India, the developing countries would have to agree to at least look at the possibility of negotiations in investment facilitation and e-commerce.

In any case, the time has come to launch a wide consultation with all stakeholders (private sector, NGOs, chambers of commerce, etc.) on all issues of importance not just in the WTO but also in the RCEP. Many of the issues, such as e-commerce and investment are common to both the WTO and the RCEP negotiations and it is time India took a clear position of what is at stake. So far, we have been content to argue that we do not want new issues in the WTO because it constricts 'policy space'.

This is good as far as it goes. But then, every international negotiation is about giving up 'policy space' and 'sovereignty' and getting something critical for national interest, be it investment or job creation. At the end of the day, the WTO is a forum where concessions are exchanged. While the developing countries including India are right in insisting on less than reciprocal concessions (based on Special and Differential Treatment), the developed countries may also expect something in return for concessions granted by them.

The Foreign Trade Policy (2015–20) has rightly underlined the importance of the WTO and the multilateral trading system for a country such as India. The question therefore is: What should India do since the WTO is showing signs of being in the most serious existential crisis since its establishment? It is the author's view that India should undertake initiatives for restoring confidence in the WTO. Wide consultations on the subject are important. Our interests, as of most other nations, are best served by an open, predictable and rule-based multilateral trading system. Only countries in a 'dominant' position can afford to go unilateral outside a multilaterally negotiated set of rules and norms of conduct. India's stakes today in the WTO are far greater than say even Western countries such as the US.

Two other specific developments in the WTO merit India's attention. One is the crisis confronting the appellate body. There is a paucity of members, thanks to the new appointments being vetoed by the US. The time has come for a coalition of developed and developing countries (say led by EU and India) to impress on the US that no matter what, the dispute settlement system of the WTO cannot be held hostage to politics. The system is what gives confidence to all countries, big or small, strong or weak, in the WTO, and this cannot be allowed to erode any further. This is an emergency and needs to be attended to without further delay. And India should take the lead in this regard, rather than allow the drift to continue. It is the efficacy and sanctity of the WTO's dispute settlement machinery that distinguishes it from all the other international arrangements.

The other issue that confronts India is perhaps even more serious. It is clear after the December 2017 WTO ministerial meeting in Argentina that a group of countries (call it coalition of the willing, if you like) are ready to launch negotiations in new areas such as e-commerce, investment facilitation and fisheries subsidies. Obviously, these, if they are launched, will be plurilateral in nature. There is a need to ensure, at a minimum, that these negotiations are open to every WTO member and that once an outcome emerges, it will be applicable to the rest of the WTO membership on an MFN basis. It is noteworthy that a number of developing countries are also willing to join hands with the developed countries to look at these new subjects. China, for example, appears to have no problem with some of these new areas. And where it does, Hong Kong, China (a WTO member in its own right) seems to cover it pretty well. This does pose problems for India, and we should be conscious of this, even while being steadfast in protecting our vital interests, such as public stockholding for food security purposes. It should also be a matter of concern that some forty-six countries, including developing ones, are quite happy to bid good bye to the Doha Round. These need not deter us, but it does underline the importance of carrying out far-reaching domestic consultations to reach definitive decisions on what constitutes fundamental national interest and what else could be used as negotiating leverage to obtain concessions from our trading partners. Especially in new areas like e-commerce and investment facilitation, it would be good to determine the redlines to be ready for all eventualities.

A nation's trade policy is not static; it is dynamic and should be recalibrated from time to time. Now may be a good time to take stock and tweak our trade policy to bring it in line with current economic attributes and the ongoing policy reforms.

Ironically, our defence and strategic partnership with the United States continues to make great strides, but the trade and investment dossier remains as thorny and as vexing as ever. The problem has aggravated since Donald Trump's ascent to power as he has displayed an unmistakable proclivity to see bilateral trade as a zero-sum game. He has done so with great élan vis-à-vis China, given the huge trade deficit the US has with it. Less understandable is why he has not spared India which, for one thing, is not anywhere close to the trade surplus that China has with the US. Furthermore, threatening to hit us with steel tariffs when our share of exports is minimal is unfair.

There is little doubt that the use of Section 301 in and of itself, without any resort to the WTO's dispute settlement system in parallel, is not in conformity with the obligations of the US in the WTO. The Chinese have taken the US to dispute settlement precisely on this issue. But it is not clear whether the issue will go forward in the WTO dispute settlement mechanism. It is not inconceivable that the Chinese might settle with the US bilaterally at some stage. Indeed, bilateral negotiations between China and the US are ongoing, albeit with very little progress so far.

This unilateral instinct of the US is neither novel nor unprecedented. Indeed in the bad old GATT days, Section 301 was used with impunity against countries such as India, Brazil and Argentina with a view to bring us on board the Uruguay Round TRIPs negotiations. But with the onset of the WTO, the US has by and large kept its commitment made in the Uruguay Round that it will not resort to unilateralism without first exhausting the WTO dispute settlement mechanism. But now reneging on this commitment, President Trump is reverting to the old mechanics of conducting international trade, going against the principles of the WTO, which the US had helped create. This poses an existential challenge for developing countries such as India which actually depend heavily on the multilateral trading system for their international trade.

It is possible that Trump steps back from the brink. However, this is far from certain. Should he go ahead with what he has threatened, then there is a real danger that it may sound the death knell of the multilateral trading system as we know it. From India's perspective, there is thus a need to engage the US bilaterally at all levels along with a plan B upon which India can fall back should the need arise. This plan B must be formulated by the ministry of commerce in close consultation with all domestic stakeholders.

It turns out that Trump was not bluffing when he said that he would penalize trading partners who were not 'playing fair' by the US. To prove this, in March 2018 he announced punitive tariffs on steel and aluminium (25 per cent and 10 per cent respectively) on EU, Canada, China and India. All countries, including India, protested at this move, but to no avail. What was particularly galling to trading partners such as Canada and EU was that Trump justified it on grounds of 'national security'! Canada argued that it could never pose a national security threat to the US and that this was an absurd argument.[23] Again, this had no effect on Trump who went against all the above trading partners at the G7 meeting held in early June 2018 in Canada. The meeting ended in failure with US not agreeing to a joint statement. So far India has played it well. The minister of commerce travelled to Washington from 10–12 June 2018 and had detailed talks on this issue with his US counterpart. After waiting for a decent amount of time and realizing that the US would not change course with regard to India, on 13 June 2018, India announced its own retaliatory tariffs which in WTO parlance would be 'suspension of equivalent concessions' in response to the ones imposed by the US. Again the WTO was kept in the picture. India's retaliation would apply to some thirty items of US exports such as almonds, dry fruits, chocolates, shrimps, motor cycles, heavy machinery, etc., worth USD 240 million, which was India's calculation of the loss it suffered due to the tariffs on steel and aluminium.[24] This was the right thing to do since India could not have just kept quiet and accepted these tariffs when every other trading partner of the US was protesting.

The good news is that US officials from the commerce department met with their Indian counterparts again in September 2018—this time in New Delhi. There has emerged a consensus on both sides that a dialogue must continue to resolve the lingering thorns that continue to act as an irritant in this important bilateral relationship. From an Indian perspective, it would be good to have a list of items where we can make reciprocal concessions to the US so as to defuse the matter and prevent it from deteriorating into a full-blown trade war which we can ill afford. The challenge is to ensure that our trade, investment and IPRs with the US do not derail a vitally important strategic relationship for India.

Acknowledgements

During a nearly four decade long career in the Indian Foreign Service, I had a ringside view of what goes on in the world of decision-making at the highest levels. Ever so often, one also got a peek into the minds of those responsible for taking important decisions, ostensibly in 'national interest'. Fairly early in a long career, I started noticing behavioural traits, often among my own colleagues, that could only be described as delusional. These were perfectly normal individuals, willing to risk taking decisions that they knew could only have negative, adverse and even disastrous consequences.

I felt I owed it to myself to study this phenomenon in detail and, if possible, write a book on this subject. I saw first-hand how delusional politics and decision-making go hand-in-hand and are perhaps the biggest bane in our professional lives.

I owe a deep debt of gratitude to many of my professional colleagues with whom I enjoyed long conversations, both in the world of diplomacy and outside. There are too many to permit individual mention. And yet, in respect of some, a mere acknowledgment in a passing reference will not suffice.

I first met Mohan Kumar, now Dr Mohan Kumar, chairman of RIS, when he was posted to the Permanent Mission of India to the UN in Geneva as a third secretary language trainee.

Since we were a small delegation, I requested him to read out India's statement at a meeting of the Committee on Subsidies and Countervailing Measures, which I was chairing. He has not looked back since that day, acquiring exceptional domain knowledge on trade policy. He went on to serve as India's ambassador to France, and also acquired a PhD from Sciences Po, Paris. Dr Kumar is now one of India's finest minds on international trade. The chapter 'Politics of Trade Policy' in this book is based on extensive discussions with him for which I place my gratitude on record. We agree on most issues concerning India and the multilateral trading system, though I suspect Dr Kumar would want to frame his recommendations in more cautious terms.

A book covering such a vast array of subjects would not have been possible without a little bit of help. I must, therefore, start by acknowledging the support of Ariun Enkhsaikhan, my former colleague at the International Peace Institute (IPI). She was my proverbial 'brother in arms' from the beginning of the process. She has the energy, dedication and academic rigour that every author wishes in a research assistant. Thank you, Ariun.

Having been inducted into the council of ministers in September 2017, I realized early on that the rigours of the job would involve severe time constraints. I decided to poach Shubh Soni from a Delhi-based think tank to join my staff. Shubh is brilliant. He not only helped fill the gaps but also assisted in putting the final touches to this book. His ability to put my thoughts in words in a relatively short time frame is greatly appreciated.

I also owe a big thanks to Premanka Goswami and his team at Penguin Random House for being patient with me. As I mentioned in the author's note, the book was scheduled for October 2017, but was pushed back by a year due to my induction into the council of ministers.

This book would not have been possible without the continuing inspiration and support of Lakshmi, my partner and soulmate of forty-four years. She went through the manuscript on multiple occasions, often finding gaps that my research team and I had missed. She is a wordsmith par-excellence, and this book has greatly benefited from her inputs.

While I was writing my first book, *Perilous Interventions*, my lovely daughters, Himayani and Tilottama, were fully engaged in the process. They read my manuscript and provided detailed feedback. The second time around, they were so busy with their own professional preoccupations that they left me to my own devices. Both of them, and my son-in-law, Hari, have, however, been a great source of inspiration and encouragement.

My eternal gratitude to all those who were part of this journey. Responsibility for the views expressed and for errors, that still remain, is entirely mine.

Notes

The Setting

1. Suhasini Haidar, 'Trump Makes Sense to a Grocery Store Owner', *The Hindu*, 29 January 2017, http://www.thehindu.com/books/%E2%80%98Trump-makes-sense-to-a-grocery-store-owner%E2%80%99/article17109351.ece.

2. The remarks were made at a private meeting at the Club de Madrid. The South Asian PM was Jigme Yoezer Thinley, Prime Minister of Bhutan (2008–13), http://nextgenerationdemocracy.org/wp-content/uploads/2017/07/Z-Program-NGD-Asia-Oceania-DILI-July-2607.pdf.

3. Perry Bacon Jr. and Dhrumil Mehta, 'Republicans Are Coming Home To Trump', FiveThirtyEight, 16 February 2018, https://fivethirtyeight.com/features/republicans-are-coming-home-to-trump/.

4. Nida Najar, 'A Conversation with: Author Sanjaya Baru', India.Blogs.Nytimes.com, 16 April 2014, https://india.blogs.nytimes.com/2014/04/16/a-conversation-with-author-sanjaya-baru/.

5. Arun Jaitley, a senior lawyer, played a critical role in the BJP's 2014 election campaign. One of India's leading political strategists, he has been in active politics for over forty-five years, starting out as a student leader in the Akhil Bharatiya Vidyarthi Parishad (ABVP) during his Delhi University days. He went on to become the president of Delhi University Students Union in 1974, and during the dark days of the 1975 Emergency, he was one of the most

prominent voices in the Opposition. Post the electoral victory in 2014, he was named the leader of the house, Rajya Sabha, and was sworn in as the finance minister on 26 May 2014.

6. Press Trust of India, 'Modi's Elevation a "Winning Decision": Jaitley', *The Hindu,* 15 September 2013, http://www.thehindu. com/news/national/modis-elevation-a-winning-decision-jaitley/ article5130333.ece.

7. Election Commission of India, General Elections, 2014 (16th Lok Sabha), http://eci.nic.in/eci_main/archiveofge2014/20%20 -%20Performance%20of%20National%20Parties.pdf.

8. The statement was made by Mani Shankar Aiyar on 16 January 2014, when he stated, 'There is no way he can be Prime Minister in the 21st century . . . but if he wants to come and distribute tea here we can make some room for him.' Amit Chaturvedi, 'Won't Apologize for Inviting Narendra Modi to Sell Tea: Mani Shankar Aiyar', NDTV, 17 January 2014, https://www. ndtv.com/elections-news/wont-apologise-for-inviting-narendra-modi-to-sell-tea-mani-shankar-aiyar-548095.

9. Shyam Saran, 'Of China, Terror and US Trade: Why Hillary Will Be a Safe Bet for India', *Hindustan Times,* 7 September 2016, https://www.hindustantimes.com/analysis/on-policy-terror-and-trade-india-can-gain-from-a-second-clinton-era/ story-LQPgXCbGskI5DZ6FmAFxLI.html.

10. Editorial, 'Donald Trump's Revolt', *New York Times,* 9 November 2016, https://www.nytimes.com/2016/11/09/opinion/donald-trumps-revolt.html.

Introduction

1. From the Archive, 'Nepal's Crown Prince Murders Royal Family', *Guardian,* 2 June 2001, https://www.theguardian.com/ books/2009/jun/02/archive-nepal-crown-prince.

2. PRI's The World, 'Why Nepal's Crown Prince Went on a Killing Spree', *PRI,* 1 June 2011, https://www.pri.org/stories/2011-06-01/ why-nepals-crown-prince-went-killing-spree.

3. Antoine Harari and Matteo Maillard, 'A President's Downfall, Nepotism And A Ghost Town In Sri Lanka', WorldCrunch, 16 March 2017, https://www.worldcrunch.com/world-affairs/a-presidents-downfall-nepotism-and-a-ghost-town-in-sri-lanka.

4. Wade Shepard, 'Sri Lanka's Debt Crisis Is So Bad the Government Doesn't Even Know How Much Money It Owes', *Forbes,* 30 September 2016, https://www.forbes.com/sites/wadeshepard/2016/09/30/sri-lankas-debt-crisis-is-so-bad-the-government-doesnt-even-know-how-much-money-it-owes/#78ed20c94608.

5. James Tarabay, 'With Sri Lankan Port Acquisition, China Adds Another "Pearl" to Its "String"', *CNN,* 5 February 2018, https://edition.cnn.com/2018/02/03/asia/china-sri-lanka-string-of-pearls-intl/index.html.

6. Khurram Husain, 'Exclusive: CPEC Master Plan Revealed', *Dawn,* 21 June 2017, https://www.dawn.com/news/1333101.

7. Norman Ohler, *Blitzed, Drugs in the Third Reich* (Houghton Mifflin Harcourt, 2017), translated from German by Shaun Whiteside, p. 292.

Chapter 1: The Credibility Crisis

1. Helen Thomas was an influential American journalist. She was the first female member of the White House Press Corps, the first female chief White House correspondent of the United Press International, and the first female president of the White House Correspondents' Association. Thomas died in 2013. She was often called 'the First Lady of the Press'.

2. 'The Post-Truth World: Yes, I'd Lie to You', *The Economist,* 10 September 2016, https://www.economist.com/briefing/2016/09/10/yes-id-lie-to-you.

3. Ibid.

4. Oxford Dictionary, 'Word of the Year 2016 Is…'

5. Collins Dictionary, 'Definition of Fake News'.

6. Ralph Keyes, *The Post-Truth Era: Dishonesty and Deception in Contemporary Life* (New York: St Martin's Press, 2004), p.14.

7. Lynn Vavreck, 'Why This Election Was Not About the Issues', *New York Times*, 23 November 2016.

8. Ralph Keyes, *The Post-Truth Era: Dishonesty and Deception in Contemporary Life* (New York: St Martin's Press, 2004).

9. Edward Hallett Carr, *What Is History?* (Basic Books, 2009).

10. Shaul R. Shenhav, 'Political Narratives and Political Reality', *International Political Science Review*, Vol. 27, No. 3, July 2006, p. 248.

11. William Davies, 'The Age of Post-Truth Politics', *New York Times*, 24 August 2016.

12. UK Statistics Authority, 'UK Statistics Authority Statement on the Use of Official Statistics on Contributions to the European Union', 27 May 2016.

13. Jon Henley, 'Why Vote Leave's £350m Weekly EU Cost Claim Is Wrong', *Guardian*, 10 June 2016, https://www.theguardian.com/politics/reality-check/2016/may/23/does-the-eu-really-cost-the-uk-350m-a-week.

14. Linda Qiu, 'Fact-Checking President Trump through His First 100 Days', *New York Times*, 27 April 2017, https://www.nytimes.com/2017/04/29/us/politics/fact-checking-president-trump-through-his-first-100-days.html.

15. Ralph Keyes, *The Post-Truth Era: Dishonesty and Deception in Contemporary Life* (New York: St Martin's Press, 2004), p. 15.

16. Ralph Keyes, *The Post-Truth Era: Dishonesty and Deception in Contemporary Life* (New York: St Martin's Press, 2004), p. 13.

17. Charlie Cooper, 'EU Referendum: Immigration and Brexit—What Lies Have Been Spread?', *Independent*, 20 June 2016.

18. 'Post-Truth Politics: Art of the Lie', *The Economist*, 10 September 2016, https://www.economist.com/leaders/2016/09/10/art-of-the-lie.

19. Amy Mitchell, Jeffrey Gottfried, Jocelyn Kiley and Katerina Eva Matsa, 'Political Polarization & Media Habits', Pew Research

Center, 21 October 2014, http://www.journalism.org/2014/10/21/
political-polarization-media-habits/.

20. Elisa Shearer and Jeffrey Gottfried. 'News Use Across Social
Media Platforms 2017', Pew Research Center, 7 September
2017, http://www.journalism.org/2017/09/07/news-use-across-
social-media-platforms-2017/.

21. Election Commission of India, 'Poll Dates of 14 Lok Sabha
Elections', http://eci.nic.in/eci_main1/poll_dates_of_loksabha_
elc.aspx.

22. Hilary Osborne, 'What Is Cambridge Analytica? The Firm at
the Centre of Facebook's Data Breach', *Guardian*, 18 March
2018, https://www.theguardian.com/news/2018/mar/18/what-
is-cambridge-analytica-firm-at-centre-of-facebook-data-breach.

23. Heather Timmons, 'If Cambridge Analytica Is So Smart, Why
Isn't Ted Cruz President?' *Quartz*, 21 March 2018, https://
qz.com/1234364/cambridge-analytica-worked-for-mercer-
backed-ted-cruz-before-trump/.

24. Carole Cadwalladr, 'Robert Mercer: The Big Data Billionaire
Waging War on Mainstream Media', *Guardian*, 26 February 2017,
https://www.theguardian.com/politics/2017/feb/26/robert-
mercer-breitbart-war-on-media-steve-bannon-donald-trump-
nigel-farage.

25. Carole Cadwalladr, 'The Great British Brexit Robbery: How
Our Democracy Was Hijacked', *Guardian*, 7 May 2017, https://
www.theguardian.com/technology/2017/may/07/the-great-
british-brexit-robbery-hijacked-democracy.

Chapter 2: Brexit

1. David Cameron, Resignation Speech, 24 June 2016, https://
www.nytimes.com/2016/06/25/world/europe/david-cameron-
speech-transcript.html.

2. Kim Janssen, 'Fateful O'Hare Airport Pizza Meeting Sealed
Brexit Vote Deal: British Media', *Chicago Tribune*, 24 June 2016,

http://www.chicagotribune.com/news/chicagoinc/ct-brexit-ohare-pizza-20160624-story.html.

3. Nicholas Watt, 'David Cameron Rocked by Record Rebellion as Europe Splits Tories Again', *Guardian*, 24 October 2011, https://www.theguardian.com/politics/2011/oct/24/david-cameron-tory-rebellion-europe.

4. Ewa Jasiewicz, 'Ukip's Success Lies in Talking to Workers—but Not about Class. We Can Do Better', *Guardian*, 29 May 2014, https://www.theguardian.com/commentisfree/2014/may/29/ukip-workers-class-identity-race-immigration.

5. David Cameron, 'EU Speech at Bloomberg', *Speech*, 23 January 2013.

6. Pierre Haski, 'All Eyes on Her', *Vice News*, 23 April 2017, https://news.vice.com/en_us/article/zmy7dy/the-rise-and-fall-and-possible-rise-again-of-marine-le-pen-frances-answer-to-donald-trump.

7. 'What Geert Wilders's Poor Showing Means for Marine Le Pen', *The Economist*, 18 March 2017, https://www.economist.com/leaders/2017/03/18/what-geert-wilderss-poor-showing-means-for-marine-le-pen.

8. Oliver Wright, 'The Speech that Was the Start of the End of David Cameron', *Independent*, 24 June 2016, https://www.independent.co.uk/news/uk/politics/brexit-eu-referendum-david-cameron-resignation-announcement-2013-a7101281.html.

9. Ewen MacAskill and Lawrence Donegan, 'Scots Vote for Their Own Parliament', *Guardian*, 13 September 2013, https://www.theguardian.com/theguardian/2013/sep/13/scotland-devolution-referendum-victory.

10. Claire Phipps, 'Scottish Independence: A Guide to the Referendum to Break Away from the UK', *Guardian*, 10 September 2014, https://www.theguardian.com/politics/2014/sep/10/scottish-independence-guide-referendum-uk-yes-no.

11. Ibid.

12. Ibid.

13. Libby Brooks, Severin Carrell and the *Guardian* interactive team, 'Scottish Independence: Everything You Need to Know About the Vote', *Guardian*, 9 September 2014, https://www.theguardian.com/politics/2014/sep/09/-sp-scottish-independence-everything-you-need-to-know-vote.

14. Libby Brooks, 'Scottish Referendum: Magnitude of the Question Galvanizes Debate', *Guardian*, 8 June 2014, https://www.theguardian.com/politics/2014/jun/08/scottish-independence-referendum-galvanises-debate.

15. Douglas Fraser, 'Study Examines Referendum Demographics', BBC.com, 18 September 2015, http://www.bbc.com/news/uk-scotland-glasgow-west-34283948.

16. 'A Divided Britain? Inequality within and between the Regions', The Equality Trust, July 2014, https://www.equalitytrust.org.uk/divided-britain-inequality-within-and-between-regions-0.

17. Nicola Woolcock, 'St Andrews Inequality Criticized in New Rankings for Diversity, *The Times*, 5 April 2018, https://www.thetimes.co.uk/article/st-andrews-inequality-criticised-52jlj5zjf.

18. Alex Salmond: 12 April 2014 Speech to SNP Conference, http://www.ukpol.co.uk/alex-salmond-2014-speech-to-snp-conference/.

19. William Dalrymple, 'The East India Company: The Original Corporate Raiders', *Guardian*, 4 March 2015, https://www.theguardian.com/world/2015/mar/04/east-india-company-original-corporate-raiders.

20. '31 December 1600: Charter Granted to the East India Company', History.com, https://www.history.com/this-day-in-history/charter-granted-to-the-east-india-company.

21. Ibid.

22. Ainslie Embree, 'British East India Company Raj', *Encyclopedia of India*, ed. Stanley Wolpert, Vol. 1, 2006.

23. William Dalrymple, 'The East India Company: The Original Raiders', *Guardian*, 4 March 2015, https://www.theguardian.com/world/2015/mar/04/east-india-company-original-corporate-raiders.

24. Ibid.

25. 'British Empire', *New World Encyclopedia*, http://www. newworldencyclopedia.org/entry/British_Empire#The_impact_ of_the_First_World_War.

26. 'Atlantic Charter', *Encyclopedia Britannica*, https://www. britannica.com/event/Atlantic-Charter.

27. 'Yalta Conference', History.com, https://www.history.com/ topics/world-war-ii/yalta-conference.

28. Council on Foreign Relations: The UN Security Council, Cfr.org, https://www.cfr.org/backgrounder/un-security-council.

29. Jeremy Rifkin, *The European Dream: How Europe's Vision of the Future is Quietly Eclipsing the American Dream* (New York: TarcherPerigee, 2005).

30. Harold Macmillan, 'Britons Have Never Had It So Good', Speech, 1957.

31. Stephen Nickell and John Van Reenen, 'Technological Innovation and Economic Performance in the United Kingdom', April 2001, http://cep.lse.ac.uk/pubs/download/dp0488.pdf.

32. Alan Travis, 'Ministers Saw Law's "Racism" As Defensible', *Guardian*, 1 January 2002, https://www.theguardian.com/ politics/2002/jan/01/uk.race.

33. David Owen, 'Ethnic Minorities in Great Britain: Patterns of Population Change: 1981–91', 1991 Census Statistical Paper No. 10, https://warwick.ac.uk/fac/soc/crer/research/publications/ nemda/nemda1991sp10.pdf.

34. G.K. Shaw, 'Fiscal Policy Under the First Thatcher Administration 1979–1983', *FinanzArchiv/Public Finance Analysis, New Series*, Bd. 41, H. 2, 1983, https://www.jstor.org/ stable/40911873?seq=1#page_scan_tab_contents.

35. Jeremy Rifkin, *The European Dream: How Europe's Vision of the Future is Quietly Eclipsing the American Dream* (New York: TarcherPerigee, 2005).

36. Timo Lochocki, 'How the United Kingdom Independence Party's One Seat Has the Power to Change British and European Politics', *Policy Brief,* The German Marshall Fund of the United States, Vol. 2, http://www.gmfus.org/file/5884/download.

37. 'The Nigel Farage Story', BBC News, 4 July 2016, http://www. bbc.com/news/uk-politics-36701855.

38. 'The Nigel Farage Story', BBC News, 4 July 2016, http://www. bbc.com/news/uk-politics-36701855.

39. 'Vote 2014: UK European Election Results', BBC News, http:// www.bbc.com/news/events/vote2014/eu-uk-results.

40. Patrick Wintour and Nicholas Watt, 'Ukip Wins European Elections with Ease to Set off Political Earthquake', *Guardian*, 25 May 2014, https://www.theguardian.com/politics/2014/ may/26/ukip-european-elections-political-earthquake.

41. Nicholas Watt, 'David Cameron Rocked by Record Rebellion as Europe Splits Tories Again', *Guardian*, 24 October 2011, https:// www.theguardian.com/politics/2011/oct/24/david-cameron-tory-rebellion-europe.

42. Brian Wheeler, 'The David Cameron Story', BBC News, 12 September 2016, http://www.bbc.com/news/uk-politics-eu-referendum-36540101.

43. Michael Ashcroft and Isabel Oakeshott. *Call Me Dave: The Unauthorized Biography of David Cameron* (London, UK: Biteback Publishing, 2015).

44. Margaret Thatcher, 'House of Commons Speech: EEC Membership (Referendum)', Speech, 11 March 1975.

45. Francis Elliott and James Hanning, 'The Many Faces of Mr Cameron', *Daily Mail*, 17 March 2007, http://www.dailymail. co.uk/news/article-442913/The-faces-Mr-Cameron.html.

46. Matt Dathan, 'David Cameron and Boris Johnson Told They're Elitist and Out of Touch because They Went to Eton', *Independent*, 5 May 2015, https://www.independent.co.uk/news/ uk/politics/generalelection/general-election-2015-watch-david-cameron-and-boris-johnson-being-told-theyre-elitist-and-out-of-10226546.html.

47. Michael Ashcroft and Isabel Oakeshott, *Call Me Dave: The Unauthorized Biography of David Cameron* (London, UK: Biteback Publishing, 2015).

48. Ibid.

49. 'Bullingdon Club: The Secrets of Oxford University's Elite', *Week*, 10 April 2017, http://www.theweek.co.uk/65410/bullingdon-club-the-secrets-of-oxford-universitys-elite-society.

50. Rowena Mason, 'David Cameron Publicly Denies Lord Ashcroft Pig Allegation for First Time', *Guardian*, 27 September 2015, https://www.theguardian.com/politics/2015/sep/27/david-cameron-denies-lord-ashcroft-allegations-call-me-dave-dead-pig.

51. Carol Brennan, 'Cameron, David', in *Newsmakers: 2012 Cumulation*, edited by Laura Avery (Detroit: Gale, 2012), pp. 91–4.

52. David Cameron, 'Speech to the Conservative Conference 2005', Speech, 4 October 2005.

53. 'Cameron Chosen As New Tory Leader,' BBC News, 6 December 2005, http://news.bbc.co.uk/2/hi/uk_news/politics/4502652.stm.

54. David Cameron, 'Speech to the Conservative Conference 2005', Speech, 4 October 2005.

55. Germania Rodriguez, 'Brexit Is a Warning to Young American Voters', *National Memo*, 24 June 2016, http://www.nationalmemo.com/brexit-is-a-warning-to-young-american-voters/.

56. Simon Shuster/Margate, 'The U.K.'s Old Decided for the Young in the Brexit Vote', *Time*, 24 June 2016, http://time.com/4381878/brexit-generation-gap-older-younger-voters/.

57. Nigel Farage, 'Nigel Farage: My Public School Had a Real Social Mix, but Now Only the Mega-rich Can Afford the Fees', *Telegraph*, extracted from *The Purple Revolution: The Year that Changed Everything* (London: Biteback Publishing, 2015), 14 March 2015, https://www.telegraph.co.uk/news/politics/nigel-farage/11467039/Nigel-Farage-My-public-school-had-a-real-social-mix-but-now-only-the-mega-rich-can-afford-the-fees.html.

58. Nick Cohen, 'Nigel Farage Is a phoney. Scrutinise Him and He'll Crumble', *Guardian*, 26 April 2014, https://www.theguardian.

com/commentisfree/2014/apr/26/nigel-farage-phoney-scrutinise-him-ukip.

59. David Cameron, Resignation Speech, 24 June 2016.

60. 'Theresa May's Full Announcement on Calling Snap Election', BBC News, 18 April 2017, http://www.bbc.com/news/av/uk-politics-39627177/theresa-may-s-full-announcement-on-calling-snap-election.

61. Russell Goldman, 'Key Points about a Snap Election in Britain', *New York Times*, 18 April 2017, https://www.nytimes.com/2017/04/18/world/europe/britain-snap-election-brexit-theresa-may-questions.html.

62. Theresa May, Speech, 28 April 2016.

63. James Masters, 'Northern Ireland Party Agrees to Prop up Theresa May's UK Government,' *CNN*, 26 June 2017, https://edition.cnn.com/2017/06/26/europe/theresa-may-dup-deal/index.html.

64. Ben Chapman, 'UK Now the Worst-performing Advanced Economy in the World Post-Brexit Vote Slump', *Independent*, 1 June 2017, https://www.independent.co.uk/news/business/news/uk-worst-performing-advanced-economy-world-post-brexit-slump-election-pound-sterling-a7766286.html.

65. Oliver Staley and Jenny Anderson, 'London's Future As a Global Financial Center Is Now in Doubt', *Quartz*, 24 June 2016, https://qz.com/716128/londons-future-as-a-global-financial-center-is-now-in-doubt/.

66. 'Cities with the Most Fortune 500 Companies', Worldatlas.com, https://www.worldatlas.com/articles/cities-with-the-most-company-headquarters.html.

67. Richard Partington, 'UK Businesses Told to Expect Workforce Crisis after Brexit', *Guardian,* 29 March 2018, https://www.theguardian.com/global/2018/mar/29/uk-businesses-workforce-crisis-brexit-young-workers.

68. 'Sturgeon: Hard Brexit "Dead in the Water"', BBC.com, 30 January 2018, http://www.bbc.com/news/uk-scotland-scotland-politics-42865430.

69. Ibid.

70. Chris McCall, 'Brexit "Will Not Be Constitutional Game Changer" for SNP', *Scotsman*, 31 January 2018, https://www.scotsman.com/news/politics/brexit-will-not-be-constitutional-game-changer-for-snp-1-4678181.

71. Andrew Whitaker, '"Scotland Is the Powerbroker When It Comes to Brexit": Labour Grandee Says Scottish Government Is Key to Forcing Second EU Referendum', *Sunday Herald*, 14 January, http://www.heraldscotland.com/news/15826834.___Sturgeon_is_key_to_securing_second_EU_referendum_____says_Lord_Adonis/.

72. 'Divided Over Brexit, Northern Ireland Marks Year with No Government', AFP, 9 January 2018, https://mg.co.za/article/2018-01-09-divided-over-brexit-nireland-marks-year-with-no-government.

73. Adapted from a statement made by Roberto Savio, IPS founder and president emeritus, on 14 December 2017, at the Geneva Centre for Human Rights Advancement and Global Dialogue, as a panellist on 'Migration and Human Solidarity, a Challenge and an Opportunity for Europe and the MENA Region'.

74. William James, 'UK's May to Pitch Status Quo Brexit Transition to Parliament', Reuters, 18 December 2017, https://www.reuters.com/article/us-britain-eu-may/uks-may-to-pitch-status-quo-brexit-transition-to-parliament-idUSKBN1EC009.

75. British Empire Overview, http://www.nationalarchives.gov.uk/education/empire/intro/overview2.htm.

Chapter 3: Trump and the Global Delusional Order

1. Katie Reilly, 'Read Hillary Clinton's "Basket of Deplorables" Remarks about Donald Trump supporters', *Time*, 10 September 2016, http://time.com/4486502/hillary-clinton-basket-of-deplorables-transcript/.

2. Barack Obama, Speech at the White House Correspondents' Dinner, 30 April 2011, https://obamawhitehouse.archives.

gov/blog/2011/05/01/president-s-speech-white-house-correspondents-dinner.

3. Ibid.

4. Michael, D. Shear, 'Obama Releases Long-Form Birth Certificate.' *New York Times*, 27 April 2011, https://www.nytimes.com/2011/04/28/us/politics/28obama.html.

5. Arlie R. Hochschild, *Strangers in their Own Land: Anger and Mourning on the American Right* (New York: The New Press, 2016).

6. '2008 Presidential Election Map', *New York Times*, 9 December 2008, https://www.nytimes.com/elections/2008/results/president/map.html.

7. '2012 Presidential Election Map', *New York Times*, 29 November 2012, https://www.nytimes.com/elections/2012/results/president.html.

8. Adam Gopnik, 'Trump and Obama: A Night to Remember', *New Yorker*, 12 September 2015, https://www.newyorker.com/news/daily-comment/trump-and-obama-a-night-to-remember.

9. Roxanne Roberts, 'I Sat Next to Donald Trump at the Infamous 2011 White House Correspondents' Dinner', *Washington Post*, 28 April 2016, https://www.washingtonpost.com/lifestyle/style/i-sat-next-to-donald-trump-at-the-infamous-2011-white-house-correspondents-dinner/2016/04/27/5cf46b74-0bea-11e6-8ab8-9ad050f76d7d_story.html?noredirect=on&utm_term=.6d8faaadd375.

10. Maggie Haberman and Alexander Burns, 'Donald Trump's Presidential Run Began in an Effort to Gain Stature', *New York Times*, 12 March 2016, https://www.nytimes.com/2016/03/13/us/politics/donald-trump-campaign.html.

11. Ibid.

12. Tim Meko, Denise Lu and Lazaro Gamio, 'How Trump Won the Presidency with Razor-thin Margins in Swing States', *Washington Post*, 11 November 2016, https://www.washingtonpost.com/graphics/politics/2016-election/swing-state-margins/.

13. 'Political Polarization in the American Public', Pew Research Center, 12 June 2014, http://www.people-press.org/2014/06/12/political-polarization-in-the-american-public/.

14. Ibid.

15. Arlie R. Hochschild, *Strangers in Their Own Land: Anger and Mourning on the American Right* (New York: The New Press, 2016), p.35.

16. Ibid, p. 47.

17. Ibid, p 14.

18. Ibid, p. 106.

19. David Brooks, 'The G.O.P. Rejects Conservatism', *New York Times*, 27 June 2017, https://www.nytimes.com/2017/06/27/opinion/the-gop-rejects-conservatism.html.

20. John B. Judis, *The Populist Explosion: How the Great Recession Transformed American and European Politics* (New York: Columbia Global Reports, 2016), p. 20.

21. Arlie R. Hochschild, *Strangers in Their Own Land: Anger and Mourning on the American Right* (New York: The New Press, 2016), p. 137.

22. 'Trump, Clinton Voters Divided in Their Main Source for Election News', Pew Research Center, 18 January 2017, http://www.journalism.org/2017/01/18/trump-clinton-voters-divided-in-their-main-source-for-election-news/.

23. Arlie R. Hochschild, *Strangers in Their Own Land: Anger and Mourning on the American Right* (New York: The New Press, 2016), p. 15.

24. 'Aftermath: Sixteen Writers on Trump's America: Essays by Toni Morrison, Atul Gawande, Hilary Mantel, George Packer, Jane Mayer, Jeffrey Toobin, Junot Diaz and More', *New Yorker*, 21 November 2016, https://www.newyorker.com/magazine/2016/11/21/aftermath-sixteen-writers-on-trumps-america.

25. Stephen Wertheim, 'Quit Calling Donald Trump an Isolationist. He's worse than That', *Washington Post*, 17 February 2017, https://www.washingtonpost.com/posteverything/wp/

2017/02/17/quit-calling-donald-trump-an-isolationist-its-an-insult-to-isolationism/?utm_term=.35ae89d313de.

26. Donald Trump and Tony Schwartz, *The Art of the Deal* (New York: Random House, 1987), p. 72.

27. Michael E. Miller, '50 Years Later, Disagreements over Young Trump's Military Academy Record', *Washington Post*, 9 January 2016, https://www.washingtonpost.com/politics/decades-later-disagreement-over-young-trumps-military-academy-post/2016/01/09/907a67b2-b3e0-11e5-a842-0feb51d1d124_story.html?utm_term=.c080a90b0559.

28. Ibid.

29. Tony Schwartz, 'I Wrote "The Art of the Deal" with Trump. His Self-sabotage Is Rooted in His Past', *Washington Post*, 16 May 2017, https://www.washingtonpost.com/posteverything/wp/2017/05/16/i-wrote-the-art-of-the-deal-with-trump-his-self-sabotage-is-rooted-in-his-past/?utm_term=.3e861ad417bd.

30. Konstantin Kilibarda and Daria Roithmayr, 'The Myth of the Rust Belt Revolt', *Slate*, 1 December 2016, http://www.slate.com/articles/news_and_politics/politics/2016/12/the_myth_of_the_rust_belt_revolt.html.

31. Russell Berman, 'The Invisible Democratic Majority', *Atlantic*, 8 April 2015, https://www.theatlantic.com/politics/archive/2015/04/democrats-dont-vote/389898/.

32. Thomas Frank, *Listen, Liberal: Or, What Ever Happened to the Party of the People?* (New York: Metropolitan Books, 2016).

33. Tom Leonard and David Gardner, 'Republican Tsunami: Democrats Lose Control of the House as Voters Slam Obama with Worst Losses for 62 Years', *Daily Mail*, 3 November 2010, https://www.dailymail.co.uk/news/article-1326053/MID-TERM-ELECTIONS-2010-Democrats-lose-House-Republican-tsunami.html.

34. Musa Al-Gharbi, 'The Democratic Party Is Facing A Demographic Crisis', The Conversation, 2 March 2017, http://theconversation.com/the-democratic-party-is-facing-a-demographic-crisis-72948.

35. 'Presidential Election Results: Donald J. Trump Wins', *New York Times*, 9 August 2017, https://www.nytimes.com/elections/results/president.

36. 'President Map', *New York Times*, 29 November 2012, https://www.nytimes.com/elections/2012/results/president.html.

37. 'President Map', *New York Times*, 2008, https://www.nytimes.com/elections/2008/results/president/map.html.

38. Nate Cohn, 'A 2016 Review: Turnout Wasn't the Driver of Clinton's Defeat', *New York Times*, 28 March 2017, https://www.nytimes.com/2017/03/28/upshot/a-2016-review-turnout-wasnt-the-driver-of-clintons-defeat.html.

39. Jonathan Martin and Patrick Healy, 'Championing Optimism, Obama Hails Clinton as His Political Heir', *New York Times*, 27 July 2016, https://www.nytimes.com/2016/07/28/us/politics/dnc-biden-kaine-obama.html.

40. Musa Al-Gharbi, 'The Democratic Party Is Facing A Demographic Crisis', The Conversation, 2 March 2017, http://theconversation.com/the-democratic-party-is-facing-a-demographic-crisis-72948.

41. 'General Election: Trump vs Sanders', RealClear Politics, https://realclearpolitics.com/epolls/2016/president/us/general_election_trump_vs_sanders-5565.html.

42. John B. Judis, *The Populist Explosion: How the Great Recession Transformed American and European Politics* (New York: Columbia Global Reports, 2016), p. 15.

43. Ibid.

44. Clare Foran, 'Bernie Sanders's Big Money', *Atlantic*, 1 March 2016, https://www.theatlantic.com/politics/archive/2016/03/bernie-sanders-fundraising/471648/.

45. Margaret Talbot, 'The Populist Prophet', *New Yorker*, 12 October 2015, https://www.newyorker.com/magazine/2015/10/12/the-populist-prophet.

46. John B. Judis, *The Populist Explosion: How The Great Recession Transformed American and European Politics* (New York: Columbia Global Reports, 2016).

47. Margaret Talbot, 'The Populist Prophet', *New Yorker*, 12 October 2015, https://www.newyorker.com/magazine/2015/10/12/the-populist-prophet.

48. 'Trump Appears to Mock Reporter's Disability', *Los Angeles Times*, http://www.latimes.com/85160455-157.html.

49. Katie Reilly, 'Here Are All the Times Donald Trump Insulted Mexico', *Time*, 31 August 2016, http://time.com/4473972/donald-trump-mexico-meeting-insult/.

50. Jay Willis, 'The Professor Who Predicted Donald Trump's Presidency Is Convinced He Will Be Impeached', *GQ*, 17 April 2017, https://www.gq.com/story/allan-lichtman-interview-trump-impeachment.

51. 'Official 2016 Presidential General Election Results', Federal Election Commission, https://transition.fec.gov/pubrec/fe2016/federalelections2016.pdf.

52. 'Judge Blocks Trump's Transgender Military Ban', BBC News, 30 October 2017, http://www.bbc.com/news/world-us-canada-41808561.

53. Sophie Tatum, 'White House Announces Policy to Ban Most Transgender People from Serving in Military', *CNN*, 24 March 2018, https://edition.cnn.com/2018/03/23/politics/transgender-white-house/index.html.

54. Statement by President Trump on the Paris Climate Accord, 1 June 2017, https://www.whitehouse.gov/briefings-statements/statement-president-trump-paris-climate-accord/.

55. Statement by President Trump on Jerusalem, 6 December 2017, https://www.whitehouse.gov/briefings-statements/statement-president-trump-jerusalem/.

56. 'President Donald J. Trump Is Ending United States Participation in an Unacceptable Deal', WhiteHouse.gov, 8 May 2018, https://www.whitehouse.gov/briefings-statements/president-donald-j-trump-ending-united-states-participation-unacceptable-iran-deal/.

57. Joseph Carroll, '1/3 of Americans Say US Supreme Court Is "Too Conservative"', Gallup, 2 October 2007, https://news.

gallup.com/poll/28861/onethird-americans-say-us-supreme-court-too-conservative.aspx. Further, Justice Neil Gorsuch, appointed by President Trump in January 2017, has lived up to conservative expectations (Richard Wolf, 'Justice Gorsuch Confirms Conservatives' Hopes, Liberals' Fears in First Year on Supreme Court', *USA Today*, 8 April 2018, https://www.usatoday.com/story/news/politics/2018/04/08/justice-gorsuch-confirms-conservatives-hopes-liberals-fears-first-year-supreme-court/486630002/). Moreover, given Justice Anthony Kennedy has announced his retirement, Trump's hand has been further strengthened ('Anthony Kennedy Retiring from Supreme Court', CNBC, 27 June 2018, https://www.cnbc.com/2018/06/27/anthony-kennedy-retiring-from-supreme-court.html).

58. Quint Forgey, 'Democrats' Edge over GOP in Midterms Waning, Poll Finds', Politico, 16 April 2018, https://www.politico.com/story/2018/04/16/poll-midterms-2018-democrats-republicans-526287.

59. Chris Megerian, 'Pivotal Moments in Mueller's Trump Investigation: 5 Guilty Pleas, 17 Indictments, and More', *Los Angeles Times*, 17 May 2018, http://www.latimes.com/projects/la-na-mueller-investigation-one-year/.

60. Andrew Prokop, 'Michael Cohen: Trump's Fix-it Guy and FBI Raid Subject Explained', Vox, 13 June 2018, https://www.vox.com/policy-and-politics/2018/4/11/17218010/michael-cohen-raid-fbi-trump-mueller-explained.

61. James Mann, 'The Adults in the Room', *New York Review of Books*, 26 October 2017, https://www.nybooks.com/articles/2017/10/26/trump-adult-supervision/.

62. Mark Landler and Katie Rogers, 'John Kelly Tells Aides He Will Remain White House Chief of Staff Through 2020', *New York Times*, 31 July 2018, https://www.nytimes.com/2018/07/31/us/politics/john-kelly-job-white-house-trump.html.

63. David Smith, 'Your Worst Nightmare: A Successful Donald Trump Presidency', *Guardian,* 3 July 2017, https://www.theguardian.com/us-news/2017/jul/03/donald-trump-winning-oval-office-twitter.

64. Roberto Savio, 'Shedding Diplomacy, Roberto Savio Speaks about Fear as a Tool to Gain Power', Inter Press Service, 14 December 2017, http://www.ipsnews.net/2017/12/shedding-diplomacy-robertosavio-speaks-fear-tool-gain-power/.

65. Ibid.

66. Drew Desilver, 'US Trails Most Developed Countries in Voter Turnout', Pew Research Center, 21 May 2018, http://www.pewresearch.org/fact-tank/2017/05/15/u-s-voter-turnout-trails-most-developed-countries/.

67. 'Stark Partisan Divisions Over Russia Probe, Including Its Importance to the Nation', Pew Research Center, 7 December 2017, http://www.people-press.org/2017/12/07/stark-partisan-divisions-over-russia-probe-including-its-importance-to-the-nation/#views-of-muellers-investigation-into-russian-involvement-in-2016-election.

68. Steven Shepard, 'Trump Voters: We'd Do It Again', Politico, 9 November 2017, https://www.politico.com/story/2017/11/09/trump-voters-polling-election-244644.

69. Michael Wolff. 'Donald Trump Didn't Want to Be President', *New York Magazine*, 3 January 2018, http://nymag.com/daily/intelligencer/2018/01/michael-wolff-fire-and-fury-book-donald-trump.html.

70. Michelle Cottle, 'Wolff Trapped', *New Republic*, 30 August 2004, https://newrepublic.com/article/67746/wolff-trapped.

71. 'Trump Bannon Row: Who Is Author Michael Wolff?', BBC News, 5 January 2018, http://www.bbc.com/news/world-us-canada-42565013.

72. Michelle Cottle, 'Wolff Trapped', *New Republic*, 30 August 2004, https://newrepublic.com/article/67746/wolff-trapped.

73. Jane Mayer, 'Christopher Steele, the Man behind the Trump Dossier', *New Yorker*, 12 March 2018, https://www.newyorker.com/magazine/2018/03/12/christopher-steele-the-man-behind-the-trump-dossier.

74. Statement by FBI Director James B. Comey on the Investigation of Secretary Hillary Clinton's Use of a Personal E-mail System,

FBI.gov, 5 July 2016, https://www.fbi.gov/news/pressrel/press-releases/statement-by-fbi-director-james-b-comey-on-the-investigation-of-secretary-hillary-clinton2019s-use-of-a-personal-e-mail-system.

75. 'FBI Letter Announcing New Clinton Review', Politico, 28 October 2016, https://www.politico.com/story/2016/10/full-text-fbi-letter-announcing-new-clinton-review-230463.

76. Sharon LaFraniere, Mark Mazzetti and Matt Apuzzo. 'How the Russia Enquiry Began: A Campaign Aide, Drinks and Talks of Political Dirt', *New York Times*, 30 December 2017, https://www.nytimes.com/2017/12/30/us/politics/how-fbi-russia-investigation-began-george-papadopoulos.html.

77. 'James Comey's Interview with ABC News Chief Anchor George Stephanopoulos', ABC News, 15 April 2018, https://abcnews.go.com/Site/transcript-james-comeys-interview-abc-news-chief-anchor/story?id=54488723.

78. Nate Silver, 'The Comey Letter Probably Cost Clinton the Election', FiveThirtyEight, 3 May 2017, https://fivethirtyeight.com/features/the-comey-letter-probably-cost-clinton-the-election/.

Chapter 4: The India Story

1. Bahadur Shah Zafar, 'Kitna Hai Bad-nasib Zafar Dafn Ke Liye', Rekhta, https://www.rekhta.org/couplets/kitnaa-hai-bad-nasiib-zafar-dafn-ke-liye-bahadur-shah-zafar-couplets.

2. William Dalrymple, 'The Most Magnificent Muslims', *New York Review of Books*, 22 November 2017, http://www.nybooks.com/articles/2007/11/22/the-most-magnificent-muslims/.

3. Anbarasan Ethirajan, 'Remembering the Last Mughal Emperor', BBC News, 8 November 2017, https://www.bbc.com/news/world-asia-41884390.

4. BS Web Team, Remembering the Life and Times of Annie Besant, *Business Standard*, 1 October 2015, https://www.business-standard.com/article/current-affairs/remembering-the-life-and-times-of-annie-besant-115100100808_1.html.

5. K.R.A. Narasiah, *A Reformer's Life*, *The Hindu*, 1 August 2015, http://www.thehindu.com/books/literary-review/kra-narasiah-reviews-gopal-krishna-gokhale-gandhis-political-guru/article7485201.ece.

6. Press Trust of India, 'Sultanate Gone, but We Behave like Sultans': Jairam Ramesh Admits Congress in Deep Crisis', *Hindustan Times*, 8 August 2017, https://www.hindustantimes.com/india-news/congress-facing-existential-crisis-jairam-ramesh/story-YdY3NxGKBOY2g9y4ORMaWK.html.

7. Times Now Bureau, 'Jairam Ramesh Faces Heat from Congress Leaders for His "Sultanate" Comment', TimesNowNews.com, 9 August 2017, http://www.timesnownews.com/india/article/cong-leaders-unhappy-with-jairam-ramesh%E2%80%99s-sultanate-remark/70789.

8. Press Trust of India, 'Sultanate Gone, but We Behave like Sultans': Jairam Ramesh Admits Congress in Deep Crisis', *Hindustan Times*, 8 August 2017, https://www.hindustantimes.com/india-news/congress-facing-existential-crisis-jairam-ramesh/story-YdY3NxGKBOY2g9y4ORMaWK.html.

9. Sobhana K. Nair, 'Rahul Gandhi Era Begins for Congress', *The Hindu*, 11 December 2017, http://www.thehindu.com/news/national/rahul-gandhi-is-president-of-congress/article21390722.ece.

10. 'Past Party Presidents—Motilal Nehru, Jawaharlal Nehru, Indira Gandhi, Rajiv Gandhi and Sonia Gandhi', Indian National Congress, https://www.inc.in/en/leadership/past-party-presidents.

11. Sobhana K. Nair, 'Rahul Gandhi Era Begins for Congress', *The Hindu*, 11 December 2017, http://www.thehindu.com/news/national/rahul-gandhi-is-president-of-congress/article21390722.ece.

12. BJP Presidents during Nineteen Years of Sonia Gandhi's Leadership of Indian National Congress—Kushabhau Thakre, Bangaru Laxman, K. Jana Krishnamurthy, Venkaiah Naidu, Lal Krishna Advani, Rajnath Singh, Nitin Gadkari and Amit Shah, http://www.bjp.org/en/leadership/bjp-presidents.

13. The concerned official was B.L. Joshi, a member of the Indian Police Service, who also served in the ministry of home affairs under Prime Minister Lal Bahadur Shastri and Prime Minister Indira Gandhi. He was appointed the lieutenant governor of Delhi from 2004 to 2007. From April 2007 to October 2007, he was the governor of Meghalaya; from October 2007 to July 2009 the governor of Uttarakhand; and from July 2009 to June 2014, the governor of UP.

14. Sandeep Phukan, 'There Is No Anti-incumbency in Gujarat As We Have Delivered, Says Deputy CM Nitinbhai Patel', *The Hindu*, 7 December 2017, https://www.thehindu.com/ elections/gujarat-2017/there-is-no-anti-incumbency-in-gujarat-as-we-have-delivered-says-deputy-cm-nitinbhai-patel/ article21291945.ece.

15. Trivedi Centre for Political Data, 'How Gujarat Was Won (and Lost): 28 Charts that Explain the Election Results,' Scroll.in, 20 December 2017, https://scroll.in/article/862048/how-gujarat-was-won-and-lost-28-charts-that-explain-the-election-results.

16. Vikram Gopal, 'The Anti-incumbency Factor against Siddaramaiah that No One Saw Coming in Karnataka', *Hindustan Times*, 16 May 2018, https://www.hindustantimes.com/ india-news/siddaramaiah-anti-incumbency-that-no-one-saw-coming-in-karnataka/story-I4Sp0DobJ4aWuDuLObJWuN. html.

17. *Hindustan Times*, Delhi Edition, 16 May 2018.

18. TNN, 'Won't Allow Dilution of SC/ST Act: PM Modi', *Times of India*, 14 April 2018, https://timesofindia.indiatimes. com/india/wont-allow-dilution-of-sc/st-act-pm-modi/ articleshow/63754523.cms.

19. Amitabh Tiwari, 'Karnataka Election Results: Numbers Prove BJP Won the Muslim and SC/ST Vote, Lingayat Move Backfired on Congress', FirstPost, 17 May 2018, https://www.firstpost. com/politics/karnataka-election-results-numbers-prove-bjp-won-the-muslim-and-scst-vote-lingayat-move-backfired-on-congress-4472561.html.

20. Anil Sasi, '21 States Are Now BJP-ruled, Home to 70 per cent of Indians', *Indian Express*, 5 March 2018, https://indianexpress. com/article/india/21-states-are-now-bjp-ruled-home-to-70-per-cent-of-indians-5085205/.

21. Hardeep S. Puri, 'Does India Have an Elected or Nominated PM', *New Indian Express*, 27 February 2014, http://www. newindianexpress.com/nation/2014/feb/27/Does-India-Have-an-Elected-or-Nominated-PM-580494.html.

22. Ibid.

23. Ibid.

24. The NewsWire, 'Party MPs Appeal for Reconsideration of Decision', *Outlook*, 18 May 2004, https://www.outlookindia. com/newswire/story/party-mps-appeal-for-reconsideration-of-decision/222664.

25. Ibid.

26. India is Indira, and Indira is India' declared D.K. Barooach, Congress president in 1976.

27. Prithviraj Chavan, 'Pranab Mukherjee, the Survivor', *Indian Express*, 26 July 2017, http://indianexpress.com/article/opinion/ pranab-mukherjee-the-survivor-president-congress-4767100/.

28. Josy Joseph, 'Pratibha's Pune Home a Break from Tradition', *Times of India*, 15 April 2012, https://timesofindia.indiatimes. com/india/Pratibhas-Pune-home-a-break-from-tradition/ articleshow/12668229.cms.

29. Sunetra Choudhury, 'Former President Pratibha Patil in Trouble over Gifts', NDTV, 25 September 2012, https://www.ndtv.com/india-news/former-president-pratibha-patil-in-trouble-over-gifts-500154.

30. Respect for the institutions of the state make me resist the temptation of sharing these details.

31. M.K. Gandhi, *The Story of My Experiments with Truth* (Penguin, 2001).

32. Mahatma Gandhi, Quit India Speech II at AICC Bombay 08-08-1942, Indian National Congress, https://www.inc.in/en/media/ speech/quit-india-speech-ii-at-aicc-bombay-08-08-1942.

33. He taught at DU from 1973–78.

34. The term 'bania' is derived from the Sanskrit word 'van.ij' or 'ban.ij', which means merchant. The term is used to indicate all people who are involved in money lending and similar activities. The bania are vaishya according to the Chaturvanya system and are third in hierarchy after the brahmin and the kshatriya. The bania community is spread across different states in India like Uttar Pradesh, Haryana, Gujarat, Maharashtra, Rajasthan, Madhya Pradesh, West Bengal, etc.

The term bania is also used pejoratively. Especially British colonial masters used the term to ridicule Mahatma Gandhi. In fact, Willingdon, the twenty-second viceroy and governor general of India, called Gandhi an 'astute little political Bania'.

Even Congress leaders like C.R. Das and Maulana Shaukat Ali referred to Gandhi as 'Wily Baiya'.

35. Ramachandra Guha, 'Does Gandhi Have a Caste?', *Indian Express*, 13 June 2017, http://indianexpress.com/article/opinion/columns/does-gandhi-have-a-caste-4700974/.

36. Ibid.

37. Narendra Singh Sarila, *The Shadow of the Great Game: The Untold Story of India's Partition* (New Delhi: HarperCollins, 2009).

38. Ibid.

39. Irfan Habib, 'On Parallel, Shining Paths', *Outlook*, 21 August 2017, https://www.outlookindia.com/magazine/story/on-parallel-shining-paths/299200.

40. Narendra Singh Sarila, *The Shadow of the Great Game: The Untold Story of India's Partition* (New Delhi: HarperCollins, 2009).

41. Ram Madhav, 'Coming Full Circle at 70', *Indian Express*, 15 August 2017, http://indianexpress.com/article/opinion/columns/independence-day-coming-full-circle-at-70-atal-bihari-vajpayee-hamid-ansari-muslims-india-insecure-modi-nehru-4796919/.

42. Ibid.

43. Ibid.

44. Ibid.

45. Ibid.

46. Aroon Purie, 'From the Editor-in-Chief', *India Today*, 14 July 2017, https://www.indiatoday.in/magazine/letters/story/20170724-editor-aroon-purie-donald-trump-narendra-modi-lynchings-1024011-2017-07-14.

47. Ibid.

48. Press Trust of India, 'India Has Highest Number of People Living Below the Poverty Line: World Bank', *Business Today*, 3 October 2016, http://www.businesstoday.in/current/economy-politics/india-has-highest-number-of-people-living-below-poverty-line-world-bank/story/238085.html.

49. Press Information Bureau, 'PM Salutes All the Women and Men Who Took Part in the Quit India Movement, on the 75th Anniversary; Urges People to Take Pledge for Creating a "New India" by 2022', Government of India, Prime Minister's Officer, 9 August 2017, http://pib.nic.in/newsite/PrintRelease.aspx?relid=169762.

50. Ibid.

51. Ibid.

52. Ibid.

53. Angus Maddison, 'The World Economy', Development Centre of the Organisation for Economic Co-operation and Development, 2006, https://www.stat.berkeley.edu/~aldous/157/Papers/world_economy.pdf.

54. International Monetary Fund, 'Report for Selected Countries and Subjects', IMF, April 2018, http://www.imf.org/external/pubs/ft/weo/2018/01/weodata/weorept.aspx?pr.x=48&pr.y=6&sy=2017&ey=2018&scsm=1&ssd=1&sort=country&ds=.&br=1&c=534&s=NGDPD%2CPPPGDP%2CNGDPDPC%2CPPPPPC&grp=0&a=.

55. Hardeep S. Puri, 'India Is Moving Towards a Corruption Free, Citizen-centric Economy', *Hindustan Times*, 9 December 2017, https://www.hindustantimes.com/opinion/india-is-moving-towards-a-corruption-free-citizen-centric-economy/story-Xu0RjzSkKtc8tfHuVeYKLK.html.

56. Dipak K. Dash, 'Highway Construction Doubles in 4 Years with 27km a day in 2017–18', *Times of India*, 4 April 2018, https://

timesofindia.indiatimes.com/india/highway-construction-doubles-in-4-years-with-27km-a-day-in-2017-18/articleshow/63601035.cms.

57. Press Trust of India, '4 Years of Modi: More Indians in Airplanes Now than in AC Trains, Says Govt', *Business Standard*, 29 May 2018, https://www.business-standard.com/article/economy-policy/4-years-of-modi-more-indians-in-airplanes-now-than-in-ac-trains-says-govt-118052801360_1.html.

58. Beneficiaries as of May 2018, Pradhan Mantri Jan-Dhan Yojana, https://www.pmjdy.gov.in/account.

59. Prasanta Sahu, 'Narendra Modi Government's Welfare Payments: Massive 75 pct to Be on DBT Platform in FY 19', *Financial Express*, 5 March 2018, https://www.financialexpress.com/economy/narendra-modi-governments-welfare-payments-massive-75-pct-to-be-on-dbt-platform-in-fy-19/1087398/.

60. Express Web Desk, 'Status Check of 12 New AIIMS Announced by PM Modi's Government', *Indian Express*, 3 October 2017, http://indianexpress.com/article/india/status-check-on-12-new-aiims-announced-under-pm-modis-government-4872523/.

61. 'Cabinet Approves Ayushman Bharat—National Health Protection Mission', Press Information Bureau, Government of India Cabinet, 21 March 2018, http://pib.nic.in/newsite/PrintRelease.aspx?relid=177816.

62. Prashant K. Nanda, '5 New IITs, 6 IIMs Likely to Become Operational by 2015', Livemint, 22 August 2014, http://www.livemint.com/Politics/Lges1pAU1eSNvJhWVxN45K/5-new-IITs-6-IIMs-likely-to-become-operational-by-2015.html.

63. 'In a Historic Decision, 60 Higher Educational Institutions Granted Autonomy by UGC: Shri Prakash Javadekar', Press Information Bureau, Government of India, Ministry of Human Resource Development, 20 March 2018, http://pib.nic.in/newsite/PrintRelease.aspx?relid=177751.

64. World Bank, 'Time to Resolve Insolvency', World Bank, https://data.worldbank.org/indicator/IC.ISV.DURS.

65. Press Trust of India, 'Acquisition of Bhushan Steel by Tatas Historic Breakthrough: Piyush Goyal', *Financial Express*, 18 May 2018, https://www.financialexpress.com/industry/banking-finance/ acquisition-of-bhushan-steel-by-tatas-historic-breakthrough- piyush-goyal/1173317/.

Chapter 5: Global Governance

1. 'The UN's Role in Global Governance', UN Intellectual History Project, August 2009, http://www.unhistory.org/ briefing/15GlobalGov.pdf.
2. H.H.S. Viswanathan and Shubh Soni, 'BRICS Role in Global Governance', Observer Research Foundation, 4 September 2017, http://cf.orfonline.org/wp-content/uploads/2017/09/GP-ORF_ BRICS.pdf.
3. United States Government, 'Remarks by President Trump on the Joint Comprehensive Plan of Action', WhiteHouse. gov, 8 May 2018, https://www.whitehouse.gov/briefings- statements/remarks-president-trump-joint-comprehensive- plan-action/.
4. Alec Luhn and Henry Samuel, 'Putin and Macron Question Trump's Withdrawal from Iran Deal and North Korea Summit', *Telegraph*, 24 May 2018, https://www.telegraph.co.uk/ news/2018/05/24/putin-macron-question-trumps-withdrawal- iran-deal-north-korea/.
5. Ibid.
6. Jonathan Allen, 'Trump: I'm Hoping for New Iran Deal that Is 'Better for Them'', NBC News, 12 May 2018, https://www. nbcnews.com/politics/donald-trump/trump-i-m-hoping-new- iran-deal-better-them-n873261.
7. Donald J. Trump's Tweet on 2 January 2018, https://twitter. com/realDonaldTrump/status/948355557022420992.
8. Eleanor Rose, 'Donald Trump and Kim Jong Un's War of Words: A Look Back after the US President's First Year', *Evening Standard*, 20 January 2018, https://www.standard.co.uk/news/

world/donald-trump-and-kim-jong-un-s-war-of-words-a-look-back-after-the-us-president-s-first-year-a3743791.html.

9. Robbie Gramer, 'Tillerson Open to Talks With North Korea', Foreign Policy, 12 December 2017, http://foreignpolicy. com/2017/12/12/tillerson-open-to-talks-with-north-korea-asia-state-department-china-pyongyang-nuclear-weapons-program-nonproliferation-diplomacy-pressure-campaign/.

10. Cindy Saine, 'State Department: No Change in US-North Korea Policy', VoaNews, 13 December 2017, https://www. voanews.com/a/state-department-no-change-in-us-north-korea-policy/4163203.html.

11. Ibid.

12. Alex Ward, 'Secretary of State Rex Tillerson Reportedly Called Trump a "Moron"', Vox, 4 October 2017, https://www.vox.com/ world/2017/10/4/16418538/tillerson-trump-moron-quit-boy-scout.

13. Amy Davidson Sorkin, 'Mike Pompeo and the Question of Torture', *New Yorker*, 12 January 2017, https://www.newyorker. com/news/amy-davidson/mike-pompeo-and-the-question-of-torture.

14. Sarah Childress and Priyanka Boghani, 'Trump's New CIA Director Nominee Helped Cover Up Torture', PBS.org, 13 March 2018 https://www.pbs.org/wgbh/frontline/article/ trumps-new-cia-director-nominee-helped-cover-up-torture/.

15. Jamies Lartey, 'Bombs Away: John Bolton's Most Hawkish Views on Iran, Iraq and North Korea', *Guardian*, 23 March 2018, https://www.theguardian.com/us-news/2018/mar/23/ john-bolton-north-korea-iran-iraq-who-is-he-what-does-he-believe.

16. Binoy Kampmark, 'Unsettling the Summits: John Bolton's Libya Solution', *International Policy Digest*, 21 May 2018, https:// intpolicydigest.org/2018/05/21/unsettling-the-summits-john-bolton-s-libya-solution/.

17. Jennifer Williams, 'Read the Full Transcript of Trump's North Korea Summit Press Conference', Vox, 12 June 2018, https://

www.vox.com/world/2018/6/12/17452624/trump-kim-
summit-transcript-press-conference-full-text.

18. 'President Trump Sits Down with George Stephanopoulos:
    Transcript', ABC News, 12 June 2018, https://abcnews.
    go.com/Politics/president-trump-sits-george-stephanopoulos-
    transcript/story?id=55831055.

19. Abhijit Iyer-Mitra, 'Trump-Kim Meet: The Carrots US Offers
    North Will Define the Deal's Success', *Business Standard*,
    12 June 2018, https://www.business-standard.com/article/
    economy-policy/trump-kim-meet-the-carrots-us-offers-north-
    will-define-the-deal-s-success-118061200656_1.html.

20. Ibid.

21. Democratic People's Republic of Korea.

22. 'Trump and Kim's Joint Statement', Reuters, 12 June 2018, https://
    www.reuters.com/article/us-northkorea-usa-agreement-text/
    trump-and-kims-joint-statement-idUSKBN1J80IU.

23. 'Kyoto Protocol—Targets for the First Commitment Period',
    UNFCCC, https://unfccc.int/process/the-kyoto-protocol.

24. 'Parties & Observes', UNFCCC, https://unfccc.int/parties-observers.

25. John H. Cushman Jr., 'U.S. Signs a Pact to Reduce Gases Tied
    to Warming', *New York Times*, 1998, http://www.nytimes.
    com/1998/11/13/world/us-signs-a-pact-to-reduce-gases-tied-
    to-warming.html.

26. Christie Aschwanden, 'A Lesson from Kyoto's Failure: Don't Let
    Congress Touch A Climate Deal', FiveThirtyEight, 4 December
    2015, https://fivethirtyeight.com/features/a-lesson-from-kyotos-
    failure-dont-let-congress-touch-a-climate-deal/.

27. John Vidal, Allegra Stratton and Suzanne Goldenberg, 'Low
    Targets, Goals Dropped: Copenhagen Ends in Failure',
    Guardian, 19 December 2009, https://www.theguardian.com/
    environment/2009/dec/18/copenhagen-deal.

28. Ibid.

29. Ibid.

30. '197 Nations Unite to Phase Out Potent Greenhouse Gases',
    Environmental and Energy Study Institute, 6 November 2015,

http://www.eesi.org/press-releases/view/197-nations-unite-to-phase-out-potent-greenhouse-gases.

31. 'The Paris Agreement', UNFCCC, https://unfccc.int/process-and-meetings/the-paris-agreement/the-paris-agreement.

32. Camila Domonoske, '2 Degrees, $100 Billion: The World Climate Agreement, By The Numbers', NPR, 12 December 2015, https://www.npr.org/sections/thetwo-way/2015/12/12/459502597/2-degrees-100-billion-the-world-climate-agreement-by-the-numbers.

33. 'What Is the Paris Agreement?', UNFCCC, https://unfccc.int/process-and-meetings/the-paris-agreement/what-is-the-paris-agreement.

34. Kevin Liptak and Jim Acosta, 'Trump on Paris Accord: 'We're Getting Out', CNN Politics, 2 June 2017, http://edition.cnn.com/2017/06/01/politics/trump-paris-climate-decision/index.html.

35. Valerie Volcovici, 'Exclusive: Trump's Coal Job Push Stumbles in Most States—Data', Reuters, 19 January 2018, https://www.reuters.com/article/us-usa-coal-jobs/exclusive-trumps-coal-job-push-stumbles-in-most-states-data-idUSKBN1F81AK.

36. Justin Gillis and Nadja Popovich, 'The U.S. Is the Biggest Carbon Polluter in History. It Just Walked Away From the Paris Climate Deal,' New York Times, 1 June 2017, https://www.nytimes.com/interactive/2017/06/01/climate/us-biggest-carbon-polluter-in-history-will-it-walk-away-from-the-paris-climate-deal.html?mtrref=www.google.co.in.

37. Rob Smith, 'The World's Biggest Economies in 2018', World Economic Forum, 18 April 2018, https://www.weforum.org/agenda/2018/04/the-worlds-biggest-economies-in-2018/.

38. Jan Burck, Franziska Marten, Christoph Bals, Niklas Höhne, 'Results 2018', Climate Change Performance Index, 15 November 2017, https://www.climate-change-performance-index.org/sites/default/files/documents/the_climate_change_performance_index_2018_a4.pdf.

39. Yui Hatcho, 'The Atlantic Charter of 1941: A Political Tool of Non-belligerent America', The Japanese Journal of American

Studies, 2003, http://www.jaas.gr.jp/jjas/PDF/2003/No.14-123.
pdf.

40. Daniel Boffey and Jennifer Rankin, 'Trump Rebukes Nato Leaders for Not Paying Defence Bills', *Guardian*, 25 May 2017, https://www.theguardian.com/world/2017/may/25/trump-rebukes-nato-leaders-for-not-paying-defence-bills.

41. Rob Smith, 'The World's Biggest Economies in 2018', World Economic Forum, 18 April 2018, https://www.weforum.org/agenda/2018/04/the-worlds-biggest-economies-in-2018/.

42. 'Full Text of Xi Jinping Keynote at the World Economic Forum', CGTN, 17 January 2017, https://america.cgtn.com/2017/01/17/full-text-of-xi-jinping-keynote-at-the-world-economic-forum.

43. 'GDP (Current US$)', World Bank, https://data.worldbank.org/indicator/NY.GDP.MKTP.CD?locations=CN.

44. GDP Per Capita (Current US$), World Bank, https://data.worldbank.org/indicator/NY.GDP.PCAP.CD?locations=CN.

45. Ankit Panda, 'Sri Lanka Formally Hands Over Hambantota Port to Chinese Firms on 99-Year Lease', *Diplomat*, 11 December 2017, https://thediplomat.com/2017/12/sri-lanka-formally-hands-over-hambantota-port-to-chinese-firms-on-99-year-lease/.

46. Zofeen T. Ebrahim, 'What's Happening at Pakistan's Gwadar Port?', *Diplomat*, 17 June 2017, https://thediplomat.com/2017/06/whats-happening-at-pakistans-gwadar-port/.

47. Ibid.

48. Elizabeth Roche, 'India, China Face Off Over Doklam Amid Bid to Ease Tensions', Livemint, 27 March 2018, https://www.livemint.com/Politics/Qq7p6f7p4O9ePeJDbbjGEL/There-is-nothing-like-changing-status-quo-in-Doklam-China.html.

49. Saibal Dasgupta, 'Chinese Media Accuses Sushma Swaraj of Lying, Puts Pressure on Its Own Government', *Times of India*, 21 July 2017, https://timesofindia.indiatimes.com/world/china/chinese-media-accuses-sushma-swaraj-of-lying-puts-pressure-on-its-own-government/articleshow/59703004.cms.

50. Tom Phillips, 'China Attacks International Court After South China Sea Ruling', *Guardian*, 13 July 2016, https://www.theguardian.com/world/2016/jul/13/china-damns-international-court-after-south-china-sea-slapdown.

51. 'The China–North Korea Relationship', Council for Foreign Relations, 28 March 2018, https://www.cfr.org/backgrounder/china-north-korea-relationship.

52. Owen Jones, 'Islamophobia Plays Right into the Hands of ISIS', *Guardian*, 25 November 2015, https://www.theguardian.com/commentisfree/2015/nov/25/islamophobia-isis-muslim-islamic-state-paris.

53. Nick Stockton, 'Turning Away Refugees Won't Fight Terrorism, and Might Make It Worse', Wired, 17 November 2015, https://www.wired.com/2015/11/turning-away-refugees-wont-fight-terrorism-it-might-make-it-worse/.

54. 'The PIIGS that Won't Fly', *The Economist*, 18 May 2010, http://www.economist.com/node/15838029.

55. 'GDP (Current US$)', World Bank, https://data.worldbank.org/indicator/NY.GDP.MKTP.CD?locations=RU.

56. Samir Saran, 'Being Vladimir Putin: Russia's President Gets 20th Century Geopolitics, What He Doesn't Get Is 21st Century Geoeconomics', *Times of India*, 2 March 2017, https://www.orfonline.org/research/putins-grasp-over-geopolitics-against-his-immaturity-in-geoeconomics/.

57. 'Uniting Our Strengths for Peace—Politics, Partnership and People', Report of the High-Level Independent Panel on United Nations Peace Operations, 16 June 2015, http://providingforpeacekeeping.org/project/uniting-our-strengths-for-peace-politics-partnerships-and-people-report-of-the-high-level-independent-panel-on-united-nations-peace-operations-2015/.

58. Hardeep S. Puri, 'The UN at 70—Its Relevance or India and the World', Speech by Hardeep S. Puri at Society for Policy Studies, 14 December 2015, http://hardeepsinghpuri.com/the-un-at-70-the-un-at-70-its-relevance-for-india-and-the-world/.

59. Hardeep S. Puri, 'Informal Thematic Debate On "The United Nations In Global Governance"', Permanent Mission of India, 28 June 2011, https://Www.Pminewyork.Org/Pdf/Uploadpdf/61476ind1879.Pdf.

60. Anthony Banbury, 'I Love the U.N but It Is Failing', *New York Times*, 18 March 2016, https://www.nytimes.com/2016/03/20/opinion/sunday/i-love-the-un-but-it-is-failing.html.

61. Charter of the United Nations, Chapter XV, Article 100, http://legal.un.org/repertory/art100.shtml.

62. 'Uniting Our Strengths for Peace—Politics, Partnership and People', Report of the High-Level Independent Panel on United Nations Peace Operations, 16 June 2015, http://providingforpeacekeeping.org/project/uniting-our-strengths-for-peace-politics-partnerships-and-people-report-of-the-high-level-independent-panel-on-united-nations-peace-operations-2015/.

63. Ibid.

64. Ibid.

65. Ibid.

66. Ibid.

67. 'The Challenge of Sustaining Peace', Report of the Advisory Group of Experts for the 2015 Review of the United Nations Peacebuilding Architecture, 29 June 2015, https://reliefweb.int/report/world/challenge-sustaining-peace-report-advisory-group-experts-2015-review-united-nations.

68. Ibid.

69. The five permanent members of the United Nations Security Council, namely, United States of America, Russia, United Kingdom, France and People's Republic of China, each with the power to Veto.

70. Antonio Guterres, 'Remarks to the General Assembly Taking Oath of Office', United Nations, 12 December 2016, https://www.un.org/sg/en/content/sg/speeches/2016-12-12/secretary-general-designate-ant%C3%B3nio-guterres-oath-office-speech.

71. Ana Maria Lebada, 'UN Secretary-General Issues Third Report on Management Reform', International Institute for Sustainable Development, 22 May 2018, http://sdg.iisd.org/news/un-secretary-general-issues-third-report-on-management-reform/.

72. The letter from the thirty-seven PRs is widely quoted in the New York United Nations dispatches (https://www.passblue.com/wp-content/uploads/2017/07/UN_Reform.pdf).

73. Archis Mohan, 'India and the United Nations', Ministry of External Affairs, Government of India, 20 September 2013, http://mea.gov.in/in-focus-article.htm?22231/India+and+the+United+Nations.

74. 'Preamble', United Nations, http://www.un.org/en/sections/un-charter/preamble/index.html.

75. Press Trust of India, 'India Puts in Candidacy for 2021–2022 UNSC Non-permanent Seat', *The Hindu BusinessLine*, 5 December 2013, http://www.thehindubusinessline.com/news/india-puts-in-candidacy-for-20212022-unsc-nonpermanent-seat/article5424929.ece.

Chapter 6: The Politics of Terror

1. 'Text of George Bush's Speech', *Guardian*, 21 September 2018, https://www.theguardian.com/world/2001/sep/21/september11.usa13.

2. 'Raqqa's Liberation from ISIS', US Department of State, 20 October 2017, https://translations.state.gov/2017/10/20/raqqas-liberation-from-isis/.

3. Ibid.

4. Ibid.

5. Press Trust of India, 'Raqqa Liberation Critical Milestone against ISIS: Rex Tillerson', *Indian Express*, 21 October 2017, https://indianexpress.com/article/world/raqqa-liberation-critical-milestone-against-isis-rex-tillerson-4899465/.

6. Ibid.

7. Independent Commission on Multilateralism, 'Discussion Paper on Terrorism Including Issues Related to Ideology, Identity Politics, and Organized Crime', International Peace Institute, September 2015, https://www.icm2016.org/IMG/pdf/discussion_paper_3.pdf.

8. 'Report of the High-level Panel on Threats, Challenges and Change', UN General Assembly, 2 December 2004, https://www.un.org/ruleoflaw/blog/document/the-secretary-generals-high-level-panel-report-on-threats-challenges-and-change-a-more-secure-world-our-shared-responsibility/.

9. Ibid.

10. Ibid.

11. Hardeep S. Puri, *Perilous Interventions: The Security Council and the Politics of Chaos* (New Delhi: HarperCollins, 2016).

12. Ibid.

13. FP Staff, 'You Can't Keep Snakes in Your Backyard and Expect Them to Only Bite Your Neighbour: Clinton', FirstPost, 21 October 2011, https://www.firstpost.com/world/clinton-continues-to-talk-tough-with-pakistan-113492.html.

14. 'Terrorists Linked to Organized Crime in Traffic of Nuclear, Biological Materials—UN', UN News, 28 September 2011, https://news.un.org/en/story/2011/09/389732-terrorists-linked-organized-crime-traffic-nuclear-biological-materials-un.

15. Ewen MacAskill and Julian Borger, 'Iraq War Was Illegal and Breached UN Charters, Says Annan', *Guardian*, 16 September 2004, https://www.theguardian.com/world/2004/sep/16/iraq.iraq.

16. Garikai Chengu, 'America Created Al-Qaeda and the ISIS Terror Group', Global Research, 19 September 2004, https://www.globalresearch.ca/america-created-al-qaeda-and-the-isis-terror-group/5402881.

17. Jack Moore, 'Hundreds of ISIS Fighters Are Hiding in Turkey, Increasing Fears of Europe Attacks', *Newsweek*, 27 December 2017, http://www.newsweek.com/hundreds-isis-fighters-are-hiding-turkey-increasing-fears-europe-attacks-759877.

18. Adam Weinstein, 'The Real Largest State Sponsor of Terrorism', Huffington Post, 16 March 2017, https://www.huffingtonpost.com/entry/the-real-largest-state-sponsor-of terrorism_us_58cafc26e4b00705db4da8aa.

19. 'Convention on Offences and Certain Other Acts Committed On Board Aircraft. Signed at Tokyo on 14 September 1963', http://treaties.un.org/doc/db/Terrorism/Conv1-english.pdf.

20. 'Convention for the Suppression of Unlawful Seizure of Aircraft. Signed at The Hague on 16 December 1970', https://treaties.un.org/doc/Publication/UNTS/Volume%20860/volume-860-I-12325-English.pdf.

21. 'Convention for the Suppression of Unlawful Acts against the Safety of Civil Aviation. Concluded at Montreal on 23 September 1971, http://treaties.un.org/doc/db/Terrorism/Conv3-english.pdf.

22. 'Convention on the Prevention and Punishment of Crimes against Internationally Protected Persons, including Diplomatic Agents. Adopted by the General Assembly of the United Nations, at New York, on 14 December 1973', http://treaties.un.org/doc/db/Terrorism/english-18-7.pdf.

23. 'International Convention against the Taking of Hostages. Adopted by the General Assembly of The United Nations on 17 December 1979', http://treaties.un.org/doc/db/Terrorism/english-18-5.pdf.

24. 'Convention on the Physical Protection of Nuclear Material. Adopted at Vienna on 26 October 1979 and Opened for Signature at Vienna and New York on 3 March 1980', https://treaties.un.org/doc/Publication/UNTS/Volume%201456/volume-1456-I-24631-English.pdf.

25. 'Protocol for the Suppression of Unlawful Acts of Violence at Airports Serving International Civil Aviation, Supplementary to the Convention for the Suppression of Unlawful Acts against the Safety of Civil Aviation. Concluded at Montreal on 23 September 1971', http://treaties.un.org/doc/db/Terrorism/Conv7-english.pdf.

26. 'Convention for the Suppression of Unlawful Acts against the Safety of Maritime Navigation. Concluded at Rome on 10 March', http://treaties.un.org/doc/db/Terrorism/Conv8-english.pdf.

27. '1988 Protocol for the Suppression of Unlawful Acts against the Safety of Fixed Platforms Located on the Continental Shelf', http://treaties.un.org/doc/db/Terrorism/Conv9-english.pdf.

28. 'Protocol of 2005 to the Protocol for the Suppression of Unlawful Acts against the Safety of Fixed Platforms Located on the Continental Shelf', https://www.state.gov/documents/organization/58425.pdf.

29. '1991 Convention on the Marking of Plastic Explosives for the Purpose of Detection', http://treaties.un.org/doc/db/Terrorism/Conv10-english.pdf.

30. '1997 International Convention for the Suppression of Terrorist Bombings', http://treaties.un.org/doc/db/Terrorism/english-18-9.pdf.

31. '1999 International Convention for the Suppression of the Financing of Terrorism', http://treaties.un.org/doc/db/Terrorism/english-18-11.pdf.

32. '2005 International Convention for the Suppression of Acts of Nuclear Terrorism', http://treaties.un.org/doc/db/Terrorism/english-18-15.pdf.

33. 'Resolution 1267', http://www.un.org/ga/search/view_doc.asp?symbol=S/RES/1267%281999%29.

34. 'Al-Qaida Analytical Support and Sanctions Monitoring Team', https://www.ipinst.org/wp-content/uploads/2012/06/pdfs_terrorism-directory_4-MonitoringTeam-CTCommitteeExec.pdf.

35. 'Resolution 1269', UNSCR, 1999, https://undocs.org/S/RES/1269.

36. 'Resolution 1904', 2009, https://undocs.org/S/RES/1904.

37. 'Resolution 1373', 2001, https://undocs.org/S/RES/1373.

38. 'Resolution 1535', 2004, http://www.un.org/en/ga/search/view_doc.asp?symbol=S/RES/1535%20%282004%29.

39. 'Resolution 1540', 2004, https://undocs.org/S/RES/1540.

40. 'Resolution 1566', 2004, https://www.securitycouncilreport. org/atf/cf/%7b65BFCF9B-6D27-4E9C-8CD3- CF6E4FF96FF9%7d/WG%20SRES%201566.pdf.

41. 'Resolution 1624', 2005, http://www.un.org/en/ga/search/view_ doc.asp?symbol=S/RES/1624%20%282005%29.

42. 'Resolution 2133', 2014, https://www.un.org/press/en/2014/ sc11262.doc.htm.

43. 'Resolution 2178', 2014,https://www.un.org/en/ga/search/view_ doc.asp?symbol=S/RES/2178%20%282014%29.

44. Ibid.

Chapter 7: The Politics of Trade Policy

1. Sidney Picker Jr., 'World Trade and the Law of GATT, by John H. Jackson', *Case Western Reserve Law Review*, Case Western Reserve University, 1971, https://scholarlycommons. law.case.edu/cgi/viewcontent.cgi?referer=https://www.google. co.in/&httpsredir=1&article=2869&context=caselrev.

2. 'Full Transcript: Donald Trump's Jobs Plan Speech', Politico, 28 June 2016, https://www.politico.com/story/2016/06/full- transcript-trump-job-plan-speech-224891.

3. Martin Wolf, 'Donald Trump and Xi Jinping's Battle over Globalisation', *Financial Times*, 24 January 2017, https://www. ft.com/content/74b42cd8-e171-11e6-8405-9e5580d6e5fb.

4. World Trade Organisation, 'Agreement Establishing the WTO', The WTO Agreements Series, https://www.wto.org/english/ res_e/booksp_e/agrmntseries1_wto_e.pdf.

5. Alfredo Saad-Filho, 'Growth, Poverty and Inequality: From Washington Consensus to Inclusive Growth', DESA *Working Paper No. 100*, November 2010, http://www.un.org/esa/desa/ papers/2010/wp100_2010.pdf.

6. Hardeep S. Puri, 'India's Trade Policy Dilemma and the Role of Domestic Reform', Carnegie India, 16 February 2017, http:// carnegieindia.org/2017/02/16/india-s-trade-policy-dilemma- and-role-of-domestic-reform-pub-67946.

7. Entry 14 of List I of the Seventh Schedule and Article 253 of the Constitution.

8. As per the department of industrial policy and promotion, the FDI inflow in India grew on an average of 35 per cent in the past three years—plus 28 per cent in the year 2014–15; 39 per cent in the year 2015–16;11 per cent in 2016–17; and minus 1 per cent in 2017–18 (http://dipp.nic.in/publications/fdi-statistics/archives; http://dipp.nic.in/publications/fdi-statistics); private investment, on the other hand, has not kept pace. As per the Economic Survey of India for 2016–17: 'Private investment, which had been soaring at the height of the boom, slowed sharply to a 5 per cent growth rate by 2010–11. By 2015–16, it had actually started to shrink, and in 2016–17 so far it seems to have contracted by more than 7 per cent' (http://indiabudget.nic.in/es2016-17/echapter.pdf)

9. Special Correspondent, 'India must Integrate with Global Value Chain: ADB', *The Hindu*, 28 November 2017, http://www.thehindu.com/business/india-must-integrate-with-global-value-chain-adb/article21040771.ece.

10. Press Trust of India, 'Ports Are Gateway to Prosperity: Narendra Modi', *Economic Times*, 22 October 2017, https://economictimes.indiatimes.com/news/politics-and-nation/ports-are-gateway-to-prosperity-narendra-modi/articleshow/61172647.cms.

11. 'Projects under Sagarmala', Ministry of Shipping, Government of India, 31 March 2018, http://sagarmala.gov.in/projects/projects-under-sagarmala.

12. 'World Trade Statistical Review 2017', World Trade Organization, https://www.wto.org/english/res_e/statis_e/wts2017_e/WTO_Chapter_01_e.pdf.

13. Ajay Srivastava, 'Why Global Value Chains Matter to India', *The Hindu Businessline*, 5 October 2017, https://www.thehindubusinessline.com/opinion/why-global-value-chains-matter-to-india/article9889221.ece.

14. Uri Friedman, '70% of India Has Yet to Be Built', *Atlantic*, 29 June 2014, https://www.theatlantic.com/international/

archive/2014/06/70-percent-of-india-has-yet-to-be-built/373656/.

15. Liu Hongyu, Yun W. Park and Zheng Siqi, 'The Interaction between Housing Investment and Economic Growth in China', *International Real Estate Review*, Vol. 5, No. 1, pp. 40–60, 2002, http://www.umac.mo/fba/irer/papers/past/vol5_pdf/040_060PRC.pdf.

16. 'Report for Selected Countries and Subjects', International Monetary Fund, April 2018, http://www.imf.org/external/pubs/ft/weo/2018/01/weodata/weorept.aspx?pr.x=48&pr.y=6&sy=2017&ey=2018&scsm=1&ssd=1&sort=country&ds=.&br=1&c=534&s=NGDPD%2CPPPGDP%2CNGDPDPC%2CPPPPC&grp=0&a=.

17. 'India Economic Survey: External Sector', Ministry of Finance, 29 January 2018, http://mofapp.nic.in:8080/economicsurvey/pdf/080-098_Chapter_06_Economic_Survey_2017-18.pdf.

18. 'Regional Comprehensive Economic Partnership (RCEP)', Association of Southeast Asian Nations, http://asean.org/?static_post=rcep-regional-comprehensive-economic-partnership.

19. Press Trust of India, 'India Needs to Gear up to Face Challenges of Mega Trade Pacts', *Economic Times*, 1 April 2015, https://economictimes.indiatimes.com/news/economy/foreign-trade/india-needs-to-gear-up-to-face-challenges-of-mega-trade-pacts/articleshow/46775647.cms.

20. 'Foreign Trade Policy (1 April 2015–31 March 2020]', Government of India Ministry of Commerce and Industry Department of Commerce, 30 June 2015, http://dgft.gov.in/sites/default/files/Updated_FTP_2015-2020.pdf.

21. 'Citizen Charter', Government of India Ministry of Commerce and Industry Department Of Commerce, 2 September 2018, https://dgft.gov.in/sites/default/files/dgft.gov_.in_exim_2000_citichar.pdf.

22. 'Foreign Trade Policy Statement 2017—Mid Term Review', Ministry of Commerce, December 2017, https://worldtradescanner.com/FTP-Statement-051217.pdf.

23. Edward Helmore, 'Trudeau Calls Trump's Tariffs "Insulting" to Longstanding US-Canada Alliance', *Guardian*, 3 June 2018 https://www.theguardian.com/world/2018/jun/03/justin-trudeau-donald-trump-tariffs-insulting-us-canada-alliance.

24. Subhayan Chakraborty, 'India's Retaliatory Tariffs on 30 US Items to Rake in Additional $240 mn', *Business Standard*, 18 June 2018, https://www.business-standard.com/article/economy-policy/india-s-retaliatory-tariffs-on-30-us-items-to-rake-in-additional-240-mn-118061700511_1.html.

Index

257